ROMAN SLAVERY AND ROMAN
MATERIAL CULTURE

PHOENIX

Journal of the Classical Association of Canada
Revue de la Société canadienne des études classiques
Supplementary Volume LII

EDITED BY MICHELE GEORGE

Roman Slavery and Roman Material Culture

UNIVERSITY OF TORONTO PRESS
Toronto Buffalo London

Library and Archives Canada Cataloguing in Publication

Roman slavery and Roman material culture / edited by Michele George.

(Phoenix supplementary volumes ; 52)
Includes bibliographical references and index.
ISBN 978-1-4426-4457-1

1. Slavery – Rome – History – Sources.   2. Romans – Material culture – Sources.
I. George, Michele G. (Michele Gladys), 1960–   II. Series: Phoenix.
Supplementary volume (Toronto, Ont.) ; 52

HT863.R64 2013   306.3'620945632   C2012-904188-2

University of Toronto Press acknowledges the financial assistance to its publishing
program of the Canada Council for the Arts and the Ontario Arts Council.

University of Toronto Press acknowledges the financial support of the Government
of Canada through the Canada Book Fund for its publishing activities.

CONTENTS

Illustrations follow p. 128

ACKNOWLEDGMENTS

The sixth E. Togo Salmon conference held at McMaster University in September 2007 featured an earlier version of most essays in this volume (with the exception of chapter 6). Funding for the conference was furnished by two bodies: the Social Sciences and Humanities Research Council of Canada (SSHRC), which also provided research funding for two of these papers (chapters 1 and 6), and the E. Togo Salmon Fund in Roman Studies at McMaster University, which also provided a subsidy for this volume's publication. I would like to thank both for their assistance.

For their invaluable help in the preparation of the conference and this volume, gratitude is extended to Keith Bradley, Carmen Camilleri, Sarah-Jane Evans, and Louise Savocchia. Suzanne Rancourt and Barbara Porter at the University of Toronto Press and the two editors of the Phoenix Supplementary series, Jonathan Edmondson and Alison Keith, eased the publication process and were unstinting in their support. Finally, I would like to thank the contributors to the volume for their readiness to explore the challenging world of Roman slavery.

ROMAN SLAVERY AND ROMAN
MATERIAL CULTURE

Introduction

MICHELE GEORGE

In the course of the twentieth century, through the pioneering scholarship of historians such as Moses Finley and Keith Hopkins, the study of Roman slavery evolved from its origins as an essential if problematic element in Roman economic history into a substantial subject for historical investigation in its own right.[1] Replete now with its own scholarly traditions and controversies, Roman slavery is no longer a subject limited to the economic sphere but is recognized as a fundamental social institution with multiple implications for Roman society and culture. In the course of this evolution, scholarship on Roman slavery has embraced a wide range of evidence and methodological approaches, including demography, epigraphy, and family studies; even Roman literature is now acknowledged as a valuable reservoir of attitudes about slaves.[2] Roman material culture, more commonly known by the traditional rubrics of archaeology and art history, remains however a largely untapped source for the study of slavery. The papers in this volume represent a concerted effort to explore the potential contribution of material culture to the subject by specialists in diverse areas of Roman studies and to combine the materials and methods of analysis of social history and archaeology. It brings together historians, art historians, and archaeologists to advance the interconnections among these disciplines in the study of Roman slavery, and to present the first fruits of an interdisciplinary approach to the subject.

'Archaeology and History'

Recognizing both the integral role of slavery in the ancient economy and the inadequacy of conventional historical sources on the subject, Finley followed M.I. Rostovtzeff in incorporating evidence from archaeological excavation and Roman art in his analysis of the Roman economy. Both scholars, however, used it in a supplementary manner and mostly for illustrative purposes, rather than comprehensively.[3] While Rostovtzeff himself actively engaged in archaeological excavation as director of the site of Dura-Europos, Finley expressed ambivalence about the contribution archaeology might make to ancient history. Although aimed specifically at the processual 'New Archaeology' emerging at that time in Cambridge, Finley's famous *cri de coeur* against archaeology seems to apply to all aspects of the discipline.[4] Rejecting what he perceived as archaeology's ahistoricism and devotion to 'classification and chronology' for its own sake, he called on archaeologists to produce more substantial, statistically rigorous data that were primarily relevant to historical questions. Yet, Finley was also critical of historians who paid no more than 'lip service' to archaeology and was sensitive to the reasonable limits of archaeological evidence. His own insistence that historical enquiry must proceed even in the face of 'insufficient evidence' is in tune with the archaeological process, which often falls short, in quantity or quality of data, of an evidentiary base deemed 'sufficient' by many historians.[5] This applies to slavery for both the historian and the archaeologist. The intervening years have witnessed a greater understanding of the social and cultural significance of archaeology and art history to ancient history that has moved beyond the utilitarian, statistically orientated perspective of Finley. However, many of the disciplinary boundaries that led Finley to despair of archaeology are still intact.[6]

Within the field of material culture itself, two factors common to most slave societies have impeded the study of slavery. First, there is the slave's lack of agency and resources to leave a personal legacy in the physical record, and second, there is the challenge of ascertaining legal status from the material evidence in order to distinguish slaves from the freeborn of low economic status.[7] Jerzy Kolendo's brief review of the iconographic evidence written thirty years ago set out broad categories of scenes with slaves in Roman art, the first comprising figures in chains and representations of the *servus callidus* of Roman comedy, and the second a much more general catch-all group that included ambiguous images of work, gladiatorial combat, and captives of war.[8] More recently, Leonhard Schumacher, addressing both Greek and Roman slavery, organized the visual evidence into economic categories (e.g., primary, secondary, and tertiary industries) and included consideration of some epigraphic evidence. His iconographic criteria overlap with Kolendo's to some extent, but he pays more attention to clarifying the issue of status among the ambiguous scenes. In gathering together archaeological evidence from excavations of both Greek and Roman slavery, F.H. Thompson omits completely the visual evidence as a possible source for slavery in itself, drawing on it mostly for its documentary contribution to illustrate ancient agricultural and manufacturing techniques. Several studies of aspects of Roman art, such as work scenes and sub-elite visual culture, include some mention of slaves, but the ambiguities of status make it difficult to draw conclusions that are specific to that status group. Freedmen, former slaves, have fared better, since their elevated status and economic success endowed them with the agency to build family tombs with which they could shape a public persona of their own.[9]

Arguably, field archaeology, the other major component in material culture and the one that has in fact been employed more by historians of slavery thus far, has been even less concerned with slavery than art history. The archaeology of the slave trade has received some study, although the identification of slave markets remains a point of controversy. Although the presence of slaves in the industrial and commercial sphere is certain, they are rarely mentioned when excavation of such premises is discussed but are more often subsumed by the *ingenui* with whom they worked. A similar impulse to focus on their function rather than their status is apparent in studies of Roman dining, in which slaves are often referred to as 'servants' rather than slaves.[10] Most puzzling, however, is the case of Roman villas, where traces of slavery might well be expected in the archaeological record, and for which, relatively speaking, there is copious textual evidence in the agricultural writers. Inexplicably, slaves have not always been found, or perhaps sufficiently sought, by excavators, nor is their apparent absence in archaeological remains generally recognized or discussed in excavation reports.[11]

The impetus behind the papers in this volume is to create stronger bonds between history and material culture, with the goal of finding new ways of understanding Roman slavery and the slave experience. The central question in all chapters of this book is how material culture is to be interpreted historically, whether by specialists in material culture (i.e., the archaeologist or art historian) or by the ancient historian willing to incorporate it into conventional historical scholarship.

* * * * * *

Drawing on texts, in the form of inscriptions and graffiti, the first three papers demonstrate the critical role of the specialist in adumbrating the potential and limitations of specific kinds of evidence. Christer Bruun's paper begins with epigraphy, a form of evidence which has figured in a number of important studies of Roman slavery.[12] Since slaves are only infrequently named in inscriptions with a clear status indicator such as the label *servus*, scholarship that draws on epigraphy has relied heavily on the Greek *cognomen*, and on the routine supposition that it implies slave status when appearing by itself, or that it indicates former slave status (even if in a previous generation) when it occurs in the full *tria nomina*. The almost universal acceptance of a Greek *cognomen* as a kind of label of legal status (or former slave status) provides a convenient justification for sidestepping onomastics, a highly specialized sub-field whose intricacies and daunting scholarly legacy discourage even other historians (let alone art historians and archaeologists) from serious engagement or challenge. As Bruun acknowledges, scholars of onomastics, above all Heikki Solin, have shown that Greek *cognomina* do dominate among slaves and freedmen in extant evidence by a ratio of 2:1. This suggests that it is not unreasonable to assume a servile connection for a Greek *cognomen*, but it also offers the caveat that, in the absence of the epigraphic marker L (for *libertus*), we cannot be absolutely sure. This reminder should have significant ramifications for archaeologists and art historians, who might wish to rely on a Greek *cognomen* to identify a portrait or tomb as belonging to a slave or, more often, a freedman. While it is a possibility, it is not at all a certainty, rendering arguments about taste or social identity based solely on this point somewhat precarious.[13] Moreover, as Bruun argues, this bald statistical fact does not fully account for the broad implications of onomastics, specifically naming practices and their connection to legal status. Focusing on the case of *vernae* (house-born slaves) and their nomenclature, Bruun gathers together and analyses studies which show that Latin *cognomina*, rather than Greek, were in fact preferred for *vernae* in both private and imperial households, presumably as a way of disguising a non-Roman origin and thus erasing the stigma of servile descent. He then identifies some of the manifold repercussions of these conclusions and outlines several paths for further investigation of the epigraphic material. For example, if *cognomina* are any indication at all of slave origins, the dominance of Greek names over Latin suggests that capture abroad, and not domestic slave reproduction as has been argued recently, was the main source of supply.[14] It would also mean that some portion of the Roman populace bearing Latin *cognomina*, rather than Greek, were in fact of servile ancestry, thus undermining the expedient polarity in nomenclature so often resorted to in the identification of status groups in written evidence. Latin *cognomina*, as much as or perhaps even more than Greek *cognomina*, emerge as an important if problematic piece of the puzzle. While hardly simplifying matters, Bruun's study will have an effect on how inscriptions can be used henceforth in future slavery studies.

The next two papers also utilize epigraphic evidence but differ considerably from Bruun's in focus. Instead of taking an expansive and methodological perspective, Henrik Mouritsen and Peter Keegan consider highly unusual groups of texts that were found in well-defined, closed contexts in Rome, the *columbaria* of the Statilii and Volusii, and the Palatine *paedagogium*. It is the rare combination of text and context that allows both Mouritsen and Keegan to adopt an approach akin to micro-history, as they present detailed case studies of household slavery, one as reflected in two elite tombs, another in the imperial *domus* itself. The physical context furnishes a social context, and it is in fact the unique archaeological find-spot of each corpus that permits an analysis more tailored and detailed than the broad strokes applied to inscriptions stripped of their provenance or graffiti from less contained and more public locations.[15]

Mouritsen examines the *columbaria* of two elite families, the Statilii and Volusii, to define the internal hierarchies of status within the elite *familia* and to produce a statistical analysis that focuses on the rate of manumission. In his discussion of commemorative practice and gender representation in these two cases, Mouritsen concludes that the rate of manumission, at 25 to 33 per cent, was relatively high compared to other slave societies but was far from universal, and that it was carried out on an informal basis, with no obvious rule of thumb beyond maturity (i.e., given that a slave's chance at freedom increased if he lived long enough). Through an analysis of their funerary commemoration, Mouritsen outlines the shape of these elite households, arguing, for example, that there were more male than female slaves, at least as represented in the commemorative evidence, and that a job title was applied more to male than to female slaves by a wide margin (5:1). Many freedmen in these two *domus* stayed within their former owner's *familia* even after liberty, thus mitigating the impact of manumission on the individual as well as on the stability of the household. By ascertaining that a small majority of slaves (61%) within these two *domus* were owned by *libertini* or were *vicarii*, slaves 'owned' by or in the apparent power of other slaves within the household, rather than by the elite family itself, this study provides further delineation of the complex internal hierarchies within the elite household as well as within slavery itself.

The advantages of any 'case-study' approach are offset by the fact that they are exactly that, individual instances that do not necessarily reflect the general rule. Indeed, as Mouritsen indicates, the differences between the two samples themselves highlight the caution to be exercised. There are almost twice as many epitaphs from the Statilii *columbarium* as from the Volusii, and the former household seems better to represent the upper rungs of the social hierarchy than the latter. As Mouritsen acknowledges, the numbers are defined not by demographic reality, but by commemorative practices, which presumably differed greatly between slave and free, as well as among slaves of different value within the internal domestic order. His conclusion, that manumission did not operate on any apparently rational basis and that its function as an incentive for good behaviour arose from its capricious nature, is likely to find opposition among some scholars, given that a statistical analysis of commemorative evidence cannot supply the dynamics of human behaviour that must have affected the decision to manumit in a household of this size.[16] Nevertheless, these two examples provoke numerous questions for further study, including the degree to which they reflect general practice, and the significance of manumission, for both slave and master, if it was not a predictable matter, but operated on more arbitrary lines.

Written evidence of a unique kind is explored by Keegan in his analysis of the graffiti from the Palatine *paedagogium*, which has been identified as a possible 'school for slaves' of the imperial household. In their unbroken connection between inscriber and inscription, graffiti are marked by an immediacy of expression that conveys explicit and often intimate musings. Unlike the scattered graffiti of Pompeii, however, this corpus is contained with a specific archaeological context that can be directly related to slavery. For a slave society from which there are no slave narratives, the *paedagogium* graffiti offer a rare manifestation of a direct slave voice, undiluted by the conventions of formal epigraphy. Drawing on ideas from social theory, Keegan uses this evidence as a unique entrée into a potential slave subculture, although, as members of the *familia Caesaris*, they were slaves of a very special kind. Keegan probes this collection of graffiti gingerly for elucidation about levels of literacy, ethnicity, and sexual behaviour, among other issues. Both material and message are markedly ephemeral, but the assertion of slave identity that emerges in these individual utterances still resonates. Ranging from the trivial (a list of garments fit for imperial wear), to the explicitly sexual, to hints of a nascent Christianity in the imperial *familia*, the effect of casual, spontaneous expression imparts some inkling of the slave mentality. For example, the association between slave and ass, made plain in both word and image in graffito 1.289 and echoed in the Alexamenos graffito (1.246), reasserts a link that emerges elsewhere, and serves as eloquent articulation of the slave's profound connection with physical work and low status.[17]

The three epigraphic papers illustrate the challenges of using this material for slavery. Bruun and Mouritsen push back the curtain on epigraphy, so to speak, to reveal to the non-specialist some of the mechanics of a subject that is often perceived (rightly or wrongly) as too specialized and complicated for the outsider to penetrate. Both guide the reader by providing a methodical, progressive interpretation of their evidence, pointing out the factors that determine and limit its efficacy. Bruun's paper demonstrates just how much more there is to be demanded of the epigraphic material, how much depends on the questions that are asked, and how much on the nature of the selection that is made from within the mountain of material. He underlines one of the limitations of the many conventions of funerary commemoration in particular by reminding us that terms such as *verna* that apply at one stage of life were abandoned at another (by age twenty-five), meaning that the house-born status of many slaves was later subsumed in the epigraphic corpus simply by virtue of a long life. His study also reveals how scholarship on one aspect of slavery (the onomastics of slaves) can have unanticipated, and even somewhat surprising, implications for another (the slave supply). In setting out with transparency the factors that circumscribe his study (e.g., the partial nature of the Volusii inscriptions in comparison to the corpus of the Statilii, the obscurity of the gender of some names), Mouritsen guides us through the kinds of questions that can and cannot be asked of this highly valuable set of data. Much like the elite households of the Volusii and Statilii, the *paedogogium* must have provided a family structure and milieu for the slaves who lived and trained there, many of whom were probably children or young boys. Working outside the standard epigraphic conventions and their attendant biases, Keegan faces the challenge of piecing together fragile, inconsistent, and often ambiguous echoes of the slave voice. More discussion of this corpus is necessary, on its own terms, in comparison with other Roman graffiti, as well as on a cross-cultural level, assessing it as a form of resistance and exploring issues such as motive and audience. Keegan's chapter represents a first step in the exploitation of this potentially rich subject.

The *domus* remains the locus for the next two papers, which shift from written expressions to the physical reality of the house in their examination of slaves at work and the profound conceptual connection between slaves and work. As Mouritsen and Keegan's papers underscore, there was a close association between slaves and their work, since it was as working property that they were of value to their owners. For the same reason, work was of fundamental importance to slave identity, as demonstrated by the widespread use of occupational titles in funerary commemoration not only of slaves by others but also by slaves themselves and their surviving relatives in their self-commemoration. Yet, an ambiguity about work lingers. The elite conception of physical labour was pejorative, a 'pledge of servitude,' in Cicero's oft-cited formulation (*de Off.* 1.150–1), and was grounded in a bias based on social status. Moreover, the work slaves did, and the occupational title that came with it, was not of their own choosing, but was thrust upon them by their owners. A positive perspective on their work and pride taken in it was a natural outcome for many slaves, and, given the negative elite attitude, might even be construed as a form of resistance, as Sandra Joshel has argued elsewhere.[18] In her paper in this volume, Joshel considers domestic space in house and villa from the slave's perspective, rather than from that of the slave owners, which has been the more conventional approach.[19] Joshel applies an approach developed by American slavery historian Stephanie Camp called the 'geography of containment,' a conceptualization of the attitudes and cultural customs that restricted a slave's physical mobility. Camp also posited the existence of a 'rival geography,' a reaction of resistance by the slave against the regulation of domestic space imposed by the master. Unlike Camp, who relies heavily on contemporary written sources from both slave owner and slave, Joshel is forced to adapt to the realities of the Roman situation, for which there is only the master's voice, as expressed in the agricultural writers and other elite authors. By setting the prescriptions of Cato, Varro, and Columella against extant archaeological evidence, she attempts to highlight the role of domestic space as part of the armature of social control integral to institutionalized slavery.

Human behaviour, whether of slave or master, occurred within a set of spatial contexts that were constructed to serve necessary functions; an examination of those contexts, therefore, can add a spatial dimension to our understanding of how slave and master used and even perceived the places they inhabited. Joshel is ambitious; she undertakes no less than a psychology of space for the Roman slave. Using archaeological evidence from the *villa rustica* and the *domus*, Joshel identifies the physical spaces in which slaves were active and examines how those spaces could have been monitored and regulated by the buildings' plan, structural elements such as doorways, and by human surveillance. Re-examining the instructions for slave management contained in the agricultural writers, Joshel asks how slaves might have regarded and used space within villa and *domus* and how elements such as sight lines, accessibility, and the size of both static and dynamic areas (i.e., respectively, rooms and corridors) might have affected the slave's perception of the physical context of the household. While occupational title reflects a slave's responsibilities in many cases, such as *ianitor*, *atriensis*, or *cubicularius*, it also indicates a connection to physical space. A slave did not choose his task, but satisfactory performance enhanced his worth to his owner and increased his chances of receiving rewards such as tips or better food, as well as nurturing the perpetual hope of manumission. Joshel suggests that occupational title, even though imposed on a slave and not chosen voluntarily, might well have led to a figurative as well as literal appropriation of space, thereby granting a form of agency, if only on a psychological level. Ascertaining a possible 'rival geography' for the Roman context is not difficult if the forms of resistance recorded in ancient sources are viewed from the perspective of domestic space. Theft and sloth, two common transgressions attributed to slaves, can also be viewed as forms of resistance to the slave condition, and can be better understood when they are re-imagined as responses to real domestic space and the patterns of movement – and the restriction of movement – that the physical sphere permitted.[20]

Both Noel Lenski and Michele George keep the focus on the domestic context, but move from the perception and use of space to domestic decoration. Lenski considers the connection between slaves and work within the house through the literal objectification of slaves into utilitarian objects in his examination of household artefacts with an anthropomorphic character. In the 'aesthetic of service,' he sees the labour of real slaves, especially banquet slaves, transformed into tools, light stands, and tray bearers, versions of human tools reified and rendered instrumental in another form, in many cases reflecting the degradation and physical abuse of slavery itself. Lenski introduces comparative objects from American folk art to illuminate their role in reinforcing a connection between race and subjugation even after Emancipation, and as persistent reminders of the power white masters once held over black slaves. In the Roman context, such objects, whether utilitarian or decorative, are expressions of a mentality in which slavery was both normative and flourishing. Lenski's exploration of this material is an exercise in the use of evidence for slavery that might at first glance appear less direct than conventional textual sources, and which might to some seem tangential rather than germane. In fact, the existence of such objects conveys the experience of living in such a context, for both slave and master, more directly and cogently than the rare epitaphs that include the term *'servus,'* or the occasional anecdotes that pepper the standard sources.

The resonance of slavery in the interior decor of the Roman house is also the focus for George, as she considers the motif of 'Cupid Punished' as an artefact of Roman attitudes towards slaves. Presented in a gently comic way, the imagery of Cupid enduring the punishments of a slave was a slight theme in Roman art for which great claims cannot be made; yet, as George asserts, even in minor artistic evidence the shadow of institutionalized slavery can be traced. Drawing on parallels in juridical and literary evidence, she illustrates the intimate association between slavery and punishment at ancient Rome, and its transformation into domestic decoration. Cupid's impudence in myth, and the discipline it required, is set against the elite Roman fashion for possessing and displaying for guests favoured child slaves (*deliciae*), whom ancient sources reveal shared many of the same characteristics with the recalcitrant divine boy. By setting this imagery within the broader cultural context in which it was created, viewed, and valued, George argues that it is possible to obtain greater purchase on the way in which slavery and its cruelties were fundamental to the Roman mindset. In her discussion of the potential levels of meaning inherent in this artistic theme, she advocates more careful consideration of the visual landscape in which slavery thrived, and a more subtle appreciation of art as a mechanism for the expression of deeply ingrained social mores.

Natalie Kampen's paper keeps the focus on visual culture, but moves from the household to the military sphere in the provincial context in her study of funerary commemorations of soldiers and their *libertini*. Focusing on commemorations from the northern frontier, Kampen dissects the stela of Marcus Caelius, a unique example of this body of material on which two *liberti*, Privatus and Thiaminus, are commemorated in portrait form alongside their master, Marcus Caelius. The commemoration of *libertini* by their patrons, often on the same monument, is a common practice in the period (first century CE), especially in Cisalpine Gaul, where the status distinctions within individual households are adumbrated in clear visual terms through portrait and inscription.[21] The stela of Marcus Caelius, however, is the only extant example of a soldier who is commemorated with two of his *libertini*, with both patron and freedmen explicitly represented in epigraphic and figural form. Although Kampen is candid about the difficulties of drawing conclusions from a *unicum*, she considers related stelae and inscriptions in an effort to coax out meaning from this exceptional monument. The paper is therefore a valuable model for scholars of slavery, who, confronted with a paucity of evidence, must often use singular examples, whether from material culture or texts. Privatus and Thiaminus were clearly former slaves, as shown by the inclusion of libertination in their short inscriptions, yet they are represented by formal portraits, and not simply by means of scale, as in the more generic reliefs. They were not, Kampen argues, mere dogsbodies doing menial tasks, but highly valued slaves with special skills who benefited from a close relationship with their owner Marcus Caelius. The hierarchy of social, rather than legal, status that existed within slavery itself and that is well illustrated in the capital by the phenomenon of imperial slaves (*familia Caesaris*) emerges as a feature of slaves in the army on the distant borders of the empire. Kampen's study also illuminates the way in which the military context might have served the same purposes as the domestic household in providing the slave with a family life and a situation in which affective ties could thrive.

The studies in this volume represent attempts to exploit as far as possible the extant historical material and to explore its possibilities as a way of proposing new lines of enquiry for others. In recognition of the disparate nature of much of the evidence, the authors were encouraged to raise questions as much as to draw conclusions, and to bring their own diverse perspectives to bear on the same issue. As might be expected, the results are varied, and from this experiment the strengths and weaknesses of different approaches emerge as scholars feel their way forward in the often intractable pursuit of Roman slavery, integrating evidence or methodologies new to them. Several fertile areas for future work emerge from these efforts. For example, on the epigraphic front, there is an opportunity to refine current wisdom on the precise value of Roman naming practices in discerning a servile heritage. If a simplified reading of the *cognomen* in individual cases is no longer possible, as Bruun argues, how do we proceed from here? New directions in onomastics with consequences for slavery are suggested by Bruun's chapter, including more investigation of Greek *cognomina*, which, as noted by Solin himself, become more common among freeborn citizens as time goes by. Moreover, it seems clear that the chronology and distribution of filiation and libertination, the epigraphic markers indispensable for identifying freedmen in the archaeological record with security, require more detailed study.[22] The closed context of Mouritsen's inscriptions makes the connection with slavery clear, but his portrait of two elite *familiae* offers an example for other distinct epigraphic corpora, while his conclusions about manumission and social mobility within these households compels further reflection on the long-standing question of the elusive meaning of freed status in Roman society. The graffiti that constitute Keegan's source material, although unique in their imperial associations, are in fact part of a neglected set of data that calls out for more attention; the probability that echoes of the slave voice are contained within in it illustrate its value to slavery studies. If the epigraphic material tends to be centred in Italy, the chapter by Kampen points to the value of casting a wider net in looking for slaves in the provincial context, an area which has not yet received sustained consideration.

The domestic arena, where slaves were especially ubiquitous, has been an important context for slavery studies since the appearance of scholarship on the Roman family in the 1980s.[23] In a parallel development, the theme of domestic space enjoyed a floruit in Roman archaeology, resulting in a number of social analyses of the house, some indeed including slavery.[24] Joshel's chapter demonstrates that more can be done to locate the domestic slave of Roman social history in the physical space of Roman domestic architecture. While artefact distribution in Pompeian houses has as yet proven to offer only an unreliable reading of spatial function, recent work on the artefacts themselves might offer more scope for analysis.[25] Lenski's exploration of the visual manifestations of a world in which slavery thrived enriches our perceptions of domestic decor as well as suggests new ways of looking at domestic objects. In a similar vein, George's study of the potential interpretation of an aspect of domestic decor demonstrates the value in reconstructing the visual world of ancient Rome and reflecting on its effect on all who viewed it.

The aim of this volume has been to initiate a more reciprocal relationship between history and material culture in the study of Roman slavery. A potential pathway for both, however, might lie in the comparative approach, in reaching beyond the ancient world for creative stimulus. In this volume, Joshel and Lenski borrow from American slavery to illuminate their own examination of domestic architecture and anthropomorphic items, while comparative approaches to ancient slavery by historians go back to Finley himself, and have been adopted by Keith Hopkins, Orlando Patterson, and Walter Scheidel.[26] Archaeology, however, has been slower to embrace the comparative methodology, with Andrea Carandini's study of the villa at Settefinestre still the exception to the rule.[27] The burgeoning research into plantation archaeology in the American South and the Caribbean provides an example of what can be accomplished with a wealth of sources such as archives, slave narratives, abundant artefacts and structures, as well as slave cemeteries.[28] Although this represents an *embarras de richesses* compared to the paucity of Roman material, plantation archaeology nevertheless offers models that might provoke archaeologists to examine the site plans of Roman villas in new ways, or to ask new questions of other relevant material. In using slavery studies of nineteenth-century America as her model, Joshel follows in a path relatively little trodden by scholars of the Roman world, but one that deserves more attention. Historical archaeologist Jane Webster has drawn on the concept of 'creolization' in New World slavery to uncover traces of slavery in Roman Britain, a part of the empire where, despite intensive study for over a hundred years of a range of archaeological remains, there has been relatively little consideration of slavery.[29] Inspired by New World plantation archaeology, Webster suggests several possible ways to identify slaves in the material culture of Roman Britain, including the suggestion that slave quarters, even possibly the *ergastula* of Columella, might be seen in the cellars and round houses of villas in the province. Both Webster and Joshel attempt not merely to see the physical remnants of slavery in villa architecture, but also to reconstruct an understanding of the slave experience. Another potentially instructive model from New World plantation studies comes from historical archaeologist James Delle, who has produced a spatial analysis of Jamaican coffee plantations. Delle invokes the 'panopticon' prison design of eighteenth-century British philosopher Jeremy Bentham, later elaborated and applied to contemporary society by Michel Foucault, to assess what he terms 'spatialities of movement, surveillance, and resistance' in plantation design. For example, the overseer's house, located at a critical central position, provided points of surveillance onto both the slave quarters uphill and the coffee works downhill, keeping slaves under perpetual observation. Plantation archaeology might offer archaeologists new ways to interpret the remains of Roman villas, where slaves lived in large numbers, but which, as Joshel notes, have thus far offered relatively limited evidence of their presence.[30]

The comparative approach, however, has its own limitations. Although plantation archaeology might offer useful models for the interpretation of Roman villas, only infrequently is there data similar enough in kind and quantity to provide genuine comparison or, for that matter, even appropriate or relevant contrast.[31] Historical archaeologists of the New World have a much deeper pool of evidence on which to draw, including, for example, the opportunity to learn from the physical remains of slaves themselves through the osteological examination of slave skeletons found on plantation sites, which has allowed them to draw conclusions about life expectancy, diet, and weaning patterns.[32] For the Roman archaeologist of slavery who peruses these studies, the sheer quantity and range of data are overwhelming, and, as should be expected from historical archaeology, highly culturally specific. Similarly, the search for remnants of slavery in prehistoric societies, generally the work of archaeologists trained in anthropological methodology, is driven by a theoretical framework that often seems too ahistorical to be of value to the classical context. In neither case is it always easy to perceive an application to Roman slavery. This is not to criticize classical archaeology for avoiding theory, nor to repudiate theoretically minded archaeologists for reaching conclusions with no firm anchor in the Roman context, but merely to acknowledge the legitimate but divergent intellectual traditions between the two. It seems timely to suggest a third mode of scholarship, that takes its inspiration as it finds it, whether in ancient history (including those texts so much disparaged by non-classicists), art history, field archaeology, or studies of other slave cultures.

Conclusion

While the comparative approach can provide an interpretative structure within which to evaluate evidence of different kinds, there is a more fundamental remedy at hand. The studies presented here offer innovative ways to deepen our understanding of Roman slavery, but, above all, they illustrate the necessity of making the slave presence central to our conception of the Roman Empire itself. Rome was a slave society; the reality of slavery is therefore an essential aspect of all things Roman. The material culture of Roman slavery is difficult to recognize in the archaeological record partly because slaves themselves were not isolated from the rest of Roman society, but were woven into its very fabric. It is in fact their integration that we see reflected in the archaeological record, not their segregation. Yet, their difference from the free (or freed) population is unambiguous; while there were modulations in the degree of difference between slaves and the free poor, the distinction in legal status was also a distinction in social status with persistent and pervasive force. It is the challenge for historians and archaeologists interested in slavery, however, to bring together whatever evidence is available and to embed slaves into their own conception of the Roman world, just as slaves were so deeply embedded in the Roman mentality.

NOTES

1 Hopkins 1978; Finley 1998 offers the best collation of Finley's perspective on the lively and sometimes polemical scholarly debates about slavery that emerged in the highly politicized scholarship of the post-war era (including editor Brent Shaw's introduction). Finley's own understanding of Roman slavery was shaped by, and developed in opposition to, the more benign view of slavery expressed by Joseph Vogt (Vogt 1974), director of the German 'Forschung zur antiken Sklaverei' project founded in 1951 in Mainz and now based in Trier. The project continues to produce comprehensive studies of slavery, including the 'Bibliographie zur antiken Sklaverei' (Bellen et al. 2003), a comprehensive listing of publications on ancient slavery that is periodically updated, and most recently the 'Bilddatenbank zur antiken Sklaverei,' a database of digitized images of slaves in ancient art. See Binsfeld 2010.

2 Slavery studies: Wiedemann 1981; Bradley 1994; demography, e.g., Scheidel 1997; 2005; epigraphy, e.g., Joshel 1992; family, e.g., Bradley 1986; literature, e.g., Segal 1968; Fitzgerald 2000; McCarthy 2000; Bradley 2000.

3 Rostovtzeff 1926; Finley 1973.

4 'Of what use … is the vast outpouring of annual reports on the year's work or the third or the fourth year's? Of what use are more and more excavations when so many older ones have not been published at all? And, finally, of what use is archaeology anyway, apart from the museum pieces that sometimes come out of the debris if it leads to nothing more than reports?' (Finley 1971: 100).

5 Finley 1998: 268–9.

6 E.g., Scheidel 2003.

7 See an issue of the journal *World Archaeology* devoted to the topic of slavery from a diachronic perspective in various cultures from around the world (including, among others, neo-Babylonian, prehistoric Eurasian, Islamic African, and colonial South African), in which the lack of evidence and its attendant challenges to interpretation are reiterated throughout (*World Archaeology* 33, no. 1 [2001]).

8 Kolendo 1979. Nicholas Himmelmann's 1971 treatment of slaves in Greek art remains one of the few focused considerations of the subject (Himmelmann 1971).

9 Schumacher 2001; Thompson 2003; Roman art: Kampen 1981; Zimmer 1982; Clarke 2003; freedmen: Zanker 1975; Kleiner 1977; Petersen 2006; George 2005. Identifying freedmen in the archaeological evidence, however, presents its own difficulties; see Bruun in this volume.

10 E.g., Dunbabin 2003a; Clarke 1998; Roller, however, does consistently identify them as slaves (Roller 2006).

11 On the relative absence of slaves in evidence from Roman villas, long a curious problem, see Samson 1989; Webster 2005; and Mattingly 2008. The villa at Settefinestre is, of course, the oft-cited exception (Carandini 1985). See also Rossiter 1978: 40–8; Roth 2007 examines the problem from the historian's perspective.

12 E.g., Kajanto 1968, Weaver 1972, Treggiari 1975, Joshel 1992, Solin 1996.

13 For 'freedmen' monuments, see Petersen 2006.

14 Scheidel 1997, 2005; see also Harris 1999; Bradley 2004.

15 For a consideration of the archaeological aspect of *columbaria*, see Granino Cecere and Ricci 2008.

16 On manumission at Rome, see Wiedemann 1985; for comparative purposes, on manumission in slave systems of the modern era, see Brana-Shute and Sparks 2009.

17 *Labora aselle quomodo ego laboraui / et proderit tibi.* 'Toil, little donkey, in the manner in which I have toiled, and you will be rewarded for it'; see Solin and Itkonen-Kaila 1966: 1.289, 1. 246; see also Keegan, infra. For the proverbial connection between the slave and the ass, see Bradley 2000.

18 Joshel 1992; elite attitudes: Garnsey 1980; D'Arms 1981; George 2006.

19 Wallace-Hadrill 1996; George 1997b, 1997a.

20 On slave resistance, see Bradley 1990.

21 Pflug 1989; George 2005.

22 Solin 1971: 125. The reference is due to C. Bruun, who is pursuing some of these onomastic questions in future research.

23 E.g., the series of conference papers on the Roman family edited by Beryl Rawson (Rawson 1986, 1991; Rawson and Weaver 1997); see also George 2005; Dasen and Späth 2010.

24 Wallace-Hadrill 1996; Wallace-Hadrill and Laurence, 1997; George 1997b, 1997a.

25 Berry 1997a, 1997b; Allison 1999, 2004, 2006.

26 Finley 1973; Hopkins 1978; Patterson 1982; Scheidel 1997, 2005, 2008; see also Bradley 1994, 2008; Dal Lago and Katsari 2008.

27 Webster 2005; see also the lively and often polemical critique of classical archaeology in Webster 2008a, along with four response articles and a counter-response by Webster in an issue of the journal *Archaeological Dialogues* (15, no. 2: 2008).

28 Handler, Lange, and Riordan 1978; Singleton 1985, 1999; Armstrong 1990, 1999.
29 Webster 2005.
30 Delle 1998: 119–67; Handler, Lange, and Riordan 1978; Singleton 1985, 1999; Armstrong 1999.
31 See Mattingly 2008; Bradley 2008.
32 New world: Armstrong 1999: 180–1. The scientific study of human remains in the Graeco-Roman world, while intriguing, is still in its infancy. For a summary of the problem in classical archaeology, with a focus on zooarchaeology, see MacKinnon 2007; for slaves, see Carandini 1985, vol. 3:278–305, especially 284–7, regarding animal bones at Settefinestre, which suggest possible differences in the diet of slaves compared to those residing in other parts of the villa, and argues against the Catonian prescription of a vegetarian servile diet (*de Agr.* 56–8). See also Prowse et al. 2007.

1

Greek or Latin? The owner's choice of names for *vernae* in Rome*

CHRISTER BRUUN

Introduction

Scholars investigating ancient societies need to make use of all available sources – archaeological, epigraphic, and literary – since no single type of evidence by itself gives a full picture. A proper understanding of one piece of evidence in reality often requires familiarity with a range of skills that have been developed by 'neighbouring' fields within the study of classical antiquity. The origins of this paper lie in an attempt to bridge the not inconsiderable gap between archaeology and epigraphy. Obviously, inscriptions are texts, but as texts they differ from their literary counterparts in many significant ways. Inscriptions are usually short, and are normally devoid of literary ambition, although they often respect a number of formulaic conventions. Even more importantly in the current context, epigraphic texts, unlike most literary sources, normally survive as first-hand evidence – the medieval tradition of textual transmission has only rarely to be reckoned with. For over two decades 'text and context' has been a standard expression in epigraphic circles,[1] and scholars have learnt to evaluate as well as to value the contribution of an inscription's context. Although sometimes only the writing remains – perhaps on a simple stone plaque or a lead pipe – in more fortunate cases the original environment can be investigated, whether it be the room in which a graffito was once scratched, or the funerary monument to which an epitaph belonged. But even inscriptions with no extant archaeological context or provenance belong to Roman material culture, for their value goes beyond a mere translation of the text. Studying the style of lettering, the stone (or other text support), and any possible other visual elements will often reveal aspects of identity and social status to which a simple transcription cannot do justice. An epigraphic text that does belong to an archaeological object or context, such as a portrait bust or a tomb, conveys important and essential information that can dramatically enhance its historical value.

Paul Zanker's seminal article from 1975 on funerary relief portraits at Rome is known to all who study Roman freedmen, their social standing, and their mentality.[2] Zanker's multidisciplinary approach, which combined archaeology, art history, epigraphy, and history, has been taken up by a new generation of scholars, who have broadened the scope of study geographically and chronologically to reach beyond the city of Rome and the late Republican and Augustan periods.[3] In Zanker's original investigation, which included around 125 funerary reliefs from Rome and its immediate surroundings, it was the inscriptions attached to approximately fifty examples that enabled Zanker to talk about 'Freigelassenenporträts' in the first place, and it was the inscriptions that led him to identify this material as a genre of its own developed for the commemoration of freedmen.[4] Yet it is important to remember that Zanker's argument was based on an *interpretation* of the extant epigraphic evidence, and that not every epitaph attached to that group of reliefs identified the deceased as a *libertus*. It is probably a little-known fact that the socio-historical and onomastic evaluation of the inscriptions that was to accompany Zanker's work (and the preliminary results of which undoubtedly informed it) was never published.[5] This is not to cast suspicion on the results that have been achieved over the last three or four decades by scholars who have built on Zanker's article, which broke new ground in scholarship that operates in the interface between archaeology and epigraphy. However, we should not forget that at a fundamental level the epigraphic foundation was tentative, rather than firm, and that those same epigraphic premises, which in fact continue to inform current scholarship and which are commonly taken for granted, require thorough study.

In this paper I focus on one practically ubiquitous method used for interpreting epigraphic evidence, namely, onomastics. Personal names represent one of the most common, most significant, and, indeed, most sought-after elements in an inscription or on a monument since names can provide an entrée to issues such as social or cultural identity, family relationships, and patronage. Yet, such identifications are often based on a few long-standing, cherished, but rarely examined assumptions about Roman names and naming practices that in fact do not necessarily remain unscathed by closer scrutiny. The heuristic nature of this paper might be heretical to some, but it is my belief that the time has come to challenge some notions about Roman names that are widely accepted but which in fact have received insufficient examination by epigraphers themselves. I will first review the current status of our understanding of Roman onomastics as it is applied to slaves and freedmen, citing several areas in which further epigraphic study is warranted. Next, I will concentrate on the names of one special group, *vernae*, or house-born slaves, who, as will become clear below, constitute a particularly interesting focal point for this kind of examination. The material discussed is not confined to one particular context or period, although the city of Rome looms large and most texts date to between the late first and the mid-third centuries, but all are funerary inscriptions and therefore constitute a uniform corpus. A study of the names of *vernae* has ramifications for two wider questions: (1) the origin of slaves in Rome during the imperial period, still a hotly debated question, and (2) the significance in Rome of the use of a Greek *cognomen* versus a Latin one, a topic familiar to anyone who has studied slaves and freedmen in Roman inscriptions, from social historian to archaeologist.

Roman Onomastics and the Names of Slaves

First, it will prove useful to survey briefly the Roman naming system, in particular with regard to the choice of *cognomina* from a linguistic point of view. During the imperial period, free men in the Roman world were identified by the *tria nomina*, a name which consisted of three main parts: *praenomen*, *nomen gentile*, and *cognomen* – as, for example, in the name Aulus Didius Gallus.[6] There was little variation among *praenomina*, which is why they came to be abbreviated, with Aulus becoming A., Publius P., etc., while people had practically no choice regarding which *gentilicium* they bore; it was either inherited from the father, or, in the case of freed slaves, taken over from the former owner.[7] The *cognomen*, the third part of a free Roman's name, was bound by different conventions and practices, giving it the strongest individual character and making it of special interest to social historians.

The individual character of the *cognomen* does not, however, mean that Romans chose their *cognomina* themselves; on the contrary, in the case of freeborn individuals (*ingenui*) it was normally bestowed on them by their parents. In such cases, the *cognomen* might be specific to the bearer, but it might also be inherited from one of the parents. The other possibility for a freeborn person was to pick up a *cognomen* at some later point during his or her life. In the case of freedmen, *liberti* or *libertae*, the general belief among scholars today is that they likewise had very little to do with the choice of *cognomen*. Roman slaves, including *vernae*, bore only one name (the question of how they acquired it will play a considerable role below), and when they were freed the assumption among modern scholars is that they retained that name, which became the *cognomen*, the third part of the *tria nomina* that characterized free individuals. Thus, when freed, Cicero's trusted slave secretary Tiro became M. Tullius Tiro, and in official contexts he should have appeared as M. Tullius M(arci) l(ibertus) Tiro.

There are almost countless Roman *cognomina*, for they could be formed in many different ways, like family names in, for instance, Indo-European languages. Scholars have divided *cognomina* according to their origin in names derived from plants, animals, geographical features, physical features, particular events, other names, etc.[8] Another way of dividing them looks to linguistic criteria, separating those with a Latin etymology, such as Primus ('first'), Felix ('happy'), or Sabinus ('the Sabine') from those with a Greek origin, such as Alexander (after the conqueror), Eutychus ('lucky'), Hermes (after the Greek god), or Onesimus ('profitable').[9]

Scholars concerned with the freedmen and commoners of Rome and Roman Italy scarcely need reminding that a Greek *cognomen* is conventionally considered typical for both freedmen and slaves in this region.[10] For this reason, whenever one encounters common Romans in inscriptions or in other contexts it is important to pay attention to the linguistic character of their *cognomina*. Categorizing *cognomina* properly is of interest to philologists and historians, and obviously to archaeologists as well, whenever they encounter an artefact or an archaeological context that is somehow connected to a Roman bearing a *cognomen*.

Ever since Theodor Mommsen's seminal 1860 article on Roman onomastics scholars have been alerted to the frequency of Greek *cognomina* in our Roman sources.[11] Today there are two generally held views in regard to the use of Greek *cognomina* in Rome and Italy; both were forcefully argued in Solin's 1971 monograph:[12]

(1) The first tenet relates to ethnicity, arguing that a Greek *cognomen* does *not* prove that a person has his or her origin in the Greek-speaking eastern parts of the Roman Empire.[13] That kind of origin is to be sure a possibility, but such a person, or his or her ancestors, may instead come from, say, Western, Central or Northern Europe, from North Africa, or from a population in the East that did not speak Greek.

(2) The second tenet relates to social history, arguing that a Greek *cognomen* is an indicator that a person is of servile origin, or in other words that the bearer of the Greek *cognomen* or a close ancestor had been a slave.[14]

Greek *Cognomina* in Latin Inscriptions

It is hardly an exaggeration to say that the notion that a Greek *cognomen* indicates 'servile origin' today has become akin to a general rule employed by scholars studying a variety of different subjects relating to Roman society and culture.[15] Indeed, simply adopting this rule is a convenient way for scholars to avoid engagement with the complexities of Roman onomastics. It is, however, important to recognize that the foundation is constituted by the work of Roman onomasticians, who work with large numbers and map out general trends and tendencies. Two figures are central when dealing with such trends: (1) the proportion of Greek names among the names born by slaves and freedmen, and (2) the proportion of Greek names in Rome at large.

The data now available through the second edition of Heikki Solin's *Namenbuch* and through his *Sklavennamen* supersede earlier surveys of the proportions of Greek and Latin *cognomina* in Rome, as well as surveys of the kind of names born by slaves and freedmen.[16] In the material that Solin included in his work on Roman slave names, around 67 per cent (18,424) are Greek names, 31.2 per cent (8,579) are Latin names, while other names (so-called barbarian ones)[17] make up a mere 1.8 per cent (506).[18] However, no one has sifted through all the existing sources (overwhelmingly epigraphical) in order to count the proportion of Greek *cognomina* versus Latin ones in the general population of the capital. In the past decades, several scholars have, however, worked with different selections of data, all finding that the Latin names are in the minority (just as among the slave names), while the figure for the Greek names (including a few 'barbarian' ones) hovers at around 60 per cent or more.[19] This figure, or rather estimate, is relatively close to the proportion of Greek *cognomina* among the slave names. This might actually lead to the suspicion that Greek names were simply fashionable in Rome, whether a person was freeborn or a slave – in which case the 'servile character' of the Greek *cognomen* would turn out to be a myth – were it not for the belief of many scholars that most of the individuals who carry Greek names in the general population were in fact freedmen (or of servile descent, whatever the exact meaning of that term is). That is to say, freedmen are believed massively to dominate the funerary inscriptions in Rome, which provide the vast majority of our sources for individuals from ancient Rome.[20]

There are further reasons for suspecting that Roman commoners who are *incerti* (this is the term commonly used for individuals who are free, but whose status – freeborn or freed slave – is not stated and thus remains uncertain) and carry Greek names are freedmen or closely related to freedmen. One reason is provided by Solin's survey of persons who expressly state that they are freeborn through the use of filiation (the inclusion of the father's *praenomen* in their nomenclature), as in M. Tullius M(arci) f(ilius) Cicero. A freed slave had no legal father and could not include filiation is his or her nomenclature. While there were only 2,508 persons in Solin's material, the

Table 1. The decrease in the number of Greek *cognomina* in successive generations among Roman commoners according to Frank 1916: 693.

Father with Greek *cognomen*: 849		Father with Latin *cognomen*: 488	
son with Greek *cognomen*: 450	son with Latin *cognomen*: 399	son with Greek *cognomen*: 53	son with Latin *cognomen*: 435

result was clear: of those who were the freeborn *filius/filia* of a Roman, 88.6 per cent bear a Latin *cognomen* (2,223 cases), while only 10.2 per cent bear a Greek one (256 cases).[21] Thus the Latin *cognomen* clearly seems to be favoured by the freeborn.[22]

Thus, there are several indications that the Greek *cognomen* was much used by slaves and freedmen at the expense of Latin ones, while freeborn individuals in Rome preferred Latin *cognomina*. In addition, several investigations of naming patterns among families of commoners in Roman Italy show that the presence of Greek names decreases from one generation to the next – the central point being that the successive generation should be considered to be freeborn. As persuasive as tables 1 and 2 may seem, however, they share a feature that provides one rationale for the present study, as we shall see.

The first to carry out this kind of generational onomastic survey and to interpret the result as proof of the undesirability of Greek *cognomina* was Tenney Frank, who presented figures based on 13,900 inscriptions in *CIL* VI 2–3. He found 1347 cases where he could identify the names of a father-son pair (see table 1), and showed that the Greek *cognomina* diminished from 64 per cent in the paternal generation to 38 per cent in the next generation.[23]

Later similar surveys were carried out by Hilding Thylander and Lily Ross Taylor.[24] Thylander studied inscriptions from Italian seaports[25] in which both the parents and a child were known (see table 2), while Taylor added material from a sample from Rome (the funerary inscriptions recorded in *CIL* VI 17478–26713).[26]

Once again the result follows the general trend of a diminishing portion for the Greek names. One important issue here is the explanation that scholars have given for this onomastic behaviour: the fact that the proportion of Greek names tends to decrease is explained as deriving from the wish of the parents to conform to society at large, to liberate their children from the stigma of bearing a Greek *cognomen*. As Solin writes, 'These statistics indicate a preconception against the use of Greek *cognomina*, namely so, that the freedmen and their descendants perceived the Greek *cognomen* as a burden, as a reminder of the status of former slave.'[27]

Table 2. Generational shifts in the use of Greek and Latin cognomina in Rome and Italy according to Thylander 1952.

cognomen of parents	place	children, Greek *cognomen*	children, Latin *cognomen*
1. both Greek	Italian ports	100 (52 %)	91
	Rome	123 (57 %)	93
2. father Greek	Italian ports	63 (48 %)	68
mother Latin	Rome	37 (35 %)	67
3. father Latin	Italian ports	22 (27 %)	60
mother Greek	Rome	37 (29 %)	90
4. both Latin	Italian ports	15 (11 %)	118
	Rome	11 (12 %)	79
Total		415	670

Yet it is obvious from both tables 1 and 2 that in the second generation there is a fair number of Roman *ingenui* who still carry a Greek *cognomen*. Even more importantly, the downward trend for Greek names is not present everywhere. There is also group 4 in table 2, which normally receives little attention. Here are registered pure 100 per cent 'Latin' couples, who generate new citizens bearing a Greek *cognomen*! Of the children born to parents with Latin names, one in ten is given a Greek *cognomen*. This seems to run contrary to the assumption of a cultural bias and of the significance of the Greek *cognomen* in Roman society.[28]

The argument just presented is one significant reason (and there are others that due to space limitations will have to wait for a later treatment) for why I believe that it is warranted to revisit the question of how decisive a criterion the Greek *cognomen* is when identifying freedmen in the Roman world. This is where the names of Roman *vernae* come into play. The nomenclature of Roman *vernae* represents a field of study that is not only rewarding in itself but that also has a bearing on the general question of the value of a Greek *cognomen* for determining Roman social status.

The Onomastics of *Vernae* in Rome

The Latin word *verna* in most cases refers to a slave born and bred in the owner's household, although *verna* can also denote a free individual, an indigenous person, or someone from Rome.[29] Among Roman slaves, *vernae* are considered normally to have enjoyed a more favourable situation than other slaves, as they grew up in their master's house, and ties of affection with different members of the household, including their owner's children, would have had a greater probability of developing.[30]

There are almost six hundred inscriptions from Rome in which the term *verna* appears with the meaning of 'home-born slave.' A few typical inscriptions read as follows (I will label the inscriptions cited in this article from A to K to make cross-referencing easier):[31]

(A) *Cassia Epinice Amandae vernae suae f(ecit) vix(it) ann(is) VIII*
     mens(ibus) III die I
     (CIL VI 11315)
     'Cassia Epinice made this for Amanda her home-born slave, who lived eight years, three months and one day'

(B) *Dis Manibus Aricino Volusiaes Phoebes verna(e) vix(it) ann(is) II*
     men(sibus) VIII fecet [sic] mater
     (CIL VI 12306)
     'To the departed spirits. For Aricinus a home-born slave of Volusia Phoebe who lived two years, eight months, his mother made (this memorial)'

(C) *D(is) M(anibus) Oniro ver(nae) dulcissimo qui v(ixit) a(nnis) IIII*
     dieb(us) XXXXIV et T. Laelio Philippo Laelia Glycera coniugi bene
     merenti et M. Ulpius Aug(usti) lib(ertus) Eutyches fecerunt
     (Via Imperiale no. 18a)
     'To the departed spirits. For Onirus a home-born slave who lived four years and forty-four days and for T. Laelius Philippus. Laelia Glycera made this for her well-deserving husband together with M. Ulpius Eutyches, imperial freedman'

(D) *Diis Manibus. Theocrito vix(it) ann(is) II mens(ibus) XI diebus XI*
     horis IIII Maelius Propinquos vernae b(ene) m(erenti)
     (Via Imperiale no. 254)
     'To the departed spirits. For Theocritus who lived two years, eleven months, eleven days, four hours, Maelius Propinquus (made this) for his well-deserving home-born slave'

(E) *D(is) M(anibus) Bassae vixit annis XV fecit M. Antonius Philocalus*
     vernae suae
     (CIL VI 15329)

'To the departed spirits. For Bassa who lived fifteen years M. Antonius Philocalus made (this memorial) for his home-born slave'

(F) *Fortis Caesar(is) n(ostri) ser(vus) ver(na) pediseq(uus) domu(u)m Palatin(arum) et Ulpia Calpe fecer(unt) sibi posterisque suis*
(*CIL* VI 8658)
'Fortis, home-born slave of our Emperor, foot servant in the Palatine residences, and Ulpia Calpe made (this funerary monument) for themselves and their offspring'

Evidently, we are dealing with funerary inscriptions erected by somebody else for the *verna* in question in five cases out of six, and this reflects the actual situation. There are practically no other sources in which home-born slaves appear, except for *vernae* in the imperial household (as in case F). The *vernae* from private households cited here all died young. In the five first examples quoted above, fifteen years is the highest recorded age, and it has been shown that in Rome *verna* is used for slaves in private households only up until the age of twenty-five.[32] This does obviously not mean that all *vernae* were dead by age twenty-five, but it indicates that there were reasons why the term *servus verna* was not used for those who lived longer.[33] There will be more to say about the pattern of commemorating *vernae* below.

The names of *vernae* have interested scholars investigating aspects of Roman slavery at several moments in the past, as part of a general investigation of home-born slaves, or simply in connection with the naming of slaves. The main question that has been asked is whether there is any difference between the names born by the *vernae* and by the general population of slaves and freedmen. We saw above that in Rome Greek names dominate by about 2:1 among slaves and freedmen in general. Two studies show the opposite trend among the *vernae*.

In his investigation of the names of *vernae* from Rome and in a corpus comprising 575 individuals, Solin found 249 cases of Greek names versus 326 Latin ones (see table 3). The proportion among these 575 slaves is 43.3 per cent Greek names versus 56.7 per cent Latin ones, when the expected outcome is roughly 69 per cent non-Latin to 31 per cent Latin names (that is the overall distribution of names among slaves and freedmen in Solin's *Sklavennamen*; see n. 19).[34]

Solin used his result to answer a different question than the one that is at issue here, namely, to prove that Greek names could be given to slaves *born in Rome*. Although he had to concede that this occurred with lesser frequency than in the slave population as a whole, Solin's figures were enough to show that a Greek *cognomen* is not proof of its bearer's origin in

Table 3. The linguistic character of the names born by vernae compared to all the slave names in Rome (numbers from Solin 1971 and Solin 2001; cfr. n. 19 above).

Slave / freedman *cognomina*	Greek	Latin
among the *vernae* in Rome	43.3%	56.7%
in the total evidence from Rome	68.8% (including 1.8 'barbarian')	31.2%

the Greek-speaking part of the Mediterranean (as several scholars in previous generations had argued, and as is occasionally still assumed in some scholarly works).[35]

A few years later Elisabeth Herrmann-Otto dedicated a massive monograph to the *vernae* of the Roman world, including evidence from a much wider geographical area than Solin had done. Her study of the names of the *vernae* led, not surprisingly, to very similar results, although it was based on a less complete collection of the material from Rome itself. In addition, the author separated the *vernae* of private households from those in the *familia Caesaris*.[36] In the former group, some 37 per cent of the *vernae* had a Greek *cognomen*, against almost 63 per cent with a Latin one (see table 4). In the *familia Caesaris* (one instance appears above in the inscription labelled F) the Greek names were better represented, but even here they made up less than half of the total.[37]

All in all, the preference for Latin names over Greek ones when naming *vernae* in Rome is not in doubt (incomplete as our evidence may be). A few new examples culled from recent epigraphic corpora from Rome can be added; they show some deviation from the expected outcome, but cannot change the general trend.[38]

Of interest here is the question Herrmann-Otto asked of her material (different from the one that engaged Solin above): she was simply interested in seeing what the onomastic preferences among the *vernae* were, and in explaining the trend she detected. Although she did not dwell particularly long on the explanation, she did refer to another work by Solin, in which it had been argued that a freedman father (who often carried a Greek name) likely 'chose a Latin name for his son, as being more respectable.'[39]

As we saw above in the section, 'Greek *cognomina* in Latin inscriptions,' the common view today is that Greek *cognomina* in Rome are considered to have had a 'servile taint,' and that therefore individuals tended to avoid them, if possible. So, for instance, the social stigma that scholars see attached to Greek *cognomina* is given as the reason for why, in cases where we can follow the naming over at least two generations, the tendency is to

Table 4. The linguistic character of the names used by vernae in Herrmann-Otto's lists (1994: 414–20).

	Latin *cognomen*	Greek *cognomen*
vernae in private households	ca 300 (62.5%)	ca 180 (37.5%)
vernae in imperial ownership (only Rome and surroundings)	162 (52.2%)	148 (47.8%)
vernae in imperial ownership (overall)	211 (55.1%)	172 (44.9%)

move away from Greek names to Latin ones, as in the following case (where Helpis, 'Hope,' is Greek, Felicissima obviously Latin):

(G) *D(is) M(anibus). Bene maerenti [sic] fecit Oppia Helpis Felicissim(a)e filiae qu(a)e vixit annis XII menses [sic] nove(m)*
    (Via Imperiale no. 13)
    'To the departed spirits. For her well-deserving daughter Felicissima who lived twelve years, nine months Oppia Helpis made (this memorial)'

That this move towards Latin *cognomina* is no more than a trend, however, and not a law of nature, can easily be demonstrated. In the following example the daughter's name Olympias has an obvious Greek etymology, while the father carries a Latin name:[40]

(H) *D(is) M(anibus) Octaviae Olympiadi q(uae) v(ixit) a(nnis) XV m(ensibus) VI dieb(us) VIIII fil(iae) dulcissim(ae) fecit Octavius Victor pater*
    (Via Imperiale no. 221)
    'To the departed spirits. For Octavia Olympias who lived fifteen years, six months, nine days Octavius Victor her father made (this memorial) for his sweetest daughter.'

The explanation given for the phenomenon of switching from a Greek *cognomen* to a Latin one in the next generation is always the same: these individuals attempt to disguise the servile background of their children, which (allegedly) would have been revealed by bestowing a Greek *cognomen* on them.[41]

This situation prevails also among the *vernae*, as illustrated above in the examples labelled A, B, and E. Herrmann-Otto presents the following

Table 5. The occurrence of Greek and Latin *cognomina* among owners and their
vernae (after Herrmann-Otto 1994)

	owner has Greek *cognomen*	owner has Latin *cognomen*
verna has Greek *cognomen*	99 cases	51 cases
verna has Latin *cognomen*	114 cases	109 cases

numerical analysis of her data (see table 5). Although there are many examples to the contrary, a trend favouring Latin *cognomina* is visible:[42]

Solin's and Herrmann-Otto's surveys of the names born by the *vernae* seem to agree with the general view that, among commoners in Rome, for reasons of status it was more desirable to carry a Latin name than a Greek one. Scholars have to my knowledge not taken the discussion of *vernae* further, nor has anything in this current picture been challenged.

How Were *Vernae* Named?

It seems intuitive that there should be a difference between the names of *vernae* and other slaves in Rome, for it could be argued that *vernae* constituted a particularly favoured group. There are two reasons for this supposition. First, one can advance a general a priori argument: they were born in the owner's house, where they had a chance to form affectionate bonds with the master's family. Some *vernae* might even have been sired by the owner or a close relative of the owner, and thus there might have existed an even stronger reason for affection. Second, and perhaps more importantly, there is concrete evidence to show that such bonds in fact existed. The most common source for these slaves are funerary inscriptions, such as the ones presented above, to which a few more are added below, erected by the master (not by the parents), which proves (in these cases anyway) the particular tie between master and slave that one might have anticipated. For understandable reasons, normally a young person who received a funerary commemoration did so from his or her parents (while many probably received none). Richard Saller has shown that among individuals in Rome who died before the age of twenty-five years and received a funerary commemoration, the overwhelming majority did so from their parents: 92 per cent for the age bracket 10–14 years, 87 per cent for the age bracket 15–19 years, and 75 per cent for the age bracket 20–24 years.[43] This is not the case in four of the five funerary inscriptions mentioning *vernae* we saw above (examples A–E), nor in the following ones:

(J) *Volusia Pulchra Ursulo vernae suo karissimo posuit*
     (*CIL* VI 29563)
     'Volusia Pulchra erected this (funerary monument) for Ursulus her
     dearest home-born slave'

(K) *Ianuario vernae que vixit annos XXII menses V fecit Claudia Tryfosa*
     vernae suo
     (*CIL* VI 19633)
     'Claudia Tryfosa made (this memorial) for her home-born slave
     Ianuarius the *verna* who lived twenty-two years and five months'

But in probing the evidence for the onomastics of Roman *vernae* somewhat deeper some puzzling features emerge. Nowhere is the mechanism discussed by which a home-born slave received a Latin name. And how widespread was the practice of bestowing Latin names on home-born slaves? It stands to reason that if the owner knew that he was the father of a slave baby, he might have wanted to promote the child, in which case choosing a Latin name may have seemed a suitable action. Yet there are other possibilities that may or may not have led to the same affective relationship, possibilities that normally have not found a place in modern scholarly discussions. Would a slave grandchild of the *dominus* or *domina* have been singled out in the same way (for instance, a child sired by their teenage son)? And what about the slaves that were the property of the *domina* – when her female slaves gave birth and she suspected that her husband was the father, was it likely that these children too received 'special treatment' and a Latin name? The modern scholar, a prisoner of bourgeois values, may doubt it. Perhaps it was a happier occasion when female slaves gave birth after a casual visit by a favourite uncle or a cousin from abroad.

These eventualities all lead up to an important general question: should we in fact assume that the owner predominantly chose a Latin name for *any* slave child born within the walls of his or her *domus*, not just for those suspected of being the offspring of the owner's family? Before attempting to answer this question, we need to consider the moment at which slaves were given their names, and what influences were at play when the naming took place. Neither this question nor any of the subsequent ones addressed in this paper have to my knowledge received any previous scholarly discussion.

Freeborn Roman children were given their name very early in life, on the eighth (for girls) or ninth (boys) day of their life.[44] No information exists about the ritual of naming slave babies, or if indeed there even was one. It seems possible that it was a less solemn event, and one that had a less regular form (although this will have differed from household to household, and will have depended, among other factors, on the size of the slave *familia*).[45]

The name of a freeborn child was always chosen by the parents. For a slave child, one can imagine three possible sources for the name: the master, the *vilicus* or someone else who was supervising the slaves, and the slave parent(s) of the baby.[46] Herrmann-Otto concluded that 'the influence of the parents is slight in the naming of *vernae*,'[47] but we have practically no useful evidence; she based her statement on the few known cases where one slave parent has the same name as the young slave, or a clearly related name (such as mother Servanda, son Servatus).[48] Slave parents may equally well have chosen names for their children that did not derive from either parent's name; we cannot know. To imagine that the slave parents might have exercised some influence in naming is not impossible; although slaves could not legally marry, they could unofficially form families, and clearly the Roman legal texts assumed that family relations among slaves (parents-children, siblings, etc.) were known.[49]

We might also consider the possibility that owners did not generically favour Latin names over Greek ones, but did so only in a few cases involving their own illegitimate children (in the case of male owners) and their favourite slaves (regardless of blood ties to the owners). Undoubtedly there will have been affectionate bonds between owners and little servants or playmates. The problem here is that such pleasing qualities in a favourite slave will have become noticeable only with the passing of time, several years after the original naming took place. There are no sources that indicate that a favourite slave could be given a new (and more respectable) name, although one cannot exclude it, as name change was permitted in Roman society.[50] Therefore this line of thought points in the direction of a general trend to give home-born slaves Latin names; otherwise our evidence makes no sense.

Finally, one might also underline the fact that a large number of the funerary commemorations of *vernae* were erected by women (as in our examples A–C, J, and K above). In these cases we are unlikely to be dealing with blood ties between commemorator and slave (had the Roman *matrona* in question been the mother, it is difficult to see how the child could have remained a slave).[51] This fact also points to the likelihood that any *verna* tended to be given a Latin name.

In conclusion, the evidence from the names of *vernae* in Rome indicates that the use of Latin names in this group was much more common than in the slave population at large.[52] There are certain reasons to believe that this was a practice that could involve many other home-born slaves besides those who were identified as being blood relations of the owners. One might doubt this conclusion by pointing to the small number of inscriptions that provide our data for *vernae*, claiming that all we find in these texts are the most favoured slaves, for whom the owner was willing to spend money on a funerary monument (and who tended to carry Latin names more often than the average *verna*). Yet this counter-argument is not compelling, for what is relevant is the comparison with the general slave / freedman population, and in the latter group too our evidence is, obviously, skewed in favour of the most successful individuals, those who were most favoured by their owners, just as in the case of *vernae*.

The *Vernae* of Rome and the Roman Slave Supply

Setting out from the tentative suggestion that Latin names may have been overall more common among the home-born slaves as a group than in the slave / freedman population at large, some interesting implications emerge. Let us once more contrast the results from the onomastic study of *vernae* in Rome with the overall distribution of slave names as evident in Solin's corpus (see table 6).[53]

The fact that the large majority of (identified) slaves in fact bore Greek names now requires an explanation. Most of these slaves clearly cannot have been born in their owner's house, for in that case, as we just saw, they would mostly have carried Latin names. If the slave and freedman population of Rome consisted largely of home-born slaves our name statistics would look very different (always provided it truthfully reflects the actual situation in antiquity, which admittedly is a different matter that cannot be pursued here).

That leaves just two possibilities for explaining the origin of the majority of the slaves and freedmen we encounter in our Roman evidence: they were either purchased on the market (whether they were imported from abroad or were born somewhere in Italy),[54] or they were born in conditions where they never encountered their master and the names were given by a *vilicus* or someone else who routinely chose typical slave names, which mostly were Greek. It may be significant that *vernae* in the *familia Caesaris* carry Greek names more commonly than *vernae* in private homes, although here too the Latin names make up the majority.[55] Herrmann-Otto prefers to see this as a sign that imperial slaves, who often had an enhanced status due to their social connections, did not care about the possible stigma of a Greek *cognomen*.[56] But since that supposed feeling of unassailable superiority of an adult *servus Caesaris* cannot explain how he acquired his Greek *cognomen* in the first place, at a very tender age, it seems preferable to explain the greater frequency of Greek *cognomina* among the *vernae Caesaris* differently. It seems to me that only two parties could have been involved in the

Table 6. A comparison between the distribution of Latin and non-Latin *cognomina* among all the slaves and freedmen in Rome and among vernae.

	Greek and 'barbarian'	Latin
Cognomina of slaves and freedmen in Rome (Solin 1996)	68.8%	31.2%
Cognomina among *vernae* in Rome (Solin 1971)	43.3%	56.7%
Cognomina among *vernae* (non-imperial) (Herrmann-Otto 1994)	37.5%	62.5%

naming process of imperial slaves: the overseer and the parent(s). This may be one reason why the Greek names are somewhat more frequent.[57]

There are some interesting consequences deriving from table 6 that are relevant for the lively and ongoing debate about the sources of Roman slaves and the size of the slave population. In that debate, William Harris advocated a number of different ways in which the Roman slave population would have been reproduced, namely, besides the obvious source represented by home-born slaves, through the importation of slaves (many captured outside the borders of the Roman Empire), through self-enslavement, and through the enslavement of foundlings (made possible by widespread incidence of child exposure).[58]

A different solution was advocated by Walter Scheidel, who, based on various demographic arguments, argued that home-bred slaves must have provided the bulk of new slaves during the imperial period, as much as 80 per cent.[59] This view now seems less likely in the light of the onomastic material. The names of *vernae* in Italy have played no part in that debate to date,[60] but looking at the name statistics we have, it seems clear that our onomastic material from Rome would not have the composition it has if large numbers of *vernae*, who bore Latin *cognomina* in six cases out of ten, had regularly entered the free population of Rome after manumission.

Conclusion: The Paradoxical Character of the Latin *Cognomina*

In addition to this contribution to the debate about the Roman slave supply, the study of the naming of *vernae* in Rome points to other features relevant to the realities of slavery in Rome. It has become almost a 'factoid' in modern scholarship that there was a social stigma attached to Greek *cognomina*, because such *cognomina* were overwhelmingly born by slaves and freedmen. The sources indeed show a far greater frequency of Greek names than Latin ones among slaves and, consequently, among freedmen, but our figures can only show general tendencies, and I believe that we are far from justified in claiming that a Greek *cognomen* in each and every case is a safe indication of slave or freedman status or even of 'servile descent,' whatever that means.

Perhaps somewhat paradoxically, while setting out to examine one aspect of the use of Greek *cognomina* among the slaves of Rome, namely, the frequency of Greek names among *vernae*, this paper has come to devote much attention to Latin *cognomina*, in particular among this group of home-born slaves. We have seen that there is a distinct possibility that Latin names were more frequent among home-born slaves than were Greek names, which in Rome would mean that a certain portion of free Romans (how many depends on how one thinks slave recruitment during the Empire was structured) who were of 'servile descent' would have been using Latin names. This realization, when combined with the commonly held, though little discussed, assumption that a very large portion of the funerary monuments in Rome, Ostia, and the vicinity of the capital were erected to commemorate freedmen, leads to the following and perhaps somewhat startling and paradoxical conclusion: a Latin *cognomen* borne by a commoner in Rome is quite likely the sign of 'servile descent,' because *vernae* were predominantly given Latin names, and because most commoners we find in Roman inscriptions of the imperial period were probably freedmen and their close descendants.

Thus, while stressing against the common view that freeborn commoners are found to use Greek names in not negligible numbers, this paper proposes a re-evaluation of the use of Greek *cognomina*, a question I intend to pursue further in a future project, focusing also on the chronological dimension that I have not touched upon here.[61] This study also suggests a reassessment of the significance of the Latin *cognomina* in our epigraphic evidence. In view of the current understanding of the composition of the evidence, it seems to be less important that statistics show that Latin names became more popular in the generations that followed upon manumission. It may well be that relatively few freeborn individuals in those successive generations are in fact recorded in the surviving evidence.[62] Those who bear Latin *cognomina* in common Roman epitaphs may be either the children of freedmen or *vernae* who began their life as home-born slaves.

One further objective for future research should be to evaluate the reasons for that dwindling portion of Greek names in families in Rome as illustrated above (see tables 1–2). Are we dealing with a phenomenon that depends on social factors (such as stigma and prejudices), or are we facing a primarily linguistic phenomenon? By a linguistic phenomenon I mean a situation in which the majority of the individuals in a certain context (e.g., freedmen) use one particular language, so that it becomes natural to use names that have an etymology which is understandable in that language. Is a situation plausible in which only the quantitative relations between two languages would be at play, while there would not at the same time, primarily or partially, exist a pressure motivated by social status to choose names in one particular language?[63] And is it at all justified to attempt to separate these two potential influences on onomastic trends among the commoners in Rome, Ostia, and the rest of central Italy? It may seem unwarranted to end with a series of questions, but it is my belief that for too long scholars have been content to regard the question of the use of Greek or Latin *cognomina* as settled. The study of the names given the *vernae* has, it seems to me, opened up a number of questions that require further investigation.

NOTES

* I wish to express my gratitude to Michele George for the invitation to the conference and for her helpful comments on this paper and earlier versions. For reasons of space, the present paper only contains part of the presentation delivered at the conference; my thanks also to those who commented on the original version, and to the two anonymous readers. The research for this paper was much assisted by a Standard Research Grant from the Social Sciences and Humanities Research Council of Canada, which is gratefully acknowledged.

1 See, for example, the contributions in Solin, Salomies, and Liertz 1995 (going back to a conference in 1991).

2 Zanker 1975.

3 E.g., Wrede 1981: 29–30, 95–105, 256–8 and passim; Kockel 1993: 77 and passim; George 2005; Petersen 2006; see also Kleiner 1977. On a related type of monument, funerary altars with portraits, there is Kleiner 1987, but Kajava 1988 in a penetrating review showed how much additional and essential information is provided by a close study of the inscriptions that accompany these objects.

4 Zanker 1975: 269.

5 See Zanker 1975: 267. Some twenty years later, Kockel 1993: 56 and 77 still referred to the same expected contribution, and added that while awaiting its publication he himself would avoid pronouncing on epigraphical and historical aspects of the reliefs.

6 On the development of the Roman name system, see briefly H. Solin, 'Names, personal, Roman,' *OCD*[3], Oxford 1996: 1024–5; see also Solin 1996b (on *cognomina* only) and Solin 2002. Women rarely carried a *praenomen*, so in their case it is more accurate to talk about a two-name system.

7 In the case of illegitimate children, the *gentilicium* would be that of the mother.

8 The standard work to consult is Kajanto 1965.

9 For any arguments about the use of Latin versus Greek *cognomina* in Rome and Italy to be meaningful, one must be able to assume that the linguistic character of a *cognomen* was as easily identifiable to ancient Romans as it is to modern philologists. This is the common assumption today, recently reiterated by Solin 2009: 61–2.

10 It is if course the case that onomastic habits varied in the eastern parts of the Roman Empire, as the linguistic context was different. Kajanto's 1968 study of naming practices in several Italian cities shows some local variances but no major ones (Kajanto 1968). Still, it stands to reason that in southern Italy, where Greek was still spoken during the imperial period, the onomastic practice will have had its own peculiarities.

11 Mommsen 1864: 59–60 (originally published in *RhM* 15, 1860: 169–210).

12 Solin 1971: 146–58; repeated in, for instance, Solin 2007: 1370–1.

13 The opposite view, that a Greek *cognomen* indicated Eastern origin, was notoriously presented by Frank 1916 as part of his argument that 'inferior' Eastern elements had overrun and destroyed the Roman state. It was criticized by Gordon (1924: 106) as well as by Chantraine (1967: 132–8). Weaver (2001: 114 n. 6) is surprisingly unclear on the issue, apparently equating a Greek *cognomen* with an Eastern origin.

14 This statement can be found, for instance, in Solin 1971: 123 (with further references to scholars such as M.L. Gordon, A.M. Duff, J. Carcopino, L.R Taylor, I. Kajanto, and R. Duthoy); Frank 1916: 693; Gordon 1924: 105; Taylor 1961: 127; Garnsey 1975: 175; Mouritsen 2005: 41.

15 This was stated already in Solin 1971: 123. The list in the previous note could be continued at will; here is a random selection of other scholars from the field of Roman social history: Garnsey and Saller 1987: 125; Weaver 1991: 171–2; Abramenko 1993: 17, 51; Kleijwegt 2006: 93. Among the very few exceptions known to me are the critical comments in Breuer 1996: 24–5 in regard to the views by Abramenko on the significance of the Greek *cognomen*.

16 Earlier surveys: Frank 1916: 691–2, cited by Gordon 1924: 101–2, 106; Kajanto 1963: 57.

17 On the concept of 'barbarian' *cognomina*, see Solin 2007: 1371–3.

18 These figures are from Solin 2001: 309; I have not found them in Solin 1996a, which contains all the relevant data. An earlier set of figures for 'Sklavennamen' are found in Solin 1971: 124; the total in that inventory was some 25,000. In Solin's newer investigation (1996a), the total, as can be seen above in the text, has increased to approximately 27,500, which is somewhat more than one-fourth of all the individuals known from Rome, according to Solin's estimate (Solin 2003a: p. xxx) of the total population known to us.

19 Solin (1971: 123) cited a study of 5,680 names from Roman epitaphs which showed that only 41.5% were Latin, against 56% Greek *cognomina*, and another 2.5% barbarian *cognomina* (neither Latin nor Greek). Since in these epitaphs many individuals will have been slaves and freedmen, the proportion of Greek *cognomina* among those who were *not* should be even lower. Solin (1971: 112) estimated that some 60% of the *cognomina* in Rome are Greek. A survey of the two hundred names from the cemetery under the Autoparco in the Vatican City, published after Solin 1971, showed that ca 37% were Latin and ca 63% were non-Latin; see Helttula 1973: 147. Using less comprehensive data, Taylor (1961: 125) claimed that Frank's estimate of 70% Greek *cognomina* in Rome was too low.

20 Taylor 1961: 129–32, followed by Mouritsen 2005: 38; hinting at a similar conclusion: Kajanto 1968: 529; George 2005: 55; Eck 2007: 60–2. The same has recently been argued for Ostia by Mouritsen 2004: 287; 2005: 38.

21 Solin 1971: 124. Scholars have been keen to find explanations for why freeborn Romans would be given Greek *cognomina*; cf. Solin 1971: 124–32. To me this sometimes has the ring of special pleading (which could obviously also be employed for Latin ones); what matters are the numbers.

22 However, the chronological distribution and the degree to which this body of evidence is representative of reality are two important questions that cannot be dealt with here.

23 Frank 1916: 693. I find it remarkable that each father included in Frank's table should have recorded one and only one son. I have not studied Frank's material myself, but in other Roman inscriptions it frequently happens that a father names more than one son.

24 See Taylor 1961: 126–7; Thylander 1952: 124–5. The results were also quoted by Solin 1971: 133, who inadvertently reported that Thylander's figures referred to Ostia only. That was not the case; cf. the following note.

25 Thylander 1952: 56; besides Ostia and Portus he included over twenty-five other ports (not Pompeii). No references were given. The scattered evidence used by Thylander ranging from Pola and Tergeste to Brundisium and Tarentum makes it somewhat more difficult to evaluate his result, as the presence of the Greek language varied from port to port.

26 Taylor 1961: 126. She included the ordinary funerary inscriptions, which are arranged alphabetically according to the name of the deceased, from the letter F to S inclusively.

27 Solin 1971: 134 (my translation).

28 The inscription below labelled H shows one such case. Attempts have been made to explain this phenomenon (see Solin 1971: 126–33), but this will not concern me here. While some explanations may be valid (certain children may have been born in captivity), they also sometimes smack of special pleading, spurred

by views such as 'It would be almost incomprehensible, if the parents had given a freeborn child a completely different name, which in addition was tainted with a servile character' (Solin 1971: 133; my translation).

29 That wider meaning of *verna* is worth keeping in mind when discussing the names and the legal and social status of individuals called *vernae*. Herrmann-Otto (1994: 12) comments on the meaning of verna: 'Inschriften aus dem militärischen, aber auch aus dem zivilen Bereich bestätigen die Bedeutung des Wortes *verna* als Freier, Eingeborener und Stadtrömer' (Inscriptions from both the military and civilian sphere confirm the meaning of the word *verna* as free person, native, and Roman citizen). The *OLD*, s.v., relying less on epigraphic material, gives a slightly more restricted range of meanings. I have not consulted the so far unpublished material of the *Thesaurus Linguae Latinae*.

30 See Herrmann-Otto 1994. See also the earlier and much shorter remarks by Rawson 1986: 186–95.

31 On purpose I have chosen several of the texts presented below from one of the two major recent corpora of new inscriptions from Rome, edited by Avetta (1985) (referred to as *Via Imperiale* below) and Gregori (2001), respectively; these texts were not included in Herrmann-Otto's 1994 study.

32 Herrmann-Otto 1994: 413.

33 One may think of two reasons, partly interconnected. It may be that the expression *servus verna* had become emotionally loaded in the funerary context and was not thought appropriate for an adult. It may also be that people who tended to use the term *verna*, namely, the slave owners, were not around anymore when an adult home-born slave received his or her funerary inscription, either because the owners were dead by then or because the slave had been set free and was commemorated by the family he or she had created.

34 Solin 1971: 156–7 for this and the following. If the same naming practice had been adopted for *vernae* as for other slaves and freedmen, Solin could expect to find some 180 Latin names in the material he surveyed, but he found 326.

35 In an article on the CNN North American website dated Friday, 17 October 2008 called 'Rome workers uncover city of dead,' reference is made to the discovery of a cemetery in Rome dating back to the classical period, in which 'some slaves of Greek origin' were found. It is obvious that this information must be derived from a careless interpretation of Greek *cognomina* born by some of the people commemorated in funerary inscriptions.

36 Herrmann-Otto (1994: 38) included 581 *vernae* from 535 inscriptions in her study, all from the 'Privathaushalt,' i.e., *servi Caesaris* or *servi publici* were excluded. A mere 407 *vernae* were from Rome, compared to 575 in Solin's earlier study. Rawson (1986: 187) mentions 564 *vernae* 'attested in usable inscriptions' in *CIL* VI. 'Familia-Caesaris' is the convenient but primarily modern term for

the slaves owned by the emperor and for his freed slaves who still were connected to him by patron-client ties.

37 The results presented by the author herself in this regard are somewhat deceptive. She states that among the private *vernae*, there were 152 Greek names (46%) and 179 Latin ones (54%) (see Herrmann-Otto 1994: 64). But she is counting individual names, not the frequency by which these names are used. Fortunately, her appendix (Herrmann-Otto 1994: 414–17) lists the frequency of each name that she included in her survey, showing that among *vernae* in private ownership, some 180 (37.5%) bore a Greek *cognomen* and some 300 (62.5%) a Latin one. This sum includes also *vernae* from outside Rome. The total of 480 is less than the sum of 581 *vernae* included by the author in her study, for reasons not clear to me. In the list of *vernae* from the *familia Caesaris* (Herrmann-Otto 1994: 418–20), the percentage of Greek *cognomina* is 47.8% in Rome with surroundings (for a total of 148), and 44.9% when all of Italy is included (for a total of 172). The separation of the imperial *vernae*, and the addition of *vernae* from the Roman empire at large, likely explains why Herrmann-Otto's figures differ somewhat from Solin's.

38 See Avetta 1985: nos. 18a, 73, 108, 254, and Gregori 2001: no. 206 Of five *vernae*, four carry a Greek *cognomen*, and one a Latin name.

39 Herrmann-Otto 1994: 66, with reference to Solin 1990: 77 (the same claim can be found in many other works).

40 Cf. that in *Via Imperiale* no. 214 a couple who both have Latin *cognomina* (Martialis and Festa) erect a funerary momument for their son who carries a Greek one (Anthus), for which see Solin 2002: 1157.

41 Statistics that show how Latin names increase at the expense of Greek ones in the following generation can be found in Frank 1916: 693; Taylor 1961: 126–7; Thylander 1952: 124–5; Solin 1971: 133. On the social stigma perceived to adhere to Greek *cognomina*, see, for instance, Frank 1916: 693; Barrow 1928: 209; Solin 1971: 134; López Barja de Quiroga 1995: 335.

42 See Herrmann-Otto 1994: 64–5 for the data presented in the table.

43 Herrmann-Otto 1994: 62: many more funerary inscriptions for young and adult *vernae* were erected by the master than by *parentes* or family. See Saller 1994: 28 for commemorative practices in Rome.

44 On the naming of Roman children, see Dixon 1992: 101 with n. 11.

45 Cf. that Trimalchio's accountant reports the birth of 30 male slaves and 40 female ones on the Cuman estate in Petr. *Sat.* 53. It does not seem as if Trimalchio had been required to decide anything in regard to these infants until then, nor does he give any orders at the dinner. The text is obviously satirical, which contributes its own interpretative problems.

46 Solin 1971: 157: 'Da der Sklave als eine *res* kein Recht auf seinen Namen hatte, konnte der Herr bei seiner Benennung beliebig verfahren' (Because, as a piece

of property, the slave had no rights in his own name, the master did what he liked when naming him).

47 Herrmann-Otto 1994: 46, but cf. p. 128 and n. 57 below.

48 Among the few scholars who have drawn attention to possible cases of the naming of slave children by their parents are Thylander 1952: 149–50; and Crea 2006: 157.

49 Herrmann-Otto 1994: 68–9, 124. That blood relationships among slaves were of importance and were monitored can be deduced also from legal passages such as Gai. *Inst.* 1.19 (where close kinship is given as one reason for manumission).

50 One might compare the contracts registering slave sales in which expressions such as *puerum Apolaustum sive is quo alio nomine est*, or *puerum … nomine Abban quem <et> Eutychen sive quo alio nomine vocatur* (*CIL* III 940 = *FIRA* III no. 88 and *P. Lond.* 229 = *FIRA* III no. 132, respectively; also published in Eck and Heinrichs 1993: nos. 45 and 47), which imply the use of other names. The possibility of name change appears in *Cod. Theod.* 9.25, from 293 CE: *Sicut initio nominis cognominis praenominis … impositio privatim libera est, ita horum mutatio innocentibus periculosa non est.*

51 From the reign of Hadrian onwards, in liaisons between an unmarried free mother and a slave father the child takes the status after its mother, who either remains free or is enslaved; see Gai. *Inst.* 1.82–4, 91 and Buckland 1908: 412–13; Watson 1987: 10–12. Previously, since the *Senatus Consultum Claudianum* from 52 CE, the mother might remain free while the child was enslaved by the father's owner. Then again, and if a married woman had been guilty of an extra-marital affair with a slave, one wonders why that would have had to be declared. Such a child could happily have grown up a free individual among its siblings.

52 There is also some contradictory evidence, namely, several passages in Martial, which deal with young favourite slaves of his friends (6.28–9 *puer delicatus Glaucias*, 6.68 *puer Eutychus*, etc.). These slaves all have Greek names. To be sure, there is nothing said about whether they were bought or had been born in their owner's house. The interesting but wide question of naming in Martial cannot be pursued in this place; see Grewing 1997: 159–61, 446–8 and passim; Vallat 2006.

53 The following figures derive from Solin 1996a; 2001: 309; 1971: 156–7; and Herrmann-Otto 1994: 414–17 (cf. notes 18, 34, and 36–7 above).

54 One obviously thinks of foundlings here, on which see Harris 1994; 1999: 73–4.

55 See above n. 36.

56 Herrmann-Otto 1994: 129.

57 It is not necessary to continue speculating in this matter here, but clearly one could go on. One might for instance suggest that the parents, as chosen slaves of the emperor, were normally highly trained professionals from the East who in fact preferred Greek names. Herrmann-Otto (1994: 128) believes that the parents of imperial *vernae* had 'völlige Freiheit' (complete freedom) in the naming

of their children, but surely one cannot exclude intervention from higher up in the imperial domestic hierarchy.

58 See Harris 1999.

59 Scheidel 1997; 2005: 75 for a brief reiteration of the significance of home-born slaves in Italy. Roth 2007 has recently argued for a much greater presence of women in the Roman slave population than previously assumed, from which it naturally follows that the number of *vernae* should have been much larger too.

60 Scheidel (1997: 157) is obviously aware of Herrmann-Otto's work, which he also reviewed in *Tyche* 11 (1996): 274–8, but the onomastic question does not play a role in his discussion of her material or conclusions.

61 For some observations on the changing onomastic pattern in Rome in late antiquity, including remarks on the proportion of Greek to Latin *cognomina*, see Solin 2003b: 21–2.

62 Cf. note 20 above.

63 On the use of Greek in Rome and Italy and the question of bilingualism, see, for instance, Adams , Janse, and Swain 2002 with Leiwo 2002; Adams 2003; Leiwo 2003; and Dupont and Valette-Cagnac 2005.

2

Slavery and Manumission in the Roman Elite: A Study of the *Columbaria* of the Volusii and the Statilii*

HENRIK MOURITSEN

Introduction

The study of Roman slavery is notoriously short of reliable statistics. The sad truth is that we have little evidence for the number of slaves or the number of freed slaves, their share of the population or indeed the rate of manumission.[1] However, quantitative data are important not just to establish a general order of magnitude for these phenomena but also because a sense of scale is vital for understanding how slavery functioned. For example, the nature of manumission to a great extent depends on the rate at which it happened. In this context it is symptomatic of the dearth of reliable information that a passing rhetorical comment in Cicero's *Philippics* about the period that well-behaving captives might expect to serve has become a key text in modern discussions of Roman manumission.[2] If nothing else this illustrates how scholars have been clutching at straws to establish even the most elementary quantification.[3]

This paper sets out to explore one particular type of archaeological evidence, the urban *columbaria* inscriptions, with the aim of establishing a basic quantitative framework for the study of manumission. The fact that the chosen material is epigraphic cannot help give cause for concern, since inscriptions are notoriously difficult to turn into useful statistics. Thus, despite the apparent promise of hard quantitative data offered by the thousands of surviving inscriptions, it has become increasingly clear in recent years that the hope of extracting demographic information from this material is usually vain.[4] Apart from the problem associated with uneven transmission of the material, a fundamental difficulty relates to the fact that putting up inscriptions was neither 'instinctive' nor universal. It was a distinct cultural practice – or 'habit,' as some scholars describe it – that some sections of society embraced while others did not, or at least not all at the same time or in the same way. Inscriptions can therefore in principle provide information only about those groups in society that decided to use this particular medium of self-expression.

The study of slavery through inscriptions faces further difficulties, since the large majority of slaves are epigraphically invisible, and when they do feature we usually have few means of turning their records into useful statistics. For example, *CIL* VI.6242, a typical epitaph for a domestic slave in imperial Rome, simply says: 'Primus atriesis.' There is very little we can do with evidence like that, apart from noting his Latin name and his job as a steward. In order to extend our enquiry we would have to know who his owner was and what the rest of the household looked like. In other words, we would like a social context for Primus, and it is this requirement that draws attention to the small minority of Roman inscriptions where such information *is* available. The inscriptions from the large familial *columbaria* of the early empire hold an exceptional position among the mass of funerary inscriptions from Rome. Their value as historical sources derives entirely from the fact that they all refer to the same household. Deprived of their archaeological context they would merge with the tens of thousands of decontextualized Roman epitaphs. Thus, in the case of 'Primus atriesis' we happen to know that the inscription came from the *columbarium* of the Statilii, and this information allows us to include him in statistical analyses of status, gender, and domestic functions in that particular household. The secure archaeological provenance thus compensates for the relatively uninformative nature of the inscription itself. Also, the more concentrated a body of epigraphic evidence is – chronologically, topographically, and socially – the more likely it is to give an accurate picture of the social world to which it once belonged. For that reason this study will focus on just two of the surviving funerary complexes from Rome, the *columbaria* of the Statilii Tauri and the Volusii Saturnini, which are also the largest and best documented of the private family burials. The monuments are broadly contemporary, dating to the first century CE, but differ somewhat in terms of their transmission history and hence also in terms of our knowledge of the sites and their contents.

The *Columbaria*

The monument of the Statilii was located near the Porta Maggiore, originally on the edge of the Horti Tauriani, which belonged to the senatorial family of the Statilii Tauri.[5] The family held no fewer than five consulships (37 and 26 BCE, 11, 16, and 45 CE) and later entered the imperial circle with the marriage of Statilia Messalina to Nero in 66. The monument was first excavated in 1875–7, the inscriptions removed and the site covered over. The recording was done by Edoardo Brizio and Rodolfo Lanciani, to whom we owe our knowledge of the structure, which consisted of three chambers, N, O, and P. The overwhelming majority of the inscriptions were found in room N (381 inscriptions), which was also the oldest of the chambers. The two others were added later and differ somewhat in character. The number of inscriptions is much lower (room O features twenty-six inscriptions and room P just twenty) and they include more outsiders.[6] There are also more collective family burials, and stelae, which were not found in room N.

Caldelli and Ricci suggested that the main chamber (N) never was filled up with urns (the capacity was apparently 700 *loculi*). Presumably it was abandoned by the *familia* after the (forced) suicide of T. Statilius Taurus in 53 CE, when his estate was confiscated and his household presumably dissolved.[7] The large majority of the burials thus belong to just two generations of the Statilii family from Augustan times to 53 CE. No burial in the main chamber of the *columbarium* can be dated after Neronian times. Following Edoardo Brizio, Maria Letizia Caldelli and Cecilia Ricci argue there were no anepigraphic burials in this chamber (N), since no unmarked urns were reported by the excavator. The absence of anepigraphic burials would be puzzling, however, given the under-recording of infant burials in the material.

The *columbarium* of the Volusii Saturnini was located on the Via Appia, but little is known about the architectural structure. The inscriptions were apparently found scattered and there is no record of the actual building. The first inscriptions were recovered in 1825, followed by another excavation in 1848. The whole material has now been carefully considered and published by Marco Buonocore, to whom I refer for more detailed discussion of the material and its provenance.[8] The corpus consists of 191 inscriptions, covering a period from 20 to 97 CE.[9] It derives from the *columbarium* of the *familia* of the aristocratic Volusii Saturnini, who held consulships in 12 BCE and 3, 56, 87, and 92 CE.

The differences in excavation history suggest that the *columbarium* of the Statilii is the more complete of the two and that the material from the Volusii Saturnini represents a sample, albeit a very substantial one. We should bear in mind the possibility that this disparity may have led to distortions of the profile of the households. The two corpora record members of a funerary *collegium* attached to the aristocratic *familiae*. These *collegia* were organized with internal officials and common funds. Presumably the members paid a certain amount in return for a formal burial space in the communal tomb.[10] Some members were apparently buried and recorded by their fellow *collegiati*, while others were commemorated by their relatives or by other people closely associated with them, for example, masters or *vicarii*.[11] Most of the inscriptions are small plaques attached to the *loculus* that contained the urn, but particularly among the Volusii we also find larger stelae and altars.

Some outsiders (i.e., carriers of different *nomina*) also gained access to the sites. Presumably they had some connections with the *familiae*, as did T. Aquilius T.l. Pelorus, who was *vestiarius de horreis Volusianis*, 130. In the smaller chambers of the Statilii we find more outsiders, the reason for which remains uncertain. Some burials differ in character from the rest, since they establish a separate 'family plot' within the communal tomb providing for future burials. That is particularly common among the Volusii, where no fewer than twenty-seven inscriptions refer to secondary burials, usually with the phrase 'et sibi.' By contrast among the Statilii we find only two instances.[12]

Composition of the *Familiae*

The central concern of this paper is the rate of manumission, and I will therefore first present a set of raw statistics of the free and unfree members of the two *familiae* (see table 1). The figures are not exact, since there is considerable scope for interpretation. Often it is difficult to distinguish between homonymous individuals recorded in different inscriptions.[13] Likewise the gender of some individuals is not entirely certain. In terms of legal status it should be noted that a large proportion of the inscriptions does not give explicit status indicators such as filiation and pseudo-filiation, or use terms such as *servus* or *vicarius*. But single names may constitute a fairly reliable indicator of slave status, and a full *tria nomina* of course indicates free status. Thus, there is sufficient evidence to suggest that indication of proper status mattered considerably to those who put up the inscriptions – note for example the frequent addition of *l(ibertus/a)* to a single name among the Statilii[14] – and a single name without further status indicators is therefore unlikely to refer to a free person.[15] There are uncertain cases, but they represent a small minority that does not affect the overall picture. In a few instances we can deduce that the person probably was freeborn.[16]

The figures raise a number of questions. The first concerns the marked difference in the unfree/free ratio in the two samples, 54 per cent slaves to 46 per cent freedmen for the Volusii household and 68 per cent slaves to 32 per cent freedmen for the Statilii. We may wonder whether this reflects original disparities in the composition of the two households, differences

Table 1

	Volusii		Statilii	
Servi	113	38.1%	272	47.9%
Servae	44	14.9%	114	20.1%
Liberti	78	26.4%	115	20.2%
Libertae	56	18.9%	64	11.3%
Ingenui/ae	5	1.7%	3	0.5%
Total	296		568	

in commemoration practices, uneven transmission of material, or perhaps a combination of all three factors. While the former remains a possibility, it would be difficult to explain why two otherwise comparable households should differ to this extent in their manumission practices. The involvement of purely epigraphic factors may therefore seem on the face of it the more likely explanation.

The question of commemorative practices may be addressed by breaking the figures down into dedicators, dedicatees, and individuals referred to indirectly. The latter include masters/patrons, spouses, or other relatives, who feature as part of the identity of the deceased, for instance, 6478, 'Irena Apolloni f.,' or 6476, 'Iazemus Posidippi lib.' These figures do not include individuals who were not dependent members of the *familia* (i.e., excluding freeborn and outsiders), since the aim is to trace the impact of commemorative practices on the vital free/unfree ratio as well as the gender balance. The figures do not match those above, because some feature in several different capacities in table 2.

Broken down in this way it becomes clear that the difference in profile is largely due to more male slaves receiving commemoration among the Statilii, which in turn reflects general differences in the epigraphic and commemorative practices. Even a cursory glance at the two *columbaria* reveals a marked difference in character, content, and execution. The epitaphs recovered from the Volusii are generally of a much higher quality than those of the Statilii, and include a far greater proportion of grand and ornate monuments often with sculptural decoration. The texts themselves are generally longer, more detailed, and better cut. By contrast, the Statilian epitaphs are typically very simple plaques, with shorter, often poorly executed texts. Thus the simple name, sometimes with age or occupation, occurs very frequently in the Statilian *columbarium* but hardly ever among the Volusii.

Table 2

	Volusii		Statilii	
A. Dedicatees				
Servi	51	33.3%	203	49.4%
Servae	28	18.3%	82	19.9%
Liberti	38	24.8%	75	18.2%
Libertae	36	23.5%	51	12.4%
Total	153	(53% of A+B)	411	(84% of A+B)
B. Dedicators				
Servi	58	42%	36	44.4%
Servae	16	11.5%	19	23.4%
Liberti	38	27.5%	16	19.7%
Libertae	26	18.8%	10	12.3%
Total	138	(47% of A+B)	81	(16% of A+B)
A+B	291		492	
C. Others (patrons, masters, relatives)				
Servi	4	44.4%	35	44.3%
Servae	7	8.8%		
Liberti	3	33.3%	32	40.5%
Libertae	2	22.2%	5	6.1%
Total	9	(3% of A+B+C)	79	(14% of A+B+C)
A+B+C	300		571	

We may wonder whether 'poorer' inscriptions of this type originally were present also among the Volusii but failed to be recovered to the same extent as more conspicuous pieces. The answer will have to remain conjectural, but the extant inscriptions from the Volusii must in any case have been considerably more expensive than the average epitaph from the Statilii – and thus presumably also more exclusive.[17] Whether an original feature or the result of skewed transmission, it follows that the Statilii is likely to give us a more complete picture of the composition of the household than the Volusii. The fact that the Statilian epitaphs were much simpler suggests easier access to commemoration for the lower ranks of the household, which in turn may explain why some low-ranking jobs such as *lecticarii* and *germani*, so plentiful among the Statilii, are absent from the Volusian material.[18] Among the

Statilii these groups received very basic commemoration, often by their fellow workers or by the *collegium*. Again the impression is one of a broader epigraphic coverage than among the Volusii, and viewed from this perspective the higher ratio of slaves to freedmen that we find among the Statilii would seem to be the more realistic.

However, the comparison between the two *columbaria* also throws up another issue, for if the Statilii seem more representative of the 'bottom' end of the *familia*, the Volusii might reflect better the affluent 'top.' Are the senior slaves and freedmen under-represented among the Statilii? Was there no such 'top' among the Statilii? Did they prefer more simple burials, or were they buried elsewhere? The latter may be a distinct possibility, since we know of several Statilii buried outside the *columbarium*.[19] Some of them were found near the Porta Maggiore monument, and occasionally there seems to be a direct connection to individuals buried inside the *columbarium*.[20] This might potentially explain why so many patrons / masters who are recorded indirectly do not themselves feature in the material. While some of these may have outlived the dissolution of the household in 53 CE, that can hardly have been universal. More likely, they may have preferred funerary display outside the *columbarium*. The question is how this affects the ratio of free to unfree. While the most successful *liberti* may not be represented among the dedicatees, they would presumably feature as patrons or owners.[21] And since this category of indirectly documented individuals was made up partly of slaves with *vicarii* the possible distortion of the free / unfree balance may have been relatively limited. In the end, therefore, the most reliable figure for male slaves and freedmen may turn out to be the ration of 68 per cent slaves to 32 per cent freedmen that we find in the raw figures of the Statilii. We should bear in mind, however, that this is the figure for the entire household, perhaps excluding the poorly documented infants. It therefore does not tell us much about the chances of individual slaves gaining their freedom, a question to which we will return below.

Gender Distinctions

We may now consider whether the same ratio of free to unfree slaves applied to females in the households (see table 3). To answer that question we must first address the overall gender balance. Males represent the large majority in both households, albeit to slightly varying degrees. They conform to the gender ratio found in the smaller *columbarium* of the Arruntii.[22]

We will have to consider whether these figures reflect an actual imbalance of men and women in large Roman households of this type, which in turn

Table 3

	Volusii		Statilii		Arruntii	
Females	100	34%	179	31.4%	17	36%
Males	191	66%	390	68.6%	30	64%

Table 4

Ages	Volusii		Statilii	
0–10	8	22%	27	30%
11–20	11	31%	27	30%
21–30	7	19%	18	20%
31–40	6	17%	15	17%
41>	4	11%	3	3%
	36		90	

means looking at possible distortions that might have caused females to be under-represented in the material, above all female slaves.[23] This may seem puzzling, since especially the Statilii appear to have a broad coverage of the lower ranks of the household. We nevertheless find that far more *servi* were commemorated than *servae* (i.e., 70% *servi* to 30% *servae*), but there was one major factor that militated against equal coverage, which was the preference for commemorating young males over females.

As we know, indicating the age of the deceased was not common practice in Rome, featuring only in a minority of funerary inscriptions and with a distinct preference for certain age groups, above all older children and young adults. The two *columbaria* display an almost identical proportion of dedicatees with age at death, Statilii 25 per cent and Volusii 27 per cent, which are distributed in table 4, excluding *ingenui*.

The material is evidently skewed in favour of persons dying prematurely, older slaves and freedmen hardly ever featuring with indication of age. In this respect it is entirely typical of urban funerary epigraphy, where mature slaves tend to appear without age at death, to the extent they were commemorated at all. Stating a person's age at death reflected a sense of *mors acerba*, which apparently was felt most strongly in late childhood and early adulthood, gradually fading until the age of forty when it can no longer be traced. As a result the figures have no meaningful implications for the age

Table 5

	Volusii			Statilii		
	Males	Females		Males	Females	
1–10	5	2	28.5%	23	4	14.8%
11–20	4	7	63.6%	20	7	25.9%
21–30	2	5	71.4%	13	5	27.7%
31–40	4	2	33.3%	12	3	20%
40>	4		0	2	1	33.3%

profiles relating to either gender or status of more advanced age groups. The two *columbaria* differ in one important respect, since the figures suggest more children were recorded among the Statilii. If true, this would tie in well with the impression of cheaper and more inclusive burial practices in this *collegium*. This feature also has important implications for the gender balance, since the preponderance of males is stronger in the younger age groups than in the older ones, as indicated by table 5.[24]

The preference for commemorating boys over girls is fully in line with common epigraphic practice, as Kinuko Hasegawa's compilation of *columbaria* profiles further demonstrates.[25] The gender imbalance is most pronounced among the Statilii, however, presumably because it offered particularly good opportunities for inexpensive child commemoration. We therefore have reason to assume that the actual gender imbalance was less than the raw figures might suggest, because of the under-representation of young females. Nevertheless, we still have to accept the likelihood of a certain degree of imbalance, for although the gender gap to some extent is explicable by the absence of female children from the record, adult women generally seem to have had good access to commemoration in both households. The fact that predominantly males married outside the household would also seem to point in that direction, as will be seen below when marriage patterns are taken into account.

We may now turn to the question of the manumission rate of female slaves, for which the figures follow in table 6.

The table suggests a substantial difference in the ratio of *servae* to *libertae* in the two households. This may of course reflect more frequent manumission of female slaves among the Volusii, although such a discrepancy in the manumission practices of otherwise comparable households would be

Table 6

	Volusii		Statilii	
Servae	44	44%	114	64%
Libertae	56	56%	64	36%
	100		178	

difficult to explain.[26] Alternatively, the difference might reflect better access to commemoration for slaves – irrespective of gender – among the Statilii. Given the general gender imbalance in this material it would not be surprising if those most under-represented would have been female slaves. The significance of epigraphic factors is also suggested by the relative infrequency with which female slaves appear as dedicators among the Volusii, which may be explained by the cost involved. Most likely, therefore, we are dealing with 'missing' *servae* among the Volusii rather than the under-representation of *libertae* among the Statilii.[27] For that reason the ratio of slave to freed would probably have been much closer to that of males than the record suggests, casting doubt on the common notion that women had a better chance being freed, which this material has inspired.[28] Still, there are signs of a possible disparity in the manumission rates of men and women, since marriages between freedwomen and male slaves were more common than between freedmen and female slaves.

Age

The ratio of freed to slave gives only a very broad impression of manumission practices and tells us little about the individual slave's chances of gaining freedom. Age is the most important factor to add to the equation, since the ratio clearly shifted between different age groups. As noted, age at death was not evenly recorded, some age groups featuring disproportionately more frequently than others. However, when the decision was made whether to record the deceased's age, there is no reason to believe that his or her personal status played any important part, with the possible exception of older slaves, whose age generally was ignored.

Table 7 shows the age distribution in the two samples.

Although small in absolute terms, the secure archaelogical context of the material gives these figures a historical weight and significance that exceed that of much larger samples of disparate epigraphic evidence. The figures suggest that, while relatively early manumission did occur, most slaves

Table 7

	Volusii			Statilii		
	Slaves	Freed		Slaves	Freed	
1–10	7	1	13%	22	5	18.5%
11–20	9	2	18%	20	7	25.9%
21–30	3	4	57%	11	7	38.8%
31–40	4	2	33%	8	7	46.6%
41>	1	3	75%		3	100%

were not freed until after the age of twenty.[29] Importantly, it also indicates that even among mature members of the household, the majority were still slaves. Thus, in the 31–40 category only 43 per cent of those recorded with age were freed. Moreover, since older slaves generally are under-represented, the actual proportion of freedmen was probably well below that figure; certainly the near absence of older slaves in Roman epigraphy cannot be taken as proof of their non-existence, as has been done.[30] Manumission was, in other words, common but not universal. The process was selective and many slaves never gained their freedom. Therefore, Cicero's famous reference to the *sexennium* as the period a well-behaved *captivus* had to serve before gaining his freedom finds little support in this evidence.[31] Nevertheless, the material still reveals a strikingly high manumission rate, which was probably unparalleled by any other slave society. Thus, between a quarter and a third of the household may have been freed at any time, the incidence of freedmen naturally growing among the more advanced age groups.

Manumission and Families in the *Familiae*

How did a household with this particular profile function? Could it sustain itself given the high rate of manumission and the imbalanced gender ratio? What were the consequences for the lives of individual servants and for the organization of the household? Long-term sustainability was closely linked to slave reproduction, making the existence of slave families a matter of critical importance.[32] The gender ratio would imply that some male slaves did not have families, as also suggested by certain features of the Statilian *columbarium*, where many male slaves were commemorated by fellow workers, their masters, or by the funerary *collegium*. Another indicator is the greater frequency of males marrying outside the *familia*, a phenomenon

Table 8

	Volusii	%	Statilii	%
Male freed / female freed	12	22	9	32
Male slave / female slave	12	22	9	32
Male freed / female slave	4	7	2	7
Male slave / female freed	14	26	6 (possibly 8)	22
Male slave / female outsider	1	2		
Male freed / female outsider	7	13	2	7
Male outsider / female freed	1	2		
Male freeborn / female outsider	3	6		
	54		28 (30)	

best documented among the Volusii. For those who did have families the question of manumission and personal status was obviously essential. The Volusian monument offers a far more detailed picture of family relations within the household than the Statilian because of the larger proportion of dedicators (44 per cent compared to 16), who often include information about their connection with the deceased as shown in the following tabulation of the marriage relations in the two *familiae* (see table 8).

There is a rough correlation between the two samples, the main difference being the larger number of Volusii marrying outside of the *familia*, which may be due to different commemorative cultures in the two households. It is not inconceivable that those from the Statilii who married outside the *familia* also were commemorated outside the *columbarium*. As already noted, the sample of the Volusii seems to represent better the top end of the household, and the higher figure for outside marriage found there, 22 per cent, may therefore be the more realistic. We also get a valuable hint of what may have happened in the next generation, since the three male freeborn Volusii represented in the sample all married outsiders.[33] Among those couples who married within the households, 38 per cent did not have the same legal status, and this figure may in reality have been somewhat higher since in two cases a freed couple were in fact patron and freedwoman, which means they originally held different status.[34] Given this difference in status between spouses it is not surprising that the status of children also varied, as shown by the figures in table 9.

We find more parent-child slaves among the Statilii, which probably reflects the overall profile of this *columbarium* and the greater opportunities

Table 9

	Volusii		Statilii	
Parent and child both slaves	11	31%	15	52%
Parent and child both freed	12	34%	6	21%
Parent slave / child freed	4	11%	1	3%
Parent freed / child slave	8	23%	7	24%
	35		29	

for commemoration it offered the humbler end of the domestic spectrum. Overall, the figures show that discrepancies between the status of parents and children were very common; no fewer than twenty parental relationships out of sixty-four involved differences in status (31 per cent). Importantly, fifteen out of thirty-three freed parents (or 45 per cent) had children who were still in slavery. Moreover, since it is possible that free children had a greater chance of receiving commemoration than unfree, the figure is probably best taken as a minimum.

The material demonstrates a complete integration of unfree and freed members of the *familia*. Among the more detailed records of the Volusii we find several examples of entire family units of mixed status, for instance, 7284a, where the mother is freed but the father is a slave along with the one-year old son. The same pattern recurs in 7347 and 9326, while in 7304 the father was a slave, and the mother and two adult sons freed. In 7379 the mother was a slave, and both the father and the sons were freed. This feature draws attention to one of the most striking aspects of this material, which is the fact that so many freedmen remained within the *familia* after their manumission, as also indicated by their subsequent burial in the familial *columbarium*. In many instances it would seem that strong familial bonds tied them to the patron's household, where close relatives still served as slaves.

Slave Ownership within the *familiae*

There are also indications that the integration of free and unfree within the household was not just a fortuitous side effect of the domestic structures but integral to the practice of manumission, which must have operated on the premise that freed servants as a rule would remain in the household. The most incontrovertible evidence comes from the extensive 'decentralization' of ownership within the *familia*. A large section of the household appears to have been owned not by the aristocratic family but by other servants.[35] This pattern is most fully documented among the Statilii but can also be traced among the Volusii, where twenty-four relationships of this type are recorded, involving forty-eight individuals in the household. Again the smaller number is probably best explained by epigraphic factors, since, as we saw, the lower ranks of the household are better represented among the Statilii.

In this household no fewer than 110 members were either the slaves or freedmen of other members of the household, while fifty-nine are recorded as controlling others. By contrast only sixty servants are recorded as slaves / freedmen of members of the aristocratic family, while nine simply feature with conventional pseudo-filiation T.l., giving a total of sixty-nine. Taken at face value these statistics suggest that 61 per cent were owned by other slaves or freedmen and just 39 per cent directly by the noble Statilii. Before considering the implications of this distribution we may consider whether there may be a purely epigraphic explanation. Thus it is possible that servile owners / patrons may disproportionately have included references to themselves in the commemoration of their own slaves and freedmen, but that tendency may have been counterbalanced by the fact that references to aristocratic masters / patrons presumably carried greater prestige than those to a slave / freedman. We should also bear in mind that details of ownership (current or previous) are given for less than a third of the recorded individuals (179 Statilii), and it is possible that for those without such indication, ownership by aristocratic masters was implicit. While that might seem plausible in some instances, such as that of the *germani*, the fact that the aristocratic family was extensive and included several individuals with separate staff meant that omission of ownership would not have been unambiguous.

For those reasons the figures we have may provide a broadly realistic picture of the ownership patterns within the *familia*. There are wide implications of this structure, which implies a remarkable degree of delegation in the management of the household. We can only speculate as to the rationale behind the system, but the widespread existence of *vicarii* would have presented an incentive for slaves, who could acquire under-slaves and thereby ease their own workload. It may also have been a practical means of allocating responsibilities, since those in charge not only had managerial duties but exercised legal control over the staff they supervised. This would explain the concentration of several *vicarii* in the hands of some slaves. For example, Chrestus Auctianus and Hipparchus had three *vicarii* each, the latter including two *horrearii*.[36]

While a structure of this nature might seem sensible from a management perspective, it raises obvious questions in the context of the frequent manumission also practised in the household; for what happened when a slave with *vicarii* was freed? The simple answer offered by the evidence is very little. The clearest indication of continuity is the fact that not just the freedmen themselves but also their slaves and freedmen received burial in the familial *columbarium* of the Statilii, where, for example, we find the four slaves of Statilius Alexander along with a similar number owned by Statilius Bassus. Their presence in the Statilian burial site suggests they continued to belong to the *familia* despite their master's manumission.

This feature takes us to the most intriguing individual in the entire corpus, the freedman T. Statilius Posidippus. The surviving epitaphs indicate that he had a *familia* counting at least nineteen members: nine *servi*, three *servae*, and seven *liberti*. In terms of age they cover a range from five to twenty-seven, and their professions include one *cocus*, two *cubicularii*, and four *dispensatores*.[37] One of these *dispensatores*, Eros, appears to have had several *vicarii* of his own, Faustus and Suavis, 6275 and 6276 respectively, further expanding Posidippus's *familia* to twenty-one.[38] Posidippus thus appears to have had his own sub-*familia*, but the fact that his slaves and freedmen still belonged to the greater *familia* and were buried in the family *columbarium* is significant.[39] The appearance of no fewer than four *dispensatores* further suggests that, although formally belonging to Posidippus, they probably worked directly for the aristocratic Statilii rather than their own master. Posidippus's large household may therefore to some extent have been a fiction, merely forming a subsection of the larger Statilian *familia*, into which its members were fully integrated. It is worth noting that a freedman of his standing and apparent wealth, if encountered outside of this particular context, would have been taken for an 'independent freedman.' However, while Posidippus may himself have been buried outside the *columbarium*, the close affiliation of his *familia* to that of his patron implies that he still functioned as a member of that household, as did the members of his substantial '*familia* within the *familia*.'

A similar conclusion is offered by the epitaph 6328, which records 'Iasullus Philerotis liberti Sisennae paedagogus.' The implication is that Iasullus belonged to a freedman, Phileros, but worked as a childminder for the aristocratic family, which demonstrates that the Roman elite were willing to employ slaves who were not their own but belonged to their freedmen.[40] In fact, judging from the patterns of ownership observed among the Statilii, the distinction seems to have been a mere technicality, which in turn raises the question of how the slaves and freedmen of the Statilii acquired so many *vicarii*, slaves, and freedmen of their own. One possibility might be that they were allocated to them as rewards for good work and loyal service and, certainly, in the case of Posidippus it is difficult to see how he could otherwise have acquired a *familia* of this size.[41] Since his *familia* functioned as part of the *familia* of his patron, it may be most plausibly explained as the direct result of favours granted by the Statilii. This practice would also explain why several low-ranking slaves had under-slaves: the *lecticarius* Agatho had a *vicaria*, Caliste, 6303; the freed cook Phileros had a slave who died aged five, 6248. Since neither a litter bearer nor a cook presumably could accumulate funds with which to buy slaves, the *vicarii* might have been given to them, in the case of the cook presumably to learn the trade. Similarly, among the Volusii Threptus, who worked in the nursery, 'de paedagogio,' died aged twenty and was commemorated by his *vicaria*, 30556. Again, this woman was presumably allocated to him, since he hardly would have had the time or financial opportunities to purchase her himself.

Effects of Manumission within the *Familia*

The structure of the *familia*, as indicated especially by the Statilian monument, suggests that manumission was not expected to make any real difference to the slave's position within the *familia*. The high rate of manumission, the commemoration of freedmen alongside other family servants, and the extensive use of *vicarii* all point in that direction. Given the size of their sub-*familiae* it would have made little sense to free the *ordinarii*, if that meant letting go of slaves who were integral to the running of the *familia*. The practice of manumission must therefore have been predicated on the assumption that the slave would remain in the patron's service along with his *vicarii*. What happened in the next generation must remain a matter of speculation, but most children of freedmen were probably themselves freed. Those who were not might in some cases have remained in the service of the household, as indicated by an instance from the Volusii.[42]

We may envisage a situation where the *familia* was mostly self-sustaining, but at the same time experiencing a steady, if limited, loss of labour caused by early manumission of still reproductive slaves. It is not a given, however, that this loss was conceptualized as such by the aristocratic owners. Elite households would have seen a steady influx of newly purchased slaves, who supplemented existing staff members who had died. Slave functions were often highly specialized and vacancies might occur unpredictably before homeborn apprentices had been fully trained. Slaves from the market were therefore a natural supplement to the self-regeneration of the *familia*. This might also account for some of the gender imbalance, since most of these 'luxury' slaves probably were male. There are indications in the material that part of the household was bought on the market, as in the occasional references to the foreign *natio* of some of those commemorated.[43]

We might also consider the possibility that slaves might move between *familiae* through sales or bequests. Little is know about this aspect, although the evidence offers a few clues. Thus, 7341 records siblings belonging to different *familiae*, and 7290 presents a complex set of inter-familial relationships.[44] Primigenius L. Volusi Saturnini was married to Charis, evidently another slave of the Volusii. Her brother was T. Iulius Antigonus, and he commemorated his *nutrix* Spurinnia Nice Torquatiana. The latter was freed by a different owner, but her *agnomen* Torquatiana implies she had once belonged to the Volusii. The evidence thus suggests that both Antigonus and Nice had at some point been alienated from the *familia* of the Volusii.

Manumission is sometimes interpreted as an economically rational practice that served to improve the efficiency of unfree labour.[45] Supposedly, certain economic functions that required care and dedication rather than physical effort demanded the use of the 'carrot' rather than the 'stick.' Manumission has therefore been identified as a vital performance-enhancing tool otherwise missing from the Roman system of unfree labour. Logically, it would be granted as a reward for long and devoted service, particularly to those in more responsible functions. This model is questioned by the relatively early age at which some slaves in our sample were freed, and to assess the hypothesis we may also briefly look at the domestic functions of those who were freed and those who were not. Job titles were not applied universally. Typically they served to describe the deceased rather than the dedicator, and overwhelmingly they were applied to male slaves. By contrast female slaves, freedmen, and freedwomen carry job titles much more infrequently.[46] Few members of the household commemorated themselves, and it was therefore left for others to decide how to identify the deceased. In the case of free people a full Roman name was apparently considered sufficient, while for male slaves more detail was sometimes seen as appropriate. Given the cultural specificity of these commemorative practices, we cannot conclude that the absence of work titles for most women indicates that they had none and mostly were engaged in reproduction.[47]

As a result of these patterns we know the profession of relatively fewer freedmen than slaves. However, there is sufficient evidence from job titles to suggest that the practice of manumission was not governed by any strict economic or managerial logic. Some slaves in relatively trusted positions were not freed, for example, Epaphus *a manu*, thirty-five years old, 6595, and Speratus *tabularius*, thirty years old, 6596. Neither were some slaves who controlled several *vicarii* of their own.[48] On the other hand, among those who were freed we find several who were not particularly high ranking but were probably in relatively close personal contact with their masters.[49] Proximity and personal contact seem to have been essential factors in ensuring manumission. This is perhaps not surprising given the scale of these households, which at any time must have comprised several hundred people. The Elder Pliny deplored the 'legions of slaves, a foreign rabble in one's home, so that a *nomenclator* has to be employed even in the case of one's slaves,' and contrasted it with the olden days when a single slave sufficed.[50] The lament is conventional moralizing but may still contain a kernel of truth, since some Roman aristocrats probably did not know all their domestic staff by name.

Manumission in the Elite Household

On the basis of this analysis of two elite households, we may now try to identify some general characteristics of the practice of slavery and manumission at the highest echelons of Roman society. What emerges with some clarity is the often-noted fact that domestic slavery did not serve any rational economical purpose at this social level. The Roman household could be seen as an extension of its master, and as such it also functioned as a vehicle for the expression of status, wealth, and power. The public persona of the master was reflected in the number of servants surrounding him, their quality, and the diversity of their domestic roles.[51] A large and expensive household was therefore an end in itself, rather than a means of fulfilling practical needs.[52]

In this social environment the long-term sustainability of the household was not a primary concern, precisely because the urban household was part of the elite's conspicuous expenditure rather than its economic basis. Most likely the regular purchase of new slaves with particular skills or looks was regarded as a normal part of the running costs of the household. Because many functions were so specialized and vacancies occurred unpredictably, recourse to the slave market may often have been necessary, despite the moral opprobrium generally attached to it. There were other sources of slaves, however; as one ancient writer reminds us, household staff was 'either home-born, inherited or bought,' and with the frequent dissolution of households we may envisage a continuous redistribution of elite slaves among members of the upper classes who inherited parts of each other's households.[53]

In this particular environment freedom would be awarded to a substantial proportion of the domestic slaves, mostly to those in trusted positions and working in close contact with their masters. Since freed staff as a rule were expected to remain in their patron's service, there were few adverse consequences of this display of generosity. The main disadvantage of manumission was the loss of home-born slaves, but this loss should not be overestimated. Often the new freedman already had children who would remain in slavery, and a substantial proportion of families were therefore 'mixed,' further ensuring the freedman's loyalty and continuity of service. There are few traces in our material of freeborn offspring, which might be explained by their leaving the household altogether, although that would have made little economic sense. Alternatively, the aristocratic masters may no longer have been interested in employing them as free labourers over whom they had no direct personal control and authority.

It could be argued that the rate of manumission may have been unusually high in this type of household, which had a greater certainty that their freedmen would remain and cause little trouble for their patron. The level of material comfort offered by elite households was probably unmatched by anything a freedman could expect if he had to fend for himself in the urban labour market. Moreover, we should not forget that a household on this scale in many respects represented a miniature society, a separate social world populated by close and distant relatives as well as old childhood friends.[54] Moreover, because the elite household not only expressed status but also reflected on the master himself, we may assume the treatment of most slaves generally was tolerable. And the important point to remember is that those slaves who were selected for manumission were precisely those who had already found favour with their owners.

Manumission was 'rational' in the sense that it involved limited losses for the owner, but that does not entail it was therefore part of a logical system of rewards and incentives for slaves performing particularly responsible economic roles.[55] Freedom appears to have been granted without much regard for years of service or rank and responsibilities. Some slaves were freed too young to fit the model, while others in positions where we might expect incentives to have applied apparently were not considered. There seems to have been an improvised, ad hoc aspect to manumission, which paradoxically may have increased its value as a spur for hard work and obedience. It meant that freedom was a realistic hope for virtually all domestic slaves at almost any time. Provided he or she was lucky enough to attract the master's attention and sympathy, manumission was not beyond the reach of any member of the household.

Conclusion

The rate of manumission in our two samples was probably at the upper end of the range, since the losses entailed by the practice probably were relatively limited and in any case easily sustained by the owners. So while we have no grounds for assuming that the two households for which we happen to have such extensive records were in any way exceptional among the aristocratic *familiae* in the early empire, they may not be representative of Roman households in general. In smaller households with fewer slaves manumission is likely to have been rarer and later, simply because the consequences of the slave's change of status would have been more unpredictable. Even in the face of these and other uncertainties, the secure archaeological context of the *columbaria* evidence allows us to establish a set of figures that offer a statistical view of Roman slavery and manumission in a specific historical environment.

NOTES

* I would like to thank John Pearce, Claire Holleran and Francesco Trifoli for their comments on this paper, which forms part of a larger project on Roman freedmen, generously sponsored by the Leverhulme Trust. All epigraphic references are to *CIL* VI. A fuller discussion of some of the issues raised in this paper can be found in *The Freedman in the Roman World* (Cambridge 2011).

1 Cf. Scheidel 1999 and 2005.

2 Cic. *Phil.* 8.32: 'Etenim, patres conscripti, cum in spem libertatis sexennio post sumus ingressi diutiusque servitutem perplessi quam captivi servi frugi et diligentes solent, quas vigilias, quas sollicitudines, quos labores liberandi populi Romani cause recusare debemus?' ('Indeed, members of the Senate, now after six years we have begun to entertain the hope of liberty, after enduring servitude longer than enslaved prisoners of war are wont to do if they are well behaved and conscientious, we must decline no vigils, no anxieties, no labours in the cause of the freedom of the Roman People'). Loeb translation.

3 Alföldy 1986: 286–331; contra Wiedemann 1985; Harris 1980, who also noted that according to Dio 53.25.4, *captivi* might be freed after twenty years.

4 Cf. Mouritsen 2005, with further references to modern scholarship.

5 The monument has been carefully studied by Caldelli and Ricci 1999, on whose results the description of the structure is based. Hasegawa's book (Hasegawa 2005), which deals with the same material in some detail, appeared while I was preparing this paper. As will become apparent, our results differ substantially on several points.

6 Room N (1–381) 6482, 6485, 6413, 6495, 6583, 6517, 6487, 6520, 6223, 6516, room O (382–407) 6608, 6598, 6597, 6605, 6621, room P (408–426) 6629, 6631, 6622, 6623, 6637, 6626, 6639. For these outsiders see below p. 46.

7 Caldelli and Ricci 1999: 19, suggested that the two other chambers were added after the family's fortunes revived in 66 CE. Hasegawa (2005: 55f) argued that members of more than one aristocratic household were represented in the Statilian *columbarium*, but the supporting evidence remains weak, undermined

    not least by the *contubernia* between members of supposedly separate house-
    holds and by apparent the abandonment of the site in 53 CE.

 8 Buonocore 1984. For the family, see Eck 1972, and AA.VV. 1982.

 9 Buonocore 1984: 44. Some inscriptions were reused later, e.g., 7327 (no. 43), 7284b (no. 113).

10 See the discussion in Manzella 2008: 307–17, with references.

11 We have little evidence for the internal workings of these *collegia*, and the fact that commemoration relied on membership and payment obviously has the potential to skew the epigraphic profile. However, there is nothing in the surviving body of material to suggest any *systematic* under-representation of specific sections of the household, apart from infants and younger female slaves, cf. the discussion below. Otherwise the evidence would seem to indicate a surprisingly wide coverage of all types of domestic staff, including the most humble.

12 Buonocore 1984: 222, no. 130. Statilii: 6214, 6612. Four more inscriptions, 6482, 6629, 6637, and 6516 provide for further burials, but they all commemorate outsiders, suggesting this category tended to establish a family burial when they gained access to the site.

13 For example, I assume that the two 'Heracleo' in 6220 and 6543 are identical, since the name is otherwise not recorded in the *columbarium*. Likewise, the 'Malchio' in 6573 and 6374, and the 'Pansa' in 6220 and 6326. There are also grounds for believing that 6433, 'Egloge Hilari,' and 6480, 'Iucunda Hilari,' may refer to the same person, since the appearance and layout of the two inscriptions are very similar, cf. Caldelli and Ricci 1999: figs. 181f. On the other hand, it is entirely possible that some of the many documented 'Felices' (18) and 'Erotes' (14) may in fact be identical. Hasegawa reaches a total for the Statilii of 657 individuals and 301 for the Volusii, but it is not clear on what basis (Hasegawa 2005). Westermann (1955: 88) gave a total of 428 slaves and freedmen for the *familia Statiliorum*, divided into 192 *servi*, 84 *servae*, 100 *liberti*, 62 *libertae*.

14 6217, 6220 (four times), 6225, 6345, 6407, 6481, 6489, 6515, 6581.

15 Given that the inscriptions all belong to a very specific social context where the free / unfree distinction would have been vitally important, it seems *a priori* unlikely that those composing the epitaphs could have ignored this aspect, *pace* Weaver 2001: 104. Indicating the deceased's free status could be done very easily, simply through the addition of an 'L' or 'Lib,' a practice also noted by Eck (1978: 282), in the 'Testamentum Dasumii.' Therefore, in inscriptions such as 'Primus atriesis,' where the dedicators even included a job title, the unfree status of Primus is overwhelmingly likely. The main uncertainty relates to indirectly recorded individuals, where occasionally free status is not indicated, e.g., 6410, 6479, but they represent a very small group (only nineteen individuals), which does not affect the overall distribution. Hasegawa (2005: 54) overestimates the problem posed by the *incerti*, also suggesting that the decline in the use of

status indicators reflected 'a degree of ambivalence in conceptions and conditions of freedom in this period.' In fact, the material reveals a keen awareness of the importance of status.

16 Since women often were freed before the end of their reproductive years, there may have been more freeborn in the material than we are able to identify. But only in one case does it seem likely that a person without filiation was freeborn, T. Statilius Gamillus, who died just one year old, 6541. Another candidate is T. Statilius Crescens filius, son of T. Statilius Tauri l. Spinther, 6301, but filiation was often used informally to indicate relationship rather than status. The lack of clear indicators of freeborn status may suggest that the most important distinction within the *familia* was that between the free and the unfree.

17 The Volusii Saturnini were famous for their wealth, cf. Tac. *Ann.* 14.56.1, and D'Arms (1981: 69f) argued for their extensive involvement in commercial activities. Some of this wealth is likely to have 'trickled' down and benefited at least some of their freedmen, who may have been unusually affluent. Still, while that may account for the many ornate monuments in the *columbarium*, it does not explain the complete absence of the simple types of burial, which dominate among the Statilii.

18 There are no *germani* among the Volusii and only one *lecticarius*, whereas the corresponding figures for the Statilii are 11 and 14, although the absence of *germani* among the Volusii may, as Prof. Werner Eck has suggested to me, be due to political factors. There are also six *pedisequi / ae* among the Statilii and none in the Volusii, along with five *atrienses* and three *ostiarii*.

19 Caldelli and Ricci 1999: appendix 3, 135–43. They assume (53–66) that these burials belong to the interval between the closure of chamber N and the building of O and P. Supposedly, the confiscation of the Statilian estate meant that burial in the *columbarium* was no longer possible. However, they also accept there was continued access to the *columbarium*, and the fact that the external burials were located in close proximity to the monuments does not suggest the estate was entirely off limits for the *familia*.

20 E.g., 6208 by the wife (outsider) of T. Statilius Chrestus, possibly the owner of slaves in the *columbarium*); 10386, for Statilia Storge, wife of Statilius Mystes decur.; 26760 for T. Statilius Tauri l. Eleutherus by Statilia Storge, *conliberta*; 26787 for Statilia T. Hilari l. Iucunda, cf. 6480 Iucunda Hilari, but both dedicatees. Caldelli and Ricci (1999) identify the patron with 6373 T. Statilius T.l. Hilarus Cor. vest., but there are also other possibilities, e.g., 6460.

21 As we shall see, the possibility that some freedmen might have left the service of the patron and disappeared from the record completely is fairly remote. Even the most affluent and favoured Statilian freedman, Posidippus, with twenty-one slaves and freedmen, remained firmly attached to the *familia*.

22 *CIL* VI 5931–60. Hasegawa (2005: 65), gives a different figure for the Arruntii, 57/43 per cent, with a total of sixty-one.

23 The greatest imbalance is found among the Statilii, which may be explained by the greater proportion in this *columbarium* of indirectly recorded individuals, especially *ordinarii* and *patroni*, who are overwhelmingly male. If we disregard this category, we find a ratio of 67/33 per cent, which brings it more in line with that of the two other *columbaria*.

24 The percentages in the columns are not counted vertically but indicate the share of females of the age groups.

25 Hasegawa 2005: 62–72, cf. figs. 5.1.1–3. She suggests that exposure of female children was a significant factor, but that seems highly unlikely when dealing with aristocratic households like these. The disparity is probably due partly to under-commemoration and partly to gender imbalance among purchased slaves. Moreover, the most striking under-representation is at ages 5–9, which was hardly affected by exposure.

26 The common notion that female slaves, especially after their reproductive years, became less valued as domestic labour and therefore were more readily freed seems to be based on a misunderstanding of the consequences of Roman manumission. Freeing a slave generally did not mean discontinuity of service or an end to patronal responsibilities. If slaves were no longer deemed useful in the household, the natural option was sale – or possibly abandonment – rather than manumission.

27 We may also note that the Volusii conform to the smaller sample of the Arruntii, which also reveals an almost identical ratio of slave and freed, twenty-four slaves and twenty-three freedmen, similar to that of the Volusii. It would therefore seem that the gender and status ratios may have been correlated, both under-representing slaves and women.

28 Treggiari 1975b; Madden 1996; López Barja de Quiroga 1998.

29 Some slaves appear to have been freed even below the age of eleven. Some may have been 'pets' or *delicia*, in which case their early death most certainly would have been recorded, thereby distorting the overall profile. Very early manumission was in any case the exception, and we cannot exclude the possibility that it may have been directly linked to the recipients' early deaths, since we have literary evidence for deathbed manumission of young slaves, Petr. *Sat.* 65.10f; Mart. 1.101; Pliny *Ep.* 8.16.

30 Alföldy 1986; Harper 1972; Weaver 1972.

31 This result questions some modern theories about the rate of manumission, most obviously Alföldy's suggestion (1972) that with few exceptions all urban slaves could expect to be freed before they reached middle age.

32 See Scheidel 1997; Harris 1999; Lo Cascio 2002.

33 7376, 7377. Buonocore 1984: nos. 76, 78.

34 1833a (Buonocore 1984: no. 6); 7368 (Buonocore 1984: no. 33). There is no trace of this practice in the Statilian material.

35 Merola discusses some of this material without drawing any conclusions (Merola 1990: 136–43).

36 6293 Protogenes Hipparchi *vicarius horrearius*, 6292 Felix Hipparchi *vicarius horrearius*, 6228, 6385, 6398. Hasegawa's reconstruction of the ownership of the Chresti is unconvincing (Hasegawa 2005: 59). She interprets the different *agnomina* as being one and the same slave changing name when passing from one owner to another. However, the use of *agnomina* clearly served to distinguish between homonymous slaves.

37 6246, 6261, 6262, 6274, 6277, 6278, 6279, 6410, 6415, 6415, 6426, 6475, 6476, 6479, 6493, 6498, 6525, 6535, 6574. The five-year-old Condicius Posidippi *liberti*, 6426, was not, as Hasagawa assumes, a freedman (Hasagawa 2005: 54). Their recorded ages are 5, 7, 12, 14, 20, 27.

38 The link to Posidippus is not made explicitly but the Eros *dispensator*, who owned them, is most likely identical with Eros T. Statili Posidippi ser. disp., 6274.

39 The distinct character of his *familia* is reflected by the fact that many of the epitaphs for its members are quite standardized, suggesting either that Posidippus himself organized the commemoration or it was done by the remaining members. See Caldelli and Ricci 1999: figs. 153–71 for illustrations.

40 Hasegawa 2005: 57, takes it for granted that Iasullus was the slave of Phileros, the *cubicularius Corneliae*, since Iasullus was *paedagogus* for her son Sisenna. The link is possible but not certain.

41 It is of course possible that some *vicarii* were purchased independently by the slaves themselves out of their *peculia*, although the scale of the phenomenon suggests this was not always the case. In any event, that does not alter the fact that their sub-*familiae* all appear to be completely integrated into the wider *familia*.

42 The freeborn Q. Volusius Q.f. Vel. Antigonus appears in two inscriptions in the Volusian *columbarium*, suggesting he was still a member of the *familia*, 7376, 7377; Buonocore 1984: nos. 76, 78.

43 Hasegawa 2005: 77, gives a full list of inscriptions with *natio* among the Statilii. Surprisingly, most of these instances relate to female slaves, but this may reflect epigraphic practices rather than the structure of the household.

44 Buonocore 1984: no. 57.

45 Fenoaltea 1984: 635–68; Scheidel 2008.

46 The figures for the distribution of job titles among men/women, slaves/freed, and dedicators/dedicatees are Volusii: 50 men/10 women; Statilii: 146 men/22 women; Volusii: 47 slaves/13 freed; Statilii: 143 slaves/25 freed; Volusii: 20 dedicators/43 dedicatees; Statilii: 23 dedicators/135 dedicatees. These patterns cast doubt on the notion that 'the slaves and freedmen without titles had no clearly defined work' (Flory 1978: 78–95, 80).

47 E.g., Treggiari 1975b: 395.

48 E.g., Chrestus Auctianus with three *vicarii*, 6228, 6385, 6398; Hipparchus with three under-slaves, 6292, 6293, 6392; and Chrestus Tauri with two, 6390, 6402. One also notes the slave status of Thyrsus, *medicus*, 6320; and Nothus, *librarius a manu*, 6314.

49 They include, e.g., 6330, T. Statilius Zabda, *paedagogus* Statiliae; 6331, Statilia T.l. Tyranis, *paedagoga* Statiliaes; 6301, T. Statilius Tauri l. Spinther, *supra lecticarius*, i.e., in charge of the litter bearers; 6381, Phileros lib. *unctor*; 6372, 6264, T. Statilius Phileros, Corneliaes *cubicularius*, T. Statilius Dasius Tauri l. *ad vestem*, presumably in charge of the wardrobe; 6373, T. Statilius T.l. Hilar[–] Cor. *vest.*; and 6374, T. Statilius Malchio, *ad vestem*.

50 *NH* 33.26, 'mancipiorum legiones, in domo turba externa ac iam servorum quoque causa nomenclator adhibendus.'

51 Corn. Nep. *Att.* 13, gives a rare insight into the various considerations that might inform the composition of an elite household. Atticus's exclusive use of *vernae* is construed as evidence of his modest lifestyle (rather than meanness), but at the same time the skills, training, and education of the slaves are emphasized. Atticus did therefore not lack adequate staff but merely pretty slaves (itself a sign of *luxuria*). His slaves even mastered several tasks and skills, which clearly was considered unusual. Thus, part of Cicero's attack on Piso focused on his household, where the cook and the *atriensis* were the same, and which did not even include a baker. Moreover, his serving staff was unkempt and some of them even old, *Pis.* 67, cf. Ael. Arist. *Eis Romen* 71. Likewise in Petr. *Sat.* 68.8, the stingy freedman Habinnas praises a slave who can perform many different tasks, whereas Trimalchio, keen to emulate the highest orders, has an absurd amount of specialized staff, *pace* Baldwin 1978. For the structure and ideology of the elite household, see Treggiari 1975b: 48–77.

52 Among the Statilii we find no fewer than seven *unctores*, 6263, 6343, 6377, 6378, 6380, 6381, 6382, as well as two *comoedi*, 6252, 6253, and a *symphoniacus*, 6356. The staff of the Volusii included a *citharoedus*, 7286.

53 Ps.-Quintilian, *Decl.Min.* 311.7, declared that slaves were: 'aut natus aut relictus hereditate aut emptus.' The tripartite origins of slaves is reflected in Petr. *Sat.* 47f, where the cook is asked whether he is bought or home-born, to which he answers that he is neither since he was left to him in a will. The importance of inheritances is underlined by the *ad hereditates* T. Statilius Iucundus, 6291.

54 The notion of the *familia* as a *res publica*, a place of belonging and identity, was actively fostered by the owners, cf. Pliny *Ep.* 8.16.2, 'nam servis res publica quaedam et quasi civitas domus est' ('for the house provides a slave with a country and a sort of citizenship'); Seneca *Ep.* 47.14, 'domum pusillam rem publicam esse iudicaverunt' ('they held that a household was a miniature *res publica*').

55 The complex internal structure of the household, based on a system of decentralized 'management' and ownership, with large numbers of servants belonging not to the aristocratic family but either to *servi ordinarii* or to freedmen, may have provided yet another means of providing incentives for loyalty and hard work.

3

Reading the 'Pages' of the *Domus Caesaris: Pueri Delicati,* Slave Education, and the Graffiti of the Palatine Paedagogium

PETER KEEGAN

Introduction

In a brief note on the interpretation of parietal inscriptions, Heikki Solin applied the term 'graffitologia' to the analytical approach that allows an informed commentary and a historically meaningful interpretation of any epigraphical text, graffiti included. Importantly, Solin noted that 'the essential difference between lapidary inscriptions and graffiti is the fact that in the case of graffiti the composer and executor of the text is the same person.'[1] This relationship between inscriber and inscription means that graffiti can open our modern eyes to a layer of lived experience in the ancient world unavailable from other approaches to history – the world of ordinary men and women, speaking their minds and their hearts, as best they can, to their family, their friends, and their contemporaries.

Graffiti, fragmentary as they are and foreign to the models of stereotypical language in the classical canon, the formal epigraphic record, and the papyrological corpora, open up good opportunities for deciphering in terms of palaeography and linguistic variation from the standard (codified) norm. Beyond textual variation, close attention can also be given to archaeological context, since the purpose of the environment can sometimes permit important deductions for reconstructing the script.[2]

But reading the inscribed spaces of a purpose-built environment in ancient Rome can do more. As Mark Grahame observed in his spatial analysis of Pompeian housing, 'buildings are "containers" for social life and without people are nothing more than empty shells.' If the historian of ancient Rome wishes to make any substantive statement about a building's social meaning, then it must be populated with the people and activities it originally contained.[3] Looking at graffiti inscribed into the material fabric of a building on the Palatine Hill occupied by a specific servile population can repopulate the otherwise empty volumes of excavated Roman space. Pierre Bourdieu tells us that a building instils a certain 'way of being' or 'habitus' into those who use it. It should be possible for the historian, by moving through a building inscribed with the material manifestations of a particular servile culture, to reconstruct something of that culture. By emphasizing material conditions and personal attitudes, the analysis and interpretation of graffiti in a built space contextualized historically as servile speak directly to one of the goals underpinning Keith Bradley's recent contribution to the study of slavery, namely, to write social history that reconstructs the reality of slavery as it was experienced by the individual.[4]

Consequently, analysing graffiti found on the walls of the Palatine Paedagogium can tell us something about the formation of social identities and cultural patterns particular to slaves under imperial Roman rule. In the first part of this chapter I examine the physical context of the Palatine Paedagogium. In addition to a descriptive survey of the building's topographical location, archaeological remains, and chronological indications, attention will be paid to the various interpretations of its functions during the imperial period at Rome, and to literary and epigraphic representations of the inhabitants of such contexts (*paedagogi* and *paedagogiani*). In the second part I consider the evidence of the numerous graffiti found in the Paedagogium as an index to the educational levels, ethnicity, and training of pre-pubescent, adolescent, and older male slaves in the imperial household. In the third part I discuss the degree to which social historians can make use of the evidence provided by the Paedagogium graffiti – for instance, to shed light on whether or not institutionalized education inculcated explicitly Roman cultural values within the social structure of Roman slavery – and whether contemporary theory serves to illuminate or obscure the material realities of Roman slavery. By situating the need to define personal and collective identity in graffiti on the walls of the Palatine Paedagogium, this study will use material culture to highlight the variety of socio-cultural relationships among the population of slaves known to some as 'pages' in the *domus Caesaris*.[5]

1. Context

Topography, Archaeology, and Dating of the Paedagogium

On the southwestern slope of the Palatine Hill from the presumed *biblio-theca Apollonis* situated south of the Flavian palace, in the area to the west of the large hemicycle of the *domus Caesaris*, are the remains of a building consisting of several rooms and a hemicycle around a central area (fig. 3.1). This edifice is generally recognized by the name of 'paedagogium' because of the phrase *exit de paedagogio* (or formulations thereof), often accompanied by a single name, which occurs twelve times in graffiti on the structure's walls.[6] In line with the primary articulation of the *domus Caesaris*, the Palatine Paedagogium is orientated northwest – southeast and is therefore more or less parallel to the Circus Maximus. The main floor of the northern section of the edifice, which is better preserved, comprises ten rooms of different size, arranged to the sides of a large semicircular chamber. These rooms open out onto a *porticus* and paved rectangular courtyard. Although the form and appearance of the remainder of the structure are less certain, from the available planimetric data it seems possible to interpret what survives as a *quadriporticus* with a large open area to the south, including a long complex of unknown function and structure. Technical data indicate that the structure, which developed on at least two levels (as indicated by the presence of a staircase near the northwest corner), was constructed originally with brickwork datable to the Domitianic period.[7]

There is still some uncertainty about the function of this building. Another building, a *paedagogium ad Caput Africae* on the Caelian Hill, has also been identified as the possible site for the imperial training school on the basis of inscriptions, and the differences between the two have given rise to several interpretations.[8] Filippo Coarelli sees the Caelian as the location for the actual school for imperial pages, while the Palatine structure might have served as their living quarters. If this were the case, one might have expected an architectural plan more typical of a building designed for residence rather than occupation: namely, a courtyard surrounded by a series of similarly sized small rooms on all four sides. Other scholarship has identified the building on the Palatine as a school for painting for those who had first served an apprenticeship at the *paedagogium ad Caput Africae*; as a prison for the Caelian slaves; as a kind of barracks for foreign soldiers redeployed from the Caelian to guard the western side of the imperial palace; as a vestibule of the palace; as a meeting place for administrative officials or *procuratores*; as a headquarters for the keepers of imperial vestments; as an infirmary connected to

the Circus Maximus; and as the *domus Gelotiana*,[9] from which the emperor
Gaius (Caligula) helped with preparations for the Circus games.[10] Questions
clearly remain about whether or not this building should be identified as a
paedagogium, and if and in what way it and the building on the Caelian may
have been related. All views, though, require the structure to be occupied by
a significant proportion of enslaved and manumitted persons. It is one of the
purposes of this chapter to work towards narrowing the range of possible
interpretations of the building's function and occupancy, and showing how
the record and context of graffiti aid in this process.

What remains of the building tells us that it was constructed originally
with brickwork datable to the Domitianic period (CE 81–96). On a plan of
the main floor of the building, two very small, symmetrical rooms (fig. 3.1, 5
and 6), located on either side of an exedra (4) contain many graffiti, while in
the other rooms the plaster has been in large part destroyed. Rooms 7 and 8,
to the east of the exedra, also contain graffiti, as do the southeast wall of corridor 15 and the northwest wall of corridor 16. Altogether, the most recent
cataloguers of these inscriptions list 369 graffiti.[11] Using relative and internal criteria to determine various relationships between the building and the
graffiti, it is possible to say that, in relative terms, the graffiti in room 6 are
Trajanic, Hadrianic, or possibly Antonine (CE 98–138 or 192), while those in
rooms 7 and 8 date to the second and third centuries AD. Applying internal
criteria case by case allows a few graffiti to be traced specifically to the time of
Septimius Severus and the Severan period.[12] The evidence provides a broad
chronology only, then, and we cannot know for certain when the building
was occupied. Nevertheless the distribution and spatial density of the graffiti in those spaces where plaster survives suggests an inscribing practice
shared over centuries by members of a population associated with activities
that took place within this building. In common with ephemeral inscriptions
preserved in other parts of Roman Italy and the wider Mediterranean world,
the Paedagogium graffiti invite us to participate in a discourse that is both
common in the oral-literate culture of Graeco-Roman antiquity and specific
to particular places within the ancient urban fabric.[13]

To contextualize the inscribed evidence that has given rise to such a range
of interpretative voices, attention will be given first to references in the ancient literary and formal epigraphic sources to the imperial buildings and
aristocratic facilities known as *paedagogia* and to slaves raised and educated
in these elite Roman establishments. Then, to negotiate the difficulty of epigraphic bias, which is encountered when looking at inscriptions generally
and graffiti particularly, this chapter will look more directly at the form and
function of graffiti inscribed by slaves and freedmen living and working in
the Palatine Paedagogium under imperial Roman rule.

Paedagogia *and* Paedagogiani *in the Ancient Sources*

The term *paedagogium* was used not only as a toponym but also as a concrete descriptive term in an early imperial literary reference and a number of inscribed sources. Retailing a dream about the phenomenon of *phantasmata*, Pliny the Younger observed that, prior to the appearance of two white-tuniced apparitions at the window of an aristocratic *uilla urbana* (perhaps his own Laurentine retreat), a young male slave was sleeping in the company of others *in paedagogio*. Given that Pliny provided a *gymnasium* for 'his own' in his villa at Laurentinum and that he was spared the shouts and festive clamour of his slaves even during the Saturnalia, we can suggest that the *paedagogium* of which he speaks comprised a number of slave children (*puer … mixtus pluribus*) who occupied the space defined by the term for an unspecified purpose, though one that might be inferred to incorporate a sense of belonging or community of some kind from its lexical associations, perhaps of organized activity, enterprise, or instruction from comparison with use of the term in epigraphic citations.[14]

As already noted, the term *paedagogium* was used by inhabitants of the Palatine building designated as such, specifically in the sense of a place to which an individual belonged and from which that individual eventually moved on (*exi(i)t de p(a)edagogio*). Commemorative inscriptions explicitly associated with the building on the Caelian refer to imperial slaves or freedmen who acted as *paedagogi* to younger male slaves. For instance, five individual epitaphs identify either *paedagogi a Kapite Africaes* or *paedagogi puerorum Kap. Afr.*, and a dedication of the second century to the emperor Caracalla lists twenty-four *paedagogi puerorum* by name. It is important to note that the latter title was used in private elite *familiae* as well as the imperial household.[15]

The evidence for the nominal staff of *paedagogia* embraces a range of conduct and duty. With respect to the imperial institution, for the individuals called *paedagogi puerorum*, Samuel Mohler suggested that the title refers to the duty of child-attendant or tutor rather than teacher. On the other hand, Keith Bradley argued that *paedagogi* of imperial and aristocratic boys and girls acted in a variety of interrelated capacities: instilling *disciplina* (dispensing academic and moral instruction); exercising *custodia* (acting in the role of companion and protector); and maintaining *decorum* (transmitting directives or precepts for public behaviour). In this view, the title given to the director of a *paedagogium* in three commemorative inscriptions (*praeceptor*) is suggestive.[16]

References to the servile objects of this organized duty of care and education – the *paedagogiani* (defined by association with place) or *pueri* (classified as the recipients of tutelary action) – can be located across a spectrum of literary genres (history, philosophy, biography, satire, and legal rescript). Paulus (*Dig.* 50.16.204) defined the term *puer* in three ways: a slave; a male; a boy. This Roman caste of servile male children is depicted in a variety of ways by the remaining sources: accompanying their *domini* on walks, travels, and hunts; serving at table and in the bathhouse; performing sexual services for their imperial and aristocratic owners. In a number of citations, the appearance of the *paedagogiani* or *pueri* is distinctive. They are sumptuously dressed and display hairstyles of uniform nature; these coiffures are very much like that of women. In addition to the elegance of their dress, hair, and deportment, this class of young male slave combines physical beauty with skill and accomplishment at their tasks.[17]

The historical range of the literary and epigraphic references to *paedagogia, paedagogi*, and *paedagogiani* encompasses in relative terms the archaeological chronology of the Palatine *paedagogium* – from the early Empire to the Severan period – and continues for at least another two centuries beyond. The first implicit reference to a servile population associated with the cultivating syllabus of the *paedagogium* dates to the late Republic. It can be found in Cicero's oration on behalf of Sextus Roscius, where he mentions the 'little slave boys' of Sulla's potent freedman, L. Cornelius Chrysogonus. These *pueruli* were 'masters of every art and every refinement, youths picked out of the most bequested households.' The latest surviving item emerges in the Digest, where Ulpian, addressing the legacy of *instructum* or *instrumentum*, considers the question of which individuals associated with the preparation and serving of food and wine should be included under this rubric. In this regard, the jurist pronounces on the incorporation of trainee slave boys into the legated *fundus instructum*, thereby outlining the appropriate exercise of care over *paedagogiani* who serve in the *triclinii* of authorized *domini*.[18]

Philo, familiar with the extravagance of the imperial *domus* from his months at Rome as the leader of a diplomatic embassy to Gaius, provides one of the most useful descriptions of the appearance of Roman slave boys in convivial contexts. In his treatise about the contemplative life, Philo comments on the beauty of the boys carrying water and pouring wine. Their faces are painted with cosmetics, their long hair is skilfully trimmed or plaited, and their tunics are of the finest fabrics and elegantly arranged. In addition to the sources cited above that support Philo's observations, we can note that slave boys serving at table are especially valued for their long, beautiful hair; they are referred to as *capillati, comati, criniti, crispuli*, and *calamistrati*.[19]

A number of iconographic documents can be added to this textual record. A painting in the *triclinium* of the Pompeian House of the Chaste Lovers (IX.12.6) depicts a boy serving wine, bringing garlands, and pouring water into a bowl. Another Pompeian *domus*, the House of the Triclinium (V.2.4), contains a banquet scene (fig. 4.3) in which slave boys take off the shoes of one guest and support another vomiting drunkenly. At Rome, in the southern side room of the *schola Praeconum*, the office of the public heralds, which has been identified as a possible adjunct to the Palatine paedagogium, are wall paintings of male figures in short tunics carrying objects appropriate to the banquet.[20] Also at Rome, in a building on the Caelian that may be part of the imperial infrastructure or an aristocratic *domus*, there is a processional scene comprising seven young male slaves, one wine-server, and six plate-bearers with a variety of foods. The wine-server and two other slaves are shown with long, flowing hair; the remainder have shorter hair. The wine-server is very well dressed in a tunic with *claui* and *orbiculi* in red and gold; the others are wearing long-sleeved tunics with ornamental shoulder patches.[21]

2. Indices of Slave Practice

Educational Levels

The inscriptions covering the walls of the Palatine Paedagogium were scratched in all probability by slaves and freedmen living or working there. The writing was inscribed for the most part with a *stylus*, or instruments sharp and stable enough to achieve a similar end, or in some instances with ink, chalk, charcoal, or paint. All the surviving items conform to the ancient Roman cursive style of writing.

At first sight, the graffiti represent a very heterogeneous orthography. Of course, with respect to the execution of cursive inscriptions, a number of factors cannot be forgotten: the ephemeral nature of the inscribed material; the ability of the writers; the instrument of execution; the surfaces for writing; and the positions for writing (from low down at the level of the floor to high up on the wall). To illustrate the importance of each of these factors, consider the consequence of surface quality on the Paedagogium inscriptions. A number of the graffiti reveal a tendency to trace curved lines with two traces rather than one. This technique resulted in the meeting point of inscribed letters being acute and the natural verticalization of signs.[22]

There is a further degree of explanation for this heterogeneity of epigraphic technique beside the mechanical. The graphic variations in the Paedagogium graffiti may reflect the diverse cultural levels of the various writers. Persons who had received only the first rudiments of elementary instruction would almost certainly have derived their style from the regular epigraphic configuration of formal inscriptions (*quadrata epigraphica*). These individuals would have been accustomed to tracing letters approaching the covered capital style. The majority of graffiti in the Paedagogium are of this type. On the other hand, persons participating in superior grades of instruction would have adopted the 'official' writing of documents, deriving from the formal epigraphic model: that is, the ancient miniscule cursive that came to be adopted for private use. Approximately 10 per cent of the Palatine inscriptions are of this type. The use of this cursive writing indicates a certain grade of instruction corresponding suggestively to the use of the building as a *paedagogium*.

Graffiti that represent the environment of the adjacent Circus Maximus and nearby Amphitheatrum Flavium confirm this educational range. Apart from two or three gladiatorial inscriptions in room 6, the remainder of graffiti with associations to the arena are located in room 8. On the northwest wall of room 8 is an image of two circus horses, each with a palm in its mouth. A message is scratched above this representation: *Pitholaus Digonus ueneti. pingit Fortunatus Afer.*[23] Since *uenetus* refers to the colour of the Blue faction, one of four *factiones* that owned and raced horses in the circus, the graffito has something to do with the personnel or animals associated with this enterprise. The first name, Pitholaus, is Greek, but male Greek names are not known as the names of horses; the second name, Digonus, is not attested in either Greek or Latin, but could stand for Dignus, which might be the name of a horse.[24] A rare signature in Latin is attached to the text.

On the same wall there is a drawing of two gladiators fighting. Above can be read the names *Antigonus / lib(ertus) MMCXII (?) Superbus lib(ertus) (pugnarum)*. To the right can be seen what appears to be a combat referee (*arbiter muneris*) with a long stick or baton, the *rudis*, in the right hand and possibly a trident in the left. Below, a message is inscribed within a *tabula ansata: Casuntius / dicet: accede.* Below the group is the name of the graffitist: *pingit / Zozzo.*[25] The gladiator named Antigonus was without doubt a *retiarius*; his uncovered head, trident, and tall shoulder guard confirm it. Although it is more difficult to identify his adversary Superbus, a visor shaped to the head, a short sword or dagger, and an elongated quadrangular shield strongly suggest that he was a *secutor*, the traditional adversary of the *retiarius*. The text can be read: 'Antigonus, freedman. MM (?). Crowns: 12. Superbus, freedman. Combats won: 1. Cassuntius declares: advance [that is, fight (hand to hand)].'[26] Again there is a signature, this time a Greek name, Zozzo.[27]

These graffiti not only attest to the literacy of the composers but also suggest a readership of their inscriptions. It is logical to infer that Fortunatus Afer and Zozzo composed and inscribed their graffiti for an intended constituency. The messages have been formulated as abbreviated textual elements accompanying inscribed visual cues. This was a primary characteristic of epigraphic intensification in the ancient world. The superscribed and enclosed words act as explanatory captions for the graphic display of victory in the circus and amphitheatre. To achieve a synthesis, the visual and symbolic syntax of these inscriptions required recognition of pattern, content, and meaning. The signatures of Fortunatus and Zozzo not only confirm an instrumental desire for recognition; they articulate a belief that their signatures would transmit authorship effectively and confidence that the servile population of the Paedagogium would understand what they wished to convey.

While it bears no signature, another graffito in room 8 registers the degree to which linguistic and visual dialogue could manifest itself and be understood.[28] Below a visual representation of a donkey turning a machine is the inscription: *Labora aselle quomodo ego laboraui / et proderit tibi* ('Toil, little donkey, in the manner in which I have toiled, and it will benefit you'). The figure represents the common type of Roman mill with a wheel whose motivating force was normally the donkey.[29] That the mill is designated to the rear and above the donkey, while normally the beast worked close to the mill, shows that the artist intended to render both elements completely visible.

There are a variety of interpretations for the text of this inscription. It may have been a joke that referred to someone of the name Asellus, or perhaps to a term of endearment for a person. Despite cinematic depictions, a slave as the motive force for a Roman mill wheel was exceptional and improbable, but the attendant implication of grinding routine seems a natural connotation. One could also want to see in the motto a quip addressed to a Christian, in relation to similar names that demonstrate the normalcy of assuming an appearance of humility. Carlo Visconti explained the graffito instead as a reference to the tribulations of military life. Tycho Wilamowitz suggested that the inscription has an iambic metre. That the graffito is able to be read as iambic may be a natural rather than an intentional occurrence. While there can be no firm solution to the problems of interpretation and scansion, the conceptual ambivalence and flexible syntax of the Asellus graffito provides further support to the contention of educational heterogeneity among the slaves and freedpersons living and working in the Palatine Paedagogium.[30]

In refining the terminology for the hands of those learning to write in Graeco-Roman Egypt, Raffaela Cribiore pointed out that writing was an art that individuals might exhibit even if they were limited to the writing of their own names. She was also able to show that there were styles of writing that could be fitted into a hierarchy, moving from formal stylized scripts for copying literary texts to various more flowing hands for private exercises. What the Paedagogium graffiti provide are reasonable and interesting suggestions of how teachers and students may have engaged in the process of learning to write in a servile environment in which the teaching of writing occurred. It may be dubious to subscribe unequivocally to the suggestion that members of the Graeco-Roman elite classes would not necessarily have had to do much writing in their own hands because of the availability of scribal slaves. Nonetheless, it is clear that the upper classes of the Roman Empire could rely on the availability of slaves suitably trained in the skills of writing and reading. Some of these slaves may have been drawn from institutions like the Palatine and Caelian *paedagogia*.[31]

Ethnicity

Roman personal names, consisting of several parts and constantly in evolution, offer material for historical interpretation. Sometimes a person's origin can be deduced on the basis of his or her name. It is dangerous, of course, to draw any direction connection between nomenclature and origins. Rather, Roman naming practices may be seen to reproduce embedded socio-political realities. Here, although Heikki Solin and Marja Itkonen-Kaila are of the opinion that the Paedagogium inscriptions do not have great historical value, onomastic study of the personal names inscribed on its walls can provide useful information about the population of the Palatine building.[32]

The names constitute principally separate *cognomina* largely of servile character. Names that are inscribed by inhabitants of the building which are typical of slaves in the Roman world include Alypus, Caetonicus, Comicus, Corinthus, Diadumenus, Doryphorus, Epitynchanus, Eugamus, Hermes, Hyacinthus, Nasta, Pallas, and Zoticus. Additionally, some *gentilicia* are used by themselves and function as *cognomina*, such as Iunio, Terini, Aelius, Domitius, Numisi, Quintio, and Valerius. With regard to the traditional structure of Roman names, there are two examples of *duo nomina* and one example of a set of *tria nomina*. The ratio of Greek to Latin names is 52:63. This ratio includes only different names, but naturally the same name could have belonged to more than one person. The ratio of all examples of Greek to Latin names is 113:139.[33]

A range so large in the use of separate names and in the Greek origin of many of them indicates the social status of the bearers of such names. While *ingenui* and *peregrini* who received the right of citizenship used Greek names, the context of the Paedagogium indicates that a Greek name should reflect servile origins. As well, it would be extraordinary if *liberti* omitted the *gentilicium*, the most manifest sign of their altered social status.

The unofficial nature of the graffiti explains why the names often provide ethnic indications without other determinants usually provided in public epigraphy, including a specific *natio* (used commonly in a more limited sense than the *gentilicium*, and sometimes identical with it), *domus* (used metonymically to denote one's native country), and so on. Names displaying an ethnic derivation are the frequent Afer, Armeni, Asiaticus, Graecus, Helen, Bithus, Daus, Gallus, and Narbonensis. Names common in North Africa, making up a significant proportion of the onomastic evidence in the graffiti, include Hadrimetinus, Ianuarius, Iugurtha, Nicaeensis, and Rogatus.

It is a difficult proposition to say in what measure the bearers of such names may be identified as belonging to the source of their toponymic, geographical, or ethnic associations. Slave names are a notoriously poor indicator of actual provenance. In other words, the individual named Corinthus may not have come originally from Corinth. By the same token, the material in the Paedagogium corroborates the contention that slaves of the imperial period in large part came from various regions of the Empire. Moreover, in the same way that 'slaves [were] either born or made,'[34] the onomastic diversity of male slave names drawn from a catalogue under Roman authority inscribes the divide between conqueror and conquered, master and slave, reproducing in substantive form the appropriative, subordinating impulses underpinning Rome's geo-political expansion. To cross the threshold of the *domus Caesaris* was to enter into one of the premier built spaces in imperial Rome within which the relationship between Roman and non-Roman was performed in name and act, accommodating and fostering the development of a series of vertical and horizontal social relationships between the centre and the periphery of the Roman Mediterranean.[35]

Training

According to Solin and Itkonen-Kaila, there are no secure examples of indications of professions connected to any of the names. However, Raffaele Garrucci records two graffiti, now lost, that provide some correlation between name and occupation: *Marin(us) ianitor* and *Ododaes custos*. Both *ianitor* and *custos* refer in a primary sense to the function of doorkeeper. It is likely that the roles of such slaves, assigned to service in the imperial palace, would have been basically similar to those of slaves and freedmen of aristocratic houses familiar from the literary sources. If this assumption is correct, then literary evidence for the kinds of service performed by *paedagogiani* can be adduced to suggest that Marinus and Ododaes had been trained in supervisory duties, gatekeeping, guest control, and protection in the imperial household. For example, Apuleius attests to the fact that a *ianitor* held custodial responsibility for the condition, conduct, and protection of household guests.[36] Epigraphic evidence relating to the *familia Caesaris* refers to the post of *custos*, a position which did not involve promotion up a regular scale or *cursus* and occupied the same category as *pedisequi, nomenclatores,* and *tabellarii* in terms of occupational status. Imperial *custodes* were non-professional workers who protected the person of the emperor and his family and the condition of the imperial household. In addition to evidence attesting the protective functions of the *custos,* a fragment of a marble tablet providing for payments to individuals involved in the supply of wine to the city of Rome refers to *custodes cuparum* (guardians of the casks). These specified persons were workers charged with looking after the *uina fiscalia* in the wine magazines attached to Aurelian's Temple of the Sun.[37] As additional support for P.R.C. Weaver's identification of *custodes* as low-status domestic staff, Ododaes *custos* may be seen to act as an individual within the larger subclerical administrative staff of the imperial household.[38]

In this regard, a graffito on the southeast wall of room 16 refers to an imperial freedman of uncertain name as a *proc(urator).* Among other duties, a *procurator* was a person given responsibility or charge of administering various positions in the imperial civil administration. Epitaphs at Rome register certain individuals, for example, as PROC VINORVM and PROC AB ORNAMENTIS. Given the literary associations of *paedagogiani* already enumerated, the person partially recorded in this graffito – [. . .]atus Aug(usti) lib(ertus) proc(urator) – may have been appointed to look after matters pertaining to either of these aspects of life in the *domus Caesaris.* Inscriptions also recognize the competency of *tricliniarchi* who served the emperor and his representatives in relation to the overall direction of service at imperial and provincial dinners. It is possible that Marinus and Ododaes were trained in specific tasks performed under the supervision of this category of imperial freedman at Rome.[39]

While the name Ododaes is recorded only once, Marinus appears a total of eight times, and on two occasions bears the *cognomen* Afer. The fact that a certain Marinus inscribed a title of employment after his name may indicate a desire to have this occupational designation recognized by his fellow slaves. Further, in the graffito already discussed in relation to evidence for educational levels, Marinus Afer is leaving the Paedagogium. This Marinus may be the same person who designated himself as *ianitor.* If this is the case, then it is also possible that it was the acquisition of an occupational title that marked Marinus's departure from the Paedagogium.[40] While it is difficult to pin down the significance of the formula *exi(i)t de p(a)edagogio,* this sequence of inferences suggests a tentative relationship between the successful completion of training in a particular category of service and movement of the trained slave from the training institution into the imperial *familia*. *Exi(i)t de p(a)edagogio* may have signified a slave's declaration of promotion from apprentice *paedagogianus* to a titled position within the imperial servile community.

The list of occupational titles inscribed in the Paedagogium is not limited to Garrucci's *ianitor* and *custos*. On the southeast wall of room 5, a certain Euphemus is named an *opi<f>er*, a slave who provided medicinal aid, which could have been entrusted to imperial slaves and freedpersons.[41] The auspicious associations of the name Euphemus may be fortuitous with respect to a functionary bringing help under the auspices of healing deities. Taken together, Euphemus *opi<f>er* should not be seen so much as support for nominative determinism – Euphemus's future career was unknown when the name was bestowed on him – but as another instance of the potential for such evidence: as part of a broader exploration of possible meanings rather than definite conclusions. On the same wall, the partial denomination Cres[ces] is followed by another word, possibly *perfusor*. Though *perfusor* is a very rare term, recurring only in a Pompeian electoral *programma*, and the interpretative solution can be viewed as internally arbitrary, the role of pouring water over bathers would not have been out of place in the imperial household.[42]

Room 6 bears witness on its north- and southeast walls to the title *episcopus* (guardian or supervisor), associated four times with the name Libanus and once following a certain Quintio, perhaps the Quinto Afer named in another Paedagogium graffito.[43] If *episcopus* was not inscribed as an insult by some *paedagogianus* to his Christian work companion – an interpretation discussed below in relation to cultural patterns – the title may designate Libanus and Quintio as performing the function of a particular type of *custos*, possibly as custodians over slaves in this building.

Two terms in the Paedagogium graffiti express the prevalent association in the literary sources of *paedagogiani* and personal service at close quarters to the emperor, his family, and the imperial retinue of aristocratic and equestrian retainers. On the west wall of room 6, the individuals Epitynchanus and Asiaticus appear to designate themselves as *pueri*; this collective term is also inscribed on the southeast wall of the same room, though in that instance without attached names. As noted previously, *pueri* existed as a clearly defined category of domestic slave and as part of the *instrumentum* of the slave-owning class. On the southeast wall of room 8, the word *iuuenes* might encompass a similar meaning.[44]

In this regard, a prevalent abbreviation among the graffiti – V () D () N () – can be interpreted as an explicit identification of collegial identity among a subgroup within the Paedagogium community. Taking account of the fact that a proportion of the servile population on the Palatine could have been a product of sexual relationships within the environment of imperial or elite *familiae*, a number of Paedagogium slave boys will have been designated as *ex ancilla natus*, that is, *uernae* or house-born slaves. The individuals Demetrius and Dolphius, for instance, identified themselves as *uerna(e)*, and an otherwise unknown person registered his occupational and social status as *uerna exit de pedagogio*. The formula V () D () N () can therefore be read as *u(erna) d(omini) n(ostri)*; for example, *Primus V () D () N ()* defines Primus as 'a house-born slave of our Lord,' namely, Imperator Caesar.[45]

But the young male slaves known as *paedagogiani* can also be recognized in the litera;ry record by their functional attributes, physical characteristics, and distinctive clothing. These identifying traits are reflected in a catalogue of personal names drawn from the Paedagogium graffiti. On the northwest wall of room 5, a person scratched the word Capillatus, a term used to describe long-haired slave boys and youths serving at banquets in a variety of roles. We have already noted other terms used in Latin literature to indicate these *serui tricliniarii: comatus, crinitus, crispulus*, and *calamistratus*. Although a common Greek appellation, the name Diadumenus, incised on the northeast wall of room 6, can also be adduced as an appropriate sobriquet in relation to the *pueri capillati*.[46]

In regard to the prestige adhering in representations of banquet-slaves, we can note that someone inscribed the name Suavis in two locations on the southeast wall of room 6. With its implications of aesthetic attraction and visual pleasure, Suavis as the personal name of an imperial *paedagogianus* aptly reflects the prominence of physical beauty in literary descriptions of long-haired young dining-slaves in the *domus Caesaris*. On the northwest wall of the same room, another person scrawled the name Venustus Afer, a *cognomen* that similarly conveys a sense of attractiveness, either in appearance or manner.[47]

Although the plaster is seriously damaged on the northwest wall of room 8, it is still possible to make out the personal names Umanus Af(er) and Urbanus. The adjectival force of these names reflects a sense of cultivated practice in keeping with the activities ascribed to *paedagogiani* retained by imperial and elite *domini*. Historians of the iconographic representation of *serui tricliniarii* in the high imperial period have noted that long-haired, finely dressed slave boys are included in banquet scenes to characterize a privileged category of servant. These names suggest something of the elegance and sophistication that would have adhered to civilized service in the imperial household.[48]

A unique graffito on the northwest wall of room 8 provides a list of clothing usually associated with the high imperial household:[49] *balagauda / Dalmatica bo ... / Dalmatica maf*[fortia] */ Dalmatica m*[afortia?] *// lacerna diui /* [b]*yrru*[s] */* [l]*acerna*[e] */ Canusini / Mutines*[es]. Comparing the items on the list with the Edict of Diocletian (19–22) shows that all names are of precious robes or their distinguishing features. Historians of textiles dating to the Roman period categorize the *paragauda* [Gk. *parayw / dhv*] primarily as the border of a tunic. Enriched with gold thread, it was traditionally worn by women, and not allowed to men except as one of the insignia of office. These borders were among the rich presents given by Furius Placidus when he was made consul in the mid-fourth century AD. Under the later emperors the manufacture of them was forbidden except in their own *gynaecea*. The term *paragauda*, probably of Oriental origin, seems also to have been converted into an adjective, and thus to have become the denomination of the tunic, which was decorated with such borders. The edict of Justinian permitted its use by men as a special distinction. Similarly, the *dalmatica mafortium* was a short mantle (*palla*) deriving from the eastern Adriatic. It was worn by women. The other items in this list could have been worn by men or women. The *lacerna* and *birrus* were woollen cloaks or mantles worn over the tunic; *Canusini* and *Mutines*[es refer to garments made of Canusian and Mutinan wool.[50]

That the catalogue pertains either specifically to women or is gender-inclusive has allowed some historians to infer the presence of at least one *uestiarius* among the Palatine population. One of the inscriptions relating to the *paedagogium ad Caput Africae* identifies a certain Marcus as *Caputafricesi deputabatur inter bestitores*, that is, an imperial slave who belonged to the training institution on the Caelium and was reckoned one of the 'keepers of the wardrobe.' In this light, the abbreviation V () D () N () has been interpreted as *u(estiarius) d(omini) n(ostri)*. References to women in the graffiti – Ulpia Phoebe; Spes – could be adduced as additional evidence supporting the contention that some of the Palatine community acted in the capacity of *uestiarii*, servicing the clothing requirements of male and female members of the imperial household. However, Spes is an isolated fragment that could signify something other than the personal name of a woman; and Ulpia Phoebe is addressed as the subject either of a wish or a declaration of affection: *Ulpia Phoebe, | di te seruent*. In other words, the likelihood is that these inscriptions contain greetings to women regarded with esteem: patronesses, perhaps; *conseruae* or *collibertae* more probably.[51]

3. Material Realities

Social Identities

The *onomasticon* of slave names inscribed on the walls of the Palatine Paedagogium contributes to our understanding of the systematic clarity with which the Roman slave-owning class distinguished property from persons.

It, and the messages associated with some of these names, can also tell us about how the imperial elite regarded a particular servile group within its extensive household *familia* and how the slaves thought about themselves and those around them.

As philologists and ancient historians have shown, Latin slave names were derived from a variety of sources. We have already noted a number of Latin, Greek, and 'barbarian' slave names that derived their force from a range of categories belonging to this onomastic system. In light of the common association in Roman contexts of servile origin with a Greek *cognomen*, some of the most frequently attested slave names in the Paedagogium are Latin – Concessus/-ianus (4); Faustus (4); Felix/-icis (21); Mari(a)nus (8); Primus (6); Victor (12) – and 'barbarian' – Afer (16); Ianuarius (6); Nicaeensis (3). A few slave names with a Greek derivation are also attested in significant numbers: Epitynchanus (11); Eutyches (6).[52]

Nine names reflect the conventional Roman practice of identifying slaves as occupying a desired position, or as somehow well off, successful, or lucky. These names are primarily Latin – Faustus, Felix, Fortunatianus, Liberalis, and Optatus – and Greek – Eulogus, Euphemus, and Eutyches; they constitute respectively 6 of the 63 Latin and 3 of the 52 Greek names, and number 41 of the overall catalogue of 252 names in the Paedagogium. While most of these names conform to the category of *Wunschnamen* (desired *nomina*), we have already seen that Euphemus is an apt moniker for an *opifer*, that is, a slave trained in the provision of medicinal remedies; possibly, in the context of the banquet, in aid of giving diners digestive relief or as palliative for intoxication. The name Liberalis, with its connotations of decency and fine or noble personal appearance, as well as a metonymic association with wine and wine-drinking, can also be viewed as a name well suited to service in the imperial *triclinia*.

As we have also seen, some names designated particular *paedagogiani* as 'talking tools.' There are other examples. The names Scarus (Latin for 'parrot-fish') and Nastas (meaning 'cake' or 'loaf' in Greek), scratched respectively once and twice on the northwest walls of rooms 5 and 7, conform to the Roman practice of assigning slave names that relate to the category of service provided. In this case, these slaves may have performed the function of carrying plates to the tables of banquets in the palace; fish and bread would certainly have featured among the variety of foods on the imperial menu.[53]

Personal names, therefore, can be used not only to corroborate many of the functions delineated in the literary record relating to imperial slave boys and youths but also to confirm the social values of the naming classes towards their property. The onomastic evidence suggests the way in which Roman society codified social difference, defining the functions and obligations of individual slaves by means of indicative *cognomina*. It also reflects the ambivalent position of a slave in the *domus Caesaris*, at one and the same time nothing more than the *instrumentum* of his imperial *dominus*, yet also a provider of essential services embodied in *nomen* and *corpus*. The personal names identified in this study open up for consideration the fact that the Paedagogium slaves had a clear concept of their position as a privileged servile population in a special relationship of dependence towards the imperial household. 'Wish' names or names connoting particular roles confirm the uniformity of rightlessness ascribed to all slaves; they can also be interpreted as expressions of the extent to which slavery in the Paedagogium could be viewed as a process rather than a permanent condition, representing both allocation of social position within a circumscribed servile population, of distinguishing function within the *domus Caesaris*, and of conferred status subsequent to manumission.[54]

Instances of homoerotic sexual display and activity can be adduced as additional evidence for the realities of a slave boy's duty as a *paedagogianus* and a basis for interpreting aspects of the servile community's attitudes about this aspect of servile life. Six of the Paedagogium graffiti consist of varieties of language used in Latin and Greek to refer to sexual acts. Four drawings describe male sexual parts and two others show a nude male figure. The vocabulary in the sexual content of these graffiti is of semantic interest, and the written and graphic representation of sexual organs and actions can reveal something about the social values of the historical period in which the graffiti were inscribed.

Drawings of the phallus in the Palatine Paedagogium can be assigned to contexts that appear to be sexual or excretory in nature, connected with fertility, or representative. An image scratched on the west wall of room 6 shows a large penis either ejaculating or urinating. A phallus on the northeast wall of the same room has been added into a drawing that Solin and Itkonen-Kaila think may be Mars. A nude male figure was chalked in outline below the inscription *Saturus Afer*. The male parts are somewhat exaggerated, perhaps alluding to the link between the name Saturus and the priapic demigod of wild places. Two naked male figures scratched on the west wall of room 6 are well endowed and could represent anything from exaggerated or idolized figures (e.g., gladiators) to heroic idealizations (e.g., emperors or gods), or something as prosaic as anonymous ordinary men in the public baths or latrines.[55] While not drawing intrinsic connections between non-literary and literary representational meanings, it is possible to read these images as part of that broader Roman cultural identification of the phallus as a marker of superordinate socio-sexual position.[56]

The evidence directly refers to penetrative sexual acts between males. On the west wall of room 6, to the right of the door, can be read Peri]*genes*

Graecus pedico. The name Perigenes is uncertain, and could record another person; for example, Diogenes. However, the orthography compares favourably with another instance of the name appearing on the southwest wall of the same room; a third instance, on the same wall, is possible. Another slave, a certain Felix, is identified as a *pedico* on the southeast wall of room 6.[57] The word *pedico* is a nominal correspondent to *pedicare* ('to penetrate anally') and designates a sodomite.[58] J.N. Adams notes that the object of the sexual act relating to the term was usually male, though sometimes female. He adds that the character of the word implied a usage that a Latin speaker might feel motivated to avoid. While the individuals who are the subjects of these graffiti possessed Greek and Latin personal names, the fact that Perigenes was identified explicitly as a Greek is inherently interesting. The message attracts additional significance when it is noted that the term *pedico* was most likely derived from Greek words related to homoerotic sexual activity (παιδικόυ / τὰ παιδικά). At least in the case of the Perigenes graffito, it is possible to infer that the inscriber wished to indicate a relationship between the act of anal intercourse and the ethnicity of the referent.[59]

In close proximity to the *Felix pedico* graffito is a message in Greek ascribing the same category of sexual congress to a certain Bassos: Βασσον πυγίζω (*Graf. Pal.* I.230). The name Bassus appears in six other graffiti: once in Greek, the remaining five times in Latinized form. David Bain identified πυγίζω as the commonest word denoting anal intercourse in Greek. Among the items featuring the name Bassos/-us, the subject of the graffiti is identified twice as an inhabitant of one of the various peninsulas and towns known as Cherronesus or Chersonesus, perhaps the Thracian Chersonese, on the northwest side of the Hellespont and once as belonging to Greece. It cannot be verified whether each of these attestations of the name Bassos/-us refers to the same person. There is a weight of probability, however, that there exists some correspondence, in which case these graffiti reflect an attitude among the inscribing population of the Paedagogium that associated and registered the practice of anal intercourse in conjunction with a person of Greek origins.[60]

Another Latin graffito adverting to the same category of sexual activity was inscribed on the southwest wall of room 15: [li]*bente(r) pedicans*. Unlike the collocation of name and ethnic background with the denomination of sexual identity in the preceding item, there are no surviving traces here of letters prior to the expression that would suggest a specific referent. However, on the northeast wall of the same room, a graffito written in Greek juxtaposes a term that may allude to a male sexual partner who plays a passive or receptive role (πόϑος = πάϑος) and two personal names (Μύδιων = Μύδωτιν Εὐτύχης). Although the reading for πόϑος is tentative, it is possible to infer an allusion to one of the two persons named in terms reminiscent of the Greek vocabulary denoting a darling or love (Gk. τὰ παιδικά; cf. Ln. *deliciae*) or a beloved youth (παιδικός).[61]

There are also two personal names, scratched on the same section of the northwest wall in room 5, that connote a sexual meaning. Era]*tust*, which can be read as Eratosthenes, may also be Eratus Ti. Cl(audi?), and hence a form of ἐραστός the referent may perhaps have been named as a beloved object of his *dominus*.[62] *Amator*, which, along with Amatus, is a known *cognomen*, can indicate an enthusiastic admirer, a devoted friend, or a lover. The indeterminate nature of these graffiti does not permit any more precise interpretation of meaning or intention on the part of the inscriber.

In no case is the sexual symbolism of the graffiti related to pedication suggestive. Each instance is direct and uses a language or graphic form that can be classified as obscene in the context of ancient Roman literature and artistic representation. In other words, the graffiti provide evidence not for the sexual practice but for understanding the terminology related to the practice.[63] However, as Christian Laes noted in a recent study of *deliciae* in the Roman household, 'it is very risky to make judgements about feelings derived from facts which can be ascribed to epigraphic habit.' While it is difficult to measure with any precision the degree to which these graffiti may have offended the Palatine slave population, interpreting the context of the sexual images in relation to the literary and iconographic record of sexual attraction to and activity associated with boys and adolescent males – free-born, manumitted, or enslaved (including imperial *paedagogiani*) – is illuminating.[64]

Literary texts that address the relationship between Roman *conuiuia* and the functions of slave boys in such contexts are permeated by the assumption that a normal Roman *dominus* will openly seek to have sexual relations with persons of either sex, including the young and adolescent male tablea ttendants. Seneca the Younger, commenting on the behaviour of the pleasure-seeking Roman elite of his day, refers to the 'shameful treatment' (*contumelia*) that unfortunate boys must expect after private dinners. He goes on: 'I shall not mention the troops of *exoleti*, ranked according to nation and colour, which must all have the same smooth skin, and the same amount of youthful down on their cheeks, and the same way of dressing their hair, so that no boy with straight hair may get among the curly-heads.'[65]

In another letter expressing his moral reservations about the mistreatment of slaves in elite households, Seneca refers to the wine server who 'must dress like a woman and wrestle with his advancing years; he cannot get away from his boyhood; he is dragged back to it; and though be has already acquired a soldier's figure, he is kept beardless by having his hair smoothed away or plucked out by the roots, and he must remain awake throughout the night, dividing his time between his master's drunkenness and his lust; in the chamber be must be a man, at the feast a boy.'[66] In a recent study of toreutic art in the early Roman Empire, John Pollini has identified as an iconographic type of the *puer delicatus* a figure depicted on Side B of the silver *scyphus* known as the Warren Cup. Given his age, good looks, and shoulder-length hair arranged in a feminine style, the identification of the younger of the two boys in the symplegma on Side B is plausible and provides historians of Roman art and society with visual confirmation of references to the pedication of *paedagogiani* in the Palatine graffiti and the literary record.[67]

As part of a detailed reconstruction of the narrative linking the two scenes on the *scyphus*, John Pollini (1999: 39) went on to speculate that the figures of young slaves represent stages in the training of *pueri delicati*: the neophyte, the apprentice, and the graduate.[68] While the conceptual aesthetic underpinning this reading of the Warren Cup narrative contradicts the generally scandalized, morally critical view of pederastic sexuality in the literary record, its relationship to the Palatine graffiti is less clear. The inscriptions that address the act of pedication provide no clear indication of an emotive register. At a basic level, the use of direct Latin and Greek terms to characterize acts of anal penetration confirms the use of obscene language among the servile population. What this vocabulary acknowledges is recognition of male-male sexual practices among imperial and elite slave boys and youths trained in household *paedagogia*. Given the likelihood that some of the Palatine *paedagogiani* would participate in sexual acts in the imperial household, the function of these graffiti may have been as an outlet for humour in the face of a humiliating but unavoidable reality of life as a young male slave in the *domus Caesaris*, or perhaps to direct abuse at a particular individual or the community of slaves more generally as a means of dealing with actual or threatened pedication.

At any rate, the literary tradition of *pueri capillati* and *exoleti*, in conjunction with related artistic representations, illuminates a number of material traces of Roman slavery inscribed on the walls of the Palatine Paedagogium. Importantly, the graffiti referring to pedication allow us to see how persons under the control of another human being and those engaged in the education and training of such individuals represented a particular facet of their social identities to each other and the broader institutional community. Seneca the Elder defined the protocols for sexual relations within the institution of slavery in terms of the Roman law of persons: loss of sexual integrity (*impudicitia*) is a 'criminal act for a free-born person, a necessity for a slave, a duty for a freedperson.' Neither Greek nor Roman legislation limited in principle an owner's rights regarding servile sexual exploitation, and there is widespread evidence for the sexual abuse of slaves. Bradley views sexual maltreatment as part of a spectrum of dehumanizing prerogatives practised by the slave-owning classes. What the graffiti representing pederastic practices add to this picture is use of terminology associated morphologically and conceptually with the actions of slaves who not only played a receptive role in sexual relations but who also asserted their active status by penetrating another. In other words, Felix, Bassos/-us, either Μύδωτις or Εὐτύχης, and a person whose name is not longer preserved, depict their sexual categories as linguistically and indicatively masculine; by the same token, Eratus, Μύδωτις or Εὐτύχης embody persons subjectively identified as passive and penetrated. While the depiction of the sexual economy of slaves in the literary tradition consistently reflects deprivation of individuality and self-respect, the Paedagogium graffiti constitute a reminder that categorical distinctions of social identity for Roman slaves played out in unexpected ways within sub-elite, servile contexts.[69]

Cultural Patterns

When studied contextually, then, graffiti usefully illuminate aspects of ancient life rarely seen in other sources. In addition to the social relationships and practices already adduced, these inscriptions refer to patterns of human activity in a servile environment and to the symbolic structures that gave such activity importance. In other words, the epigraphic evidence that survives in the Palatine Paedagogium holds information about Roman slave culture: social interaction, norms, values, belief systems, and a hierarchy of status within slavery itself. The inscribed traces of imperial Roman slavery, embedded in the material remains of a particular social group and a prescribed human institution, provide clues about the processes that produced such symbolic artefacts and gave them meaning. To illustrate how the Paedagogium inscriptions reflect such patterns, this section will look at graffiti that deal with two cultural traditions integral to imperial Rome: the *ludi* and Christianity.

The topographical and architectural relationship between the Paedagogium and adjacent Circus Maximus helps to explain references in the Palatine graffiti to chariot racing and gladiatorial combats. On the south wall of room 5, a palm was etched; and, as we have seen, on the west wall of room 6, there survives an outline that resembles the figure of an athlete. Given the proximity of a building described by Dionysius of Halicarnassus as 'one of the most beautiful and admirable structures in Rome,' which Pliny the Elder estimated was able to seat 250,000 persons, it was likely that the *paedagogiani* participated in some fashion in the *ludi circenses, munera gladiatoria,* and *uenationes* staged within its monumental spaces. Aside from those in the front row, along a portion of the podium wall reserved for senators, and other seats for the *equites* who sat behind them, the seats were not segregated as they were in the Colosseum and the theatre. As Ovid and Juvenal elaborate, men and women could sit together. The socially invisible but necessary physical presence of imperial and aristocratic *paedagogiani* accompanying their masters and mistresses to the races, combats, wild animal hunts, athletic events, and processions would not have been exceptional.[70]

Given the very visible and prominent position of the emperor and imperial elite at public spectacles in the Circus, it is not suprising to find twelve citations of the personal name Victor on the Paedagogium walls. In the same way that this name connotes a symbolic link between Circus performance and household display, the graffiti drawings of palm-bearing horses and combat between *retiarius* and *secutor* that we have already studied above retain a degree of detail reflecting eyewitness acquaintance with chariot racing and gladiatorial fighting. To these can be added the following items, all scratched on the northwest wall of room 8: the bust of a charioteer, with palms and boxes, underneath the name Gordius; the names Gordianus and Isapeodoros, followed by an invocation in Greek to win; and another image of a gladiator. The drawing and inscription relating to the charioteer may indicate the *auriga* Gordius, favourite of the emperor Elagabalus; certainly the headgear in the form of a helmet confirms the figure as a chariot driver in the Circus, and the palm branches and boxes must represent the charioteer's prizes. The inscription *Gordianus | Isapeodoros | νίκα* appears under the bust of the charioteer identified above as Gordius. It is impossible to determine a clear relationship here, nor is it feasible to identify specifically the named individuals, but the directive to prevail draws out in the graffitist a significant level of engagement with the contest, whether gladiatorial or chariot racing. With respect to the final image of a gladiator, the figure wears heavy armour, the shield is large and rectangular, and the helmet is characteristic of a *secutor*: that is, without a plume and with a long neck-flap that protects the nape. Perhaps both legs were protected by *ocrea*, but these cannot be seen clearly in the facsimile of the drawing. Again, close acquaintance with the minutiae of Circus *spectacula* was essential.[71]

Jonathan Edmondson recently argued that *ludi circenses* and *munera gladiatoria* were occasions for articulating the component elements of the Roman social order.[72] What the Palatine graffiti that treat these occasions suggest is that persons occupying a subordinate position in the hierarchy of social relations participated in the widespread registration of the arena and its combatants as touchpoints of popular culture. As potential indicators of socio-cultural identity, it is also possible to suggest that the inscribers of these graffiti drew satisfaction from the public performance of individuals of the same class and condition, and took care that their representations preserved in name and figurative detail the identity, status, and endeavour of enslaved gladiators and charioteers. This, of course, was not a phenomenon limited to servile inscribers. Gladiatorial games and venationes were highly popular topics in Roman art in general, depicted in many different media and epochs, also with reference to specific names and games.[73] With this caveat in mind, it is still possible to suggest that, by recording events and individuals in this way on the walls of the Paedagogium, the inscribing population commemorated the integrity of slave performances in the Circus Maximus that could often result in physical harm or occasionally death. If we also accept that the inscribing population was servile, then rather than relegating the performers of public spectacles to the conceptual margins of Roman society, the Palatine graffiti dispensed with conventional stigmatizing associations in the literary record to celebrate the duty of gladiators and charioteers and commemorate the dignity adhering to honourable service.[74]

Coterminous with the efflorescence of public spectacle in the Circus, arena, and theatre, one of the great turning points over the first three centuries AD was the percolation of Christianity into the socio-cultural fabric of the Graeco-Roman Mediterranean. Given the special position of Rome as a young Christian community in the thought of the apostle Paul, the extent of Christianity's rapid geographical extension in face of Jewish synagogues, Greek intelligentsia, and Roman government officials, and the fact that in fourth century AD Rome public ceremonies of Christian worship and celebration matched public celebrations of the old civic religion, we should expect to find traces at least of this pervasive historical phenomenon in the Paedagogium graffiti. However, it should already be clear that religious attestations were at a premium within the Palatine community, and those that do exist offer lip service only to the votive and dedicatory practices of the Christian and non-Christian epigraphic environments. Nevertheless, a few inscriptions require interpretation in the light of a burgeoning Christian population at Rome.

On the northeast wall of room 6 are the words *Libanus* | *episcopus*. The personal name Libanus and the term *episcopus* can be found in two locations on the southeast wall of the same room; *episcopus* also identifies a certain Quintio, on the same wall.[75] In the hierarchical lexicon of the early Christian church, an *episcopus* was an official who governed a geographical region known as a *diocese*. If this was the sense that the inscriber intended, then graffiti containing a reference to the term in relation to a specified individual can be regarded as humorous or derogatory jibes levelled against slaves professing the Christian faith by their non-Christian work companions. A Christian presence is attested in the Paedagogium, dating to the rule of Septimius Severus;[76] and the fact that the term *episcopus* was scratched after the names Libanus and Quintio by another hand supports the contention of an ulterior motive. It should be noted that *episcopus* did not occupy an exclusively Christian semantic field. The term could also refer to a civic role. In view of the earlier discussion regarding the incidence of custodial functionaries among Palatine slaves, *episcopus* may have designated Libanus and Quintio as overseers or supervisors, possibly as wardens over some element of the slave population.

The inscription that attests directly to a Christian presence on the Palatine is well known as the Alexamenos graffito (fig. 3.2), comprising a drawing and textual caption inscribed on the southeast wall of room 7. The pictorial aspect of the graffito depicts a crucified man, seen from the rear, with the head of a donkey (or horse?), and dressed in a *colobium* (an item of servile clothing) without sleeves. The cross is in the form of a T. The transverse under the feet most likely represented a *suppedaneum*, a support for the crucified person projecting from the vertical shaft of the cross. Under the crucified figure, and to the left, is a youth, also in *colobium* and seen from behind, in an act of prayer, with his right hand extending towards the man on the cross. Above the figure, and to the right, is a kind of Y, larger than the other lines comprising the graffito. Above the cross, written in badly executed Greek letters, made after the design, as deduced from the vertical of the E that can be found behind the M, is the text: Ἀλε | ξαμενὸς | αἰβετε | θεόν ('Alexamenos, worship (your) god').[77]

As testimony from other historical periods is lacking, this graffito can been dated to the Severan age, during which a Christian presence in the *domus Caesaris* is known. The drawing is therefore one of the earliest representations of the crucifixion.[78] However, Christians did not employ publicly any form of the cross prior to Constantine.[79] Since Tertullian and Minucius Felix record the assertion that Christians worshipped a god with the head of a donkey, the graffito can be interpreted as an expression of this view and not an imitation of a personal crucifixion that Alexamenos possessed.[80]

That we deal with a caricature is demonstrated by the rough aspect of the drawing and its shabby execution. The attitude of the praying youth's hands confirm this interpretation: Christians, and also non-Christians, worshipped with arms extended and raised, while here we see the left arm lowered and the right extended towards the figure on the cross with the fingers open and separate in the Roman manner of *iactare basia*.[81] If we allow for the probability that a young slave named Alexamenos worshipped the Christian god in the Palatine Paedagogium, then the graffitist who scratched this inscription was most likely ridiculing the act of prayer itself. For major derisory effect, the crucified is shown from the rear and wears servile clothing. Also the text seems mocking. In the most ancient Christian literature Christians did not use language of the type *αἰβετε τὸν θεόν* with respect to worship,[82] and *Ἀλεχαμενος* can be read as a participial form of *Ἀλέλω*, which could be a mocking designation of Christians.

The *episcopus*, *Asellus*, *Βασιλέος*, and Alexamenos graffiti suggest that Christian and non-Christian slaves trained and worked together since the late second century AD as *paedagogiani* in the imperial household. They record interactions within the servile Palatine community that recognized the historical existence of 'otherness' among its constituents and transmitted complex semiological messages attesting to the views of non-Christians towards practising Christian slaves. As a subcategory in the broader catalogue of graffiti examined in this chapter, these messages illustrate the significance of the Paedagogium inscriptions as artefacts of particular cultural values, expressing a range of attitudes that were read by fellow slaves and others sharing the same physical environment and similar lived experiences.

Conclusion

The archaeological context of the Palatine Paedagogium and its inscribed graffiti provide only partial information for assessing the nature of a specific servile population in Roman Italy. Nevertheless, while a single authoritative reconstruction is fraught with uncertainty and conjecture, it is possible to produce a range of competing probabilities with respect to a few material realities: the type and function of slaves in the community of the Palatine Paedagogium, and the nature of servile education and training. Contextualizing the material traces of graffiti in respect to the literary and epigraphic record, it is also possible to adduce characteristics of the relations between *paedagogiani* generally, particular associations among individuals, and instances of interaction between persons. These textual and graphic remainders of slave life point to a variety of social relations: membership of a larger servile environment (the *paedagogium*), subcategories of freedpersons and slaves (*paedagogi/paedagogiani*, *custodes*, *procuratores*), and a sense of inclusion or belonging to a community of persons (*pueri*, *iuuenes*, *uernae domini nostri*). In addition, the Palatine graffiti present a deposit of information about servile culture: knowledge and experience (education, literacy, *ludi*); beliefs and attitudes (Christian and non-Christian); roles and hierarchies (domestic duties, ethnic associations, pederastic practices); even material objects and possessions (*instrumenta scribendi*, clothing). As a way of entering into the realities of Roman slavery under imperial rule, contextualized inscriptions like the Paedagogium graffiti constitute a rich source of material evidence. They reward close reading and critical interpretation and provide social historians with a valuable tool for dealing directly with the ancient world.

NOTES

1 Solin 1970: 7, 12.
2 For a select overview in general studies of literacy or surveys of epigraphic practice, see, e.g., Abel and Buckley 1977; Bodel 2001; Bowman and Woolf 1994; Castellan 1978; Castleman 1982; Cooley and Cooley 2004; Cooper and Chalfant 1995; Gundaker 1998; Harris 1989; Potter 1998; for literary studies, Bove 1984; Buecheler 1894–1930; Gigante 1979; Varone 1994; for archaeological and historical observations, Bowman and Thomas 1983; Laurence 1994.
3 Grahame 2001: 1; cf. Goffman 1959; Garfinkel 1967.
4 Bourdieu 1977: 78–87; Bradley 2004.
5 For *paedagogiani* as *pagi*, see Balty 1982: 308 n.47.
6 Paedagogium: *LTUR* vol. 4, 1999: 7–8 (E. Papi); Solin and Itkonen-Kaila 1966: 72–6. Contiguous with it and, in the view of some, also identified with it is the *domus Gelotiana*, a private house attested epigraphically that was possibly incorporated into the imperial palace (*LTUR* vol. 2, 1995: 110 [E. Papi]), and the *schola Praeconum*, a structure found south of the paedagogium (and possibly connected to it by a corridor), which has been identified as the headquarters of the *praecones*, or heralds (*LTUR* vol. 4, 1999: 254–5 [E. Papi]).
7 Solin and Itkonen-Kaila 1966: 3–12. Construction typology: Lugli 1957: 600 (AD 86–92). Brickstamp chronology: *CIL* 15.118a, 1094h, 1449f; cf. Bloch 1947: 27–9.
8 Interpretations: Solin and Itkonen-Kaila 1966: 68–78 (with bibliography). Caput Africae: *CIL* 6.1052, 8982–8987: *paedagogi puerorum a Capite Africae*; cf. *CIL* 5.1039 = *ILCV* 1832. Toponym and location: Regionary Catalogue (Regio II); Itinerarium Einsieldeln (f.84a: 196 Valentini-Zucchetti II); *LTUR* vol. 1, 1993: 235 (C. Pavolini); Pavolini 1993: 29–39.
9 Suet. *Calig.* 18.3: 'commisit et subitos (ludos) cum e Gelotiana apparatum circi prospicientem pauci ex proximis maenianis postulassent' (He also undertook some games spontaneously, when a few people asked for them from the neighbouring balconies, as he was inspecting preparations in the Circus from the Gelotiana). The owner of the *domus Gelotiana* can be identified as the wealthy freedman of Augustus C. Iulius Gelos, attested in two inscriptions from Veii (*CIL* 11.3805; 6.10339 = 11.3806). Cf. Suet. *Aug.* 45.1; Cass. Dio 57.11.15. A *tesserarius* (*CIL* 6.8663: ser(uus) Caesaris de domo Gelotiana) shows that the private house was incorporated into imperial property, perhaps after the death of the owner in the Claudian or Neronian period. According to Lanciani (1979: 185–7),

the *domus Gelotiana* should be located in the area east of the *domus Caesaris*, on the summit of the Palatine and not on the south slope where it has been identified among the remains of the so-called *schola Praeconum*.

10 Coarelli 2008: 188–9.

11 *Graf. Pal.* I.1–369. All references to graffiti in Solin and Itkonen-Kaila 1966 will use the abbreviation *Graf. Pal.* I; cf. Correra (1893, 1894). Number of graffiti found by room: 66 (5); 172 (6); 32 (7); 91 (8); 5 (15); 3 (16).

12 For dating criteria and individual cases, see Solin and Itkonen-Kaila 1966: 46ff.

13 On ancient graffiti as evidence for non-elite cultural discourse, see Keegan 2010.

14 Ghost story: Plin. *Ep.* 7.27.13; Saturnalia: Plin. *Ep.* 2.17.7, 24.

15 Epitaphs: *CIL* 6.8982–6. Dedication (October, AD 198): *CIL* 6.1052. Private citations: *CIL* 6.7290, 9740; cf. *Dig.* 33.7.12.32.

16 Bradley 1991: 37–64, 71–2; Mohler 1940: 267–73. *Praeceptor CIL* 6.8977–9.

17 *Pueri* as travel companions: Julian, *Misop.* p.450 Spanh.; Sen. *Ep.* 87.10, 123.7; Amm. Marc. 29.3.3. Table slaves: *Dig.* 33.7.12.32. Bathhouse attendants: Plin. *HN* 33.40. Sexual objects: Suet. *Ner.* 28; Sen. *Ep.* 95.24; Tertul. *Apol.* 13. Clothing: Sen. *De uit. beat.* 17.2; Amm. Marc. 26.6.15, 29.3.3. Hairstyle: Mart. 3.55.30, 58.29–31; Sen. *Ep.* 95.24. Feminine appearance: Sen. *Ep.* 123.7. Combination of form and function: Plin. *HN* 33.26.

18 Cic. *Pro Rosc.* 41.120; *Dig.* 33.7.12.32.

19 Philo, *De uita contemplatiua* 50–2. *Capillati*: Petr. *Sat.* 27; Mart. 2.57.5. *Comati*: Mart. 12.70.9; 12.97.4; Suet. *Cal.* 35. *Criniti*: Sen. *Ep.* 119.14; Mart. 12.49.1. *Crispuli*: Sen. *Ep.* 95.24. *Calamistrati*: Isid. *Orig.* 10.57; Apul. *Met.* 2.19.

20 Dunbabin 2003b: 100–1, figure 52–53; *LTUR* vol. 4, 1999: 254–5 (E. Papi).

21 Dunbabin 2003b: 151–2, pl. IX and X.

22 Acute O: e.g. *Graf. Pal.* I.135; vertical E: e.g., *Graf. Pal.* I.3, 9, 16, 27, 33, and so on.

23 *Graf. Pal.* I.298.

24 Darder Lissón 1996.

25 *Graf. Pal.* I.304. For the name Zozzo, see Solin 1996b: 1358 ('Sozon').

26 The MM may be an accidental repetition (dittography) of the abbreviation for the single participle *missus*, acknowledging the defeat of the named gladiator Antigonus and his request that the *munerarius* stopped the fight and sent him alive from the arena. Its relation to the other signs is unclear.

27 Zozzo = Sozon; see Solin 1996b: 1358, dated to 200–50 CE.

28 *Graf. Pal.* I.289.

29 Varro, *RR* 1.20.4.

30 Grinding: Bradley 2000: 118. Christian: Kajanto 1963: 110ff.; Visconti 1869; Wilamowitz: *CLE* 1978.

31 Cf. e.g. *CIL* 6.9449: PVDENS M. LEPIDI L. GRAMMATICVS | PROCVRATOR ERAM LEPIDAE MORESQVE REGEBAM | DVM VIXI MANSIT CAESARIS ILLAS NVRVS | PHILOLOGVS DISCIPVLVS. Scribal slaves: McDonnell 1996; Harris 1989: 249; Horsfall 1995. Cf. Starr 1990–1; Petr. *Sat.* 75.4.

32 Solin and Itkonen-Kaila 1966: 46.

33 *Graf. Pal.* I.8, 23, 166, 231, 270, 110, 310; *duo nomina: Graf. Pal.* I. 127
   (Ulpia Phoebe), 270 (Aurelius Stephanus). *Tria nomina: Graf. Pal.* I. 126 (Ti.
   Secundinus Securus). On *cognomina* and their relationship to slave status, see
   Bruun in this volume.

34 Gai. *Inst.* 1.3.

35 Futrell 2001: 10–11.

36 Solin and Itkonen-Kaila 1966: 45; Garrucci 1879: 137; *Graf. Pal.* I.360, 361; Apul.
   Met. 1.15–16.

37 *CIL* 6.1785 = 31931; Palmer 1978: 237.

38 Weaver 1967: 4.

39 *Procurator: Graf. Pal.* I.362; *CIL* 6.8948, 31863; *tricliniarchi* e.g., *CIL* 3.536 = *ILS*
   1575; 6.1884 = *ILS* 1792; 11.3612 = *ILS* 1567.

40 *Graf. Pal.* I.78. Other personal names or fragments of names or titles attached
   to the formula *exit* only or *exi(i)t de p(a)edagogio*: Eutyches; Corinthus;
   Narbonen[sis; Umbon; *uerna*; Apollonius;]ina (*Graf. Pal.* I.9; 13, 52, 70; 34, 43;
   41; 61; 63; 66). None of these provide any indication of occupation.

41 As a noun *opifer* is not attested. In Lewis and Short it only appears as an adjective meaning 'aid-bringing.' In epigraphy the word is found in a dedication
   to Diana – *CIL* 14.3537 – and in an inscription referring to a *saltum Fortunae
   Opiferae* – *CIL* 14.3539 – both from Tibur.

42 Room 5: *Graf. Pal.* I.51; *perfusor: CIL* 4.840.

43 The word *episcopus* is attested as the technical term for a supervisor (Cicero *ad
   Att.* 7.11.5; rendered in Greek; *Dig.* 50.4.18.7).

44 Room 6: *Graf. Pal.* I.189, 230; room 8: *Graf. Pal.* I.356. On the basis of inscribed
   instances of the word *iuuenes* in this and similar contexts, Mohler (1937:
   462, 479) argued that freedmen and their sons were welcomed in *paedagogia*
   throughout the empire.

45 *Graf. Pal.* I.53, I.61, I.272, 278, 305, 317, 326, 330, 332, 342, 365.For another
   interpretation of this abbreviation, see the discussion below on *uestiarii*. On
   vernae generally, see Herrmann-Otto 1994.

46 *Capillatus: Graf. Pal.* I.2; banquet slaves: Petr. *Sat.* 27.1, 34.4, 57.9; Mart. 2,57.5,
   3.58.30, 10.62.2. Diadumenus is used in an adjectival sense by Seneca (*Ep.* 65.5) and
   Pliny the Elder (*HN* 34.55) to designate the action of tying one's hair in a band.

47 *Graf. Pal.* I.205, 234; *Graf. Pal.* I.118.

48 *Graf. Pal.* I.281, 283; Balty 1982 Dunbabin 2003a; cf. 2003b: 150–6.

49 *Graf. Pal.* I.301.

50 Reil 1913; Wilson 1938. Cf. Non. M541; Serv. *Aen.* 2.616, 4.137 (*limbus*). SHA
   Vopisc. *Aurel.* 15.4 (AD 343); 46.6; *Prob.* 4.5 (*lineae paragaudae*); *Cod.* 11.
   tit. 8 S1, 2. Lydus, *de Magistratibus* 1.17, 2.4.13 (κιτὼν λογκωτός). Cf. SHA
   Commodus 8.8 (*tunicae Dalmaticae*); *Pert.* 8.3; Dio 72.17.2 (*chiridotae
   Dalmatarum*). Sebesta and Bonfante 2001.

51 *CIL* 6.8987: ALEXANDER | AVGG. SER. FECIT | SE BIVO MARCO FILIO | DVLCISIMO CAPVTA | FRICESI QVI DEPVTA |BATVR INTER BESTITO | RES QVI VIXIT AN / NIS | XVIII MENSIBV VIIII | DIEBV. V. PERO A BOBIS |FRA.TRES BONI PER | VNVM DEVM NE QVIS | (H)VN(C) TITE. LO MOLES[TET] | POS MORT[EM MEAM]. Cf. Visconti 1868. *Graf. Pal.* I.127, 296.

52 Some of the most popular Latin and Greek slave-names (according to Solin 1996b; 2001; cf. Gordon 1924) are also attested in the Paedagogium. These include Hermes, Hilarus, and Fortunatus/-inus.

53 *Instrumenti genus uocale:* Varro, *RR* 1.17.1; rooms 5 and 6: *Graf. Pal.* I.22; 261, 262.

54 On this relationship between name and self-concept in the servile epigraphic record, see Joshel 1992: 35–61.

55 *Graf. Pal.* I.92; *Graf. Pal.* I.134; Solin and Itkonen-Kaila 1966: 31; nude male: *Graf. Pal.* I.71.; caricature / gladiators: *Graf. Pal.* I. 96, 97.

56 On the phallus as a common signifier of potency or violence in Roman sexual discourse, see Richlin 1992: 26.

57 *Graf. Pal.* I.121; *Graf. Pal.* I.74, 113; *Graf. Pal.* I.232.

58 It is important to note that *pedico* does not always act as a metonymous substitute for 'homosexual.' *Pedico/pedicator* may be used to describe men who today would be labelled 'homosexual' (or, more specifically, men who play the insertive role in penetrative acts with other males). But the literal meaning, denoting 'a man who anally penetrates,' can encompass female objects. See, e.g., Mart. 11.78.5–6, 11.99.1–2, 11.104.17–20; cf. *CIL* 10.4483 and the possibly related *CIL* 4.2184, 2194, 2248, which refer to a certain Phoebus as *pedico* and *fututor*. See also the literary equivalent of Phoebus in Martial's portrait of a certain Cantharus: 11.45.

59 Adams 1982: 123; cf. *Priap.* 3.9f. Discussing Roman perceptions of Greece and Greek cultural traditions, Williams (1999: 72) concluded that ancient writers, both Greek and Roman, displayed no preoccupation with pederasty as a distinguishing characteristic of Greek culture. Interestingly, the references to pederastic practices in the Paedagogium graffiti are outside the literary tradition that Williams surveyed.

60 *Graf. Pal.* I. 181; 65, 68, 73, 76, 113; Bain 1991: 67; Chersonese: *Graf. Pal.* I. 65: *Cherronesita*; 73: *Chersonesita*; Greece: *Graf. Pal.* I. 73: *Graecus*.

61 *Graf. Pal.* I.364. For the literary tradition linking *delicia* children to pederastic practices in the imperial household, see Laes 2003: 301–2; see also George in this volume.

62 *Graf. Pal.* I.11.

63 Richlin 1992: xvi (on the distinction between the use of sexual insults – 'male, aggressive, and bent on controlling boundaries' – and the practice of sexual acts); 57–70 (on invective in rhetoric, satire, and graffiti as a strategy of displacing personal insecurities).

64 Laes 2003: 310; see also Laes 2010; 2011: 222–68. Exoleti: Tac. *Ann.* 15.69. Tac. *Ann.* 15.37; cf. Dio 62.6.4. Suet. *Galba* 22. *SHA* (Commodus) 7.5.4. The original motivation behind the writing of these items is debatable. That literary instances of pederastic practice in the *domus Caesaris* can be interpreted as moralizing should not detract from the usefulness of the citations as historical sources.

65 Sen. *Ep.* 95.24. Williams 1999: 30–8.

66 Sen. *Ep.* 47.7.

67 Pollini 1999: 34, Side B of the Warren Cup (Pollini 1999: fig. 2; details: figs.8, 9). For the view that all protagonists in the Warren Cup depictions are Greek citizens, see Williams 2006; for a critique of this view, see Clarke 2006. For the argument that the Warren cup is a fake, see Marabini Moevs 2008; however, she also argues that the scene on Side B imitates Arretine pottery, thereby grounding the iconography (if not the Warren cup itself) in the Roman era (Marabini Moevs 2008: 7–8).

68 Pollini 1999: 39.

69 Sen. *Contr.* 4 pref.10; Wiedemann 1997: e.g. 10, 41, 104, 151f, 178f, 187, 225f, 240, 243f; cf. Bradley 1984: 118–22.

70 For gladiator, charioteer, and *uenator* inscriptions, see Langner 1999: Taf. 37–73 (fig. 769–1164); *Graf. Pal.* I.58 (palm); 97 (athlete); Dion. Hal. *Ant. Rom.* 3.68; Plin. *HN.* 36.102; Suet. *Claud.* 21.3; Tac. *Ann.* 15.53; Ov. *Am.* 3.2; *AA* 1.135–162; Juv. 11.202.

71 Victor: *Graf. Pal.* I. 99, 101, 109, 176, 310, 319, 324, 350, 351, 352, 353, 358; room 8: *Graf. Pal.* I.302, 303, 306; Gordius: Cass. Dio 79.15.1; Lampr. *Heliog.* 6.3, 12.1, 15.2. Cf. Stein, *P-W* 4.1221 and *PIR*² C 1289.

72 Edmondson 1996: 111.

73 Langner 1999: 85–9, 139–41. Between 1988 and 2004 six volumes have been published in the series entitled *Epigrafia anfiteatrale dell'Occidente romano* (Rome: Quasar). These studies of non-literary representations of arena combat and combatants support the significant, non-stigmatized position of the gladiator in popular epigraphic culture.

74 On the low regard in which gladiators were held in the literary tradition, see, e.g., Edwards 1993.

75 Northeast wall: *Graf. Pal.* I.140; *Libanus episcopus: Graf. Pal.* I.193, 213; *Quintio episcopus: Graf. Pal.* I.188. The name Quintio Afer appears on the northwest wall of room 6: *Graf. Pal.* I.110. See Solin 2006.

76 See below in relation to the Alexamenos graffito (*Graf. Pal.* I.246).

77 *Graf. Pal.* I.246; see also Sacco 1997: 192–4.

78 Christian presence: Tert. *Scap.* 4; cf. Harnack 1962: 473ff; cf. Hempel 1963: 602.

79 Cf. Bruun 1963: 95ff.

80 Tert. *Apol.* 16, *nat.* 1.4; Min. Fel. 9.3, 28.7.

81 Phaedr. 5.7.28, Mart. I.3.7, Juv. 4.118. Cf. Marti 1936: 280–1.

82 With the exception of Mart. Polyc. 17.2b; cf. W. Foerster, *ThWNT* VII.173.

4

Geographies of Slave Containment and Movement*

SANDRA R. JOSHEL

Introduction

In the mid-first century CE, Columella quotes his ancient predecessor, Cato the Elder: 'the *vilicus* should not be an *ambulator*' (1.8.7; 5.2). The slave manager of a farm should not walk around for his own pleasure or stroll about idly without purpose or aim. This sentiment against ancient slave ambling is repeated in the legal discussion of the Edict of the Aediles (21.1): 'an *erro* … does not indeed run away but frequently indulges in aimless roaming and, after wasting time on trivialities, returns home at a late hour' (*Digest* 21.1.17.14). Not as serious as trying to escape slavery, the truant's 'aimless roaming' is nonetheless undesirable from the point of view of the Roman slaveholder.

Agricultural writers and jurists instance slaveholders' concern for the mobility of their slaves. The attempt to control slaves' movements, as the historian Stephanie Camp observes, is central to many slave systems: 'At the heart of the process of enslavement is a spatial impulse: to locate bondspeople in space and to control, indeed to determine, their movements and activities.' Although her topic is the plantation South, her assumption that slavery is rooted in 'a form of captivity' finds an echo in the often-cited opinion of Florentinus.[1] Discussing the *ius gentium*, the jurist explains: '*Servi* are so-called, because generals have a custom of selling their prisoners and thereby preserving rather than killing them: and indeed they are said to be *mancipia*, because they are captives in the hand (*manus*) of their enemies' (*Digest* 1.5.4.2).

I borrow two concepts from Camp's *Closer to Freedom* to discuss Roman slaveholders' practices of slave containment and slaves' mobility and use of space. Examining slave movement in the nineteenth-century American South, Camp uses the term 'geography of containment' to refer to the 'laws, customs, and ideals [that came] together into a systematic constriction of slave movement that helped to establish slaveholders' sense of mastery.' Camp's point is not that American slaves were locked up, but rather that law, customs, and ideals enabled and legitimated certain forms of movement and not others. Not surprisingly, she argues that 'bondspeople created a 'rival geography,' by which she means 'alternative ways of knowing and using … space that conflicted with planters' ideals and demands.'[2]

In what follows, I look at a Roman 'geography of containment' by juxtaposing slave owners' views and prescriptions on slaves' movement in literature and law with the physical remains of farm buildings and urban houses. The relationship between Roman texts and archaeological remains where Roman slavery is concerned, and, in particular, the tendency to let the literary sources shape the interpretation of the material record (see below) has been the subject of serious debate.[3] Yet assertions that the archaeological record alone should or could testify to slaves' presence are equally problematic, first because we always bring assumptions and a sense about Roman culture to Roman things. Second, perhaps more important, as Martin Hall has argued, objects and words are entwined.[4] In effect, Roman legal texts, literature, and inscriptions belong to the same world as Roman objects, architecture, statues, paintings, etc. This is not to assume that we can or should fit artefacts and documents together easily to form a complete and unified picture. Rather than using texts to fill in lacks in the archaeological record or making the archaeological record stand alone, I try to set the material record and the literary record side by side and in dialogue with one another. That is, for example, Columella's concern about slave mobility and his discursive attempt to regulate slave movement can be placed beside what we find in the remains of first-century farmsteads. All this is predicated on the assumption that in slaveholding societies like ancient Rome in which slaves were everywhere and critical in producing both the income and social status of the elite, 'the material traces of slavery are inscribed into everything.'[5]

The inscription of slavery into 'everything' may tell us about slavery and slave owners but not slaves. The remains of the farm buildings, maritime villas, and urban houses reflect their owners' arrangements of space. For the reasons articulated below, slaves' use or appropriation of their owners' space will have left little in the way of observable physical marks.[6] The textual evidence in itself will not fill the gap: we lack the kind of slave testimony available to scholars of slavery in the United States. Instead, we must read the reports of Roman owners. They tell us about some slave actions, though not their motives. Most often, Roman slaveholders saw slaves' behaviour as evidence of their laziness, deceit, or criminality.

Tracing the 'rival geography' of Roman slaves, then, requires imaginative analyses of both the literary and archaeological records. Although slaveholders defined their slaves' movements in terms of their own interests, they could certainly observe the actions themselves, regardless of what they called them. I intend to take Roman slaveholders at their word and look for slaves' daily, mundane actions that so often irritated their owners. Implicit in slaveholders' words are what Camp calls 'alternative ways of knowing and using space.' Of course, slaveholders did not acknowledge – perhaps they could not even see – an alternative to their spatial arrangements and choreography of slave movements; what they saw or judged were slaves' failures and misbehaviour. We must read through their assertions to glimpse the alternative geography and choreography, one that was reactive, not revolutionary.[7]

Most often, the reported actions of slaves relied on timing. Malingering, idling, wasting time, damaging property, thieving, muttering, making noise, and being insolent, for example, all took advantage of discrete moments, particular circumstances, and transitory opportunities.[8] Because such actions seized moments and not ultimately space, they were ephemeral. In effect, without the textual record, where such actions are reported, we would have little beyond graffiti to map the rival geography.[9]

While slaves' actions did not have their *own* places, they did have a spatial dimension. If the archaeological record preserves the plans and intentions of slaveholders, architecture and decoration, at the same time, also represents what John Michael Vlach, studying the plantation South, calls the 'contexts of servitude.' Established by slaveholders, the material environment of farm building, villa, or house shaped, and was shaped by, the slaves who lived and worked in it. As Vlach observes, slave owners 'did not control those contexts absolutely.' Vlach warns us that 'appearances can be deceiving and … an apparent order on the land may not be the only order present.'[10] I hope at least to raise questions about orders on the ground other than those of the slaveholder.

Certain Roman practices and slaveholders' attitudes spell out a general physical and cultural environment of slave constraint. Many Roman slaves moved about: they accompanied their owners on short jaunts and long journeys; others, on their own, ran errands, peddled goods, managed businesses separated from their owners' domestic or commercial establishments; some acted as agents in the provinces.[11] It is important, therefore, to remember that the Roman slave system included various practices for controlling slave mobility. The material remains of chains, shackles, and fetters and literary references to chaining mark the extreme restriction of captives, fugitives, and troublesome slaves.[12] At least by the late first century BCE, and elaborated in the first and second centuries CE, Roman slave owners had legal means and tried practices for chasing down and recovering slave fugitives. Keith Bradley has given us a synthetic analysis of them and eloquently catalogued the dangers and difficulties of flight.[13] I only want to emphasize that the use of slave catchers and agents, the help of imperial and civic officials, provincial governors, and troops, and advertisements for runaways posted in public places all created fairly solid and daunting boundaries for slaves who sought to escape slavery.[14]

Roman slaveholders themselves testify to their own intense concerns about the movements of slaves. Keith Bradley has observed that 'the interest in fugitives and "troublesome" slaves displayed by those who created the historical record borders … on the obsessive.'[15] Indeed, Roman lawyers and jurists, members of the slaveholding class, evidently devoted many hours and much ink to the detailed conditions that distinguished the fugitive from the truant (*Digest* 21.1.17). The authors of the extant agricultural manuals, too, were preoccupied with the control and choreography of slave movement. In general, the literary and legal sources exhibit a tension in Roman slaveholders' geography of containment: a tension between keeping slaves put and keeping them in motion.

The Geography of Containment: The *Villa Rustica*

The most comprehensive of the extant agricultural manuals, Columella's *De Re Rustica* enjoins its readers to constrain the movements of rural slave workers and, at the same time, to foster busy slave hands and bodies.[16] The use of chains and the physical imprisonment of slaves is for Columella almost a matter of common sense. He recommends this sort of restraint for vineyard workers whose job required mental sharpness, apparently because, in the slaveholder's logic, the smart slave was a troublesome slave. Chained slaves were housed in *ergastula* (slave prisons), ideally with narrow windows to emit light, placed high enough so that the slaves could not reach them with their hands.[17]

The comings and goings of unchained slaves were patrolled by the slave *vilicus*, and the *vilicus* by the slaveholder. In the ideal *villa rustica*, the *vilicus*'s quarters were located so that he could observe his charges, and it was designed in a way that kept everyone as near as possible to make the *vilicus*'s control of movement possible.[18] No slave was supposed to leave the farm, and slave mobility on the farm was supposed to be limited by regulated paths: one of the jobs of the *vilicus* was to see that slaves cut no new footpaths.[19] If Columella's orders were followed, even the *vilicus* did not leave the estate except to do business connected with the farm. In addition, contact with outsiders was strictly regulated: there were to be no encounters with diviners and witches and no guests except his owner's friends and relations.[20]

Moreover, all slaves, from the ordinary labourer to the slave manager, were subject to constant surveillance. At the farmstead, the *vilica* kept track of weavers, cooks, provisioners, malingering field workers, and the shepherds as they milked or sheared the sheep. In the fields, foremen supervised workers and enforced discipline. The *vilicus*'s presence in the fields ensured that foremen performed their duties, and at the farmstead he oversaw the work of his wife.[21] Yet the *vilicus* himself was subject to his owner's control.[22]

At the same time, Columella, like his predecessors Cato and Varro, was at pains to keep slaves in motion. Slaveholders' ideal of the full employment of slaves meant long, busy workdays outside; a host of indoor tasks occupied slave hours when days were short, the weather bad, or the sowing finished.[23] The control of movement was to be achieved through control of time. In all three manuals, we find calculations of tasks by *iugera* and days: how many *iugera* of land can be plowed by so many workers in so many days; how many *iugera* of vines can be trimmed and dressed; how many *iugera* of meadows can be cut in a day.[24] Columella's instructions go further to outline a discipline of the slave body at work. For nearly every task, Columella prescribes in meticulous detail a choreography of slaves' bodies, arms, legs, and voices.[25]

Rather than read the archaeological remains of the *villa rustica* as a confirmation or contradiction of the agricultural manuals, I want to look at the ways in which a 'geography of containment' may have been inscribed in architecture. Whether this geography accords with or differs from the descriptions of the manuals, it seems to exhibit their dual concern with containment and control. The remains of rural farm buildings in Italy are plentiful, but so, too, are the problems of interpreting them.[26] Many of the excavated villas have been reburied, making it impossible to walk through the sites and to pursue questions unanswered in the archaeological reports. Even where farm buildings are excavated and reported in a careful, detailed, and precise manner, the translation of physical remains into lived practices is difficult. Most especially, assessments of the use of particular spaces are subject to debate, especially where slave rooms are concerned.[27] In general, as several scholars have pointed out, slave *cellae* become what owners' quarters are not. Working from the literary use of *cella* as a small cramped space for a slave, F.H. Thompson observes that archaeologists suppose that a 'row of identical rooms in the plan of a farm' signals slave quarters, especially if their floors are unpaved and their walls undecorated or plastered without further decoration. The presence of chains, fetters, or manacles reinforces the assumption.[28] Despite the difficulties of identifying slave rooms, it seems worthwhile to observe that certain patterns characterized the layout of space in many *villae rusticae*: a courtyard surrounded by small *cellae* on one or more sides; limited exits / entrances; and proximity to work areas (e.g., press rooms, storage, stables and animal stalls, threshing floors, and bakeries).[29] While exact definitions of *cellae* elude us, these sorts of spaces, in combination with other work areas, offer our best chance of understanding the kinds of spaces in which slaves would have lived and worked.

At the oft-cited example of a large estate, Settefinestre in southern Etruria, we can glimpse the historical development of the structuring of slave movement in architecture. In the first period of construction in the late first century BCE and early first century CE (fig. 4.1a), an entry courtyard (42) led to separate entrances to a *pars urbana* (43/44) and a *pars rustica* (52). The latter included stalls, a kitchen, a small bath, and press rooms. The entry courtyard (42) seems to have been a service area. Two entrances / exits opened to the outside of the villa building, the main entrance to the villa (187/188) and a corridor on the west side of the court (36) that led to the upper level of the garden portico. The rooms on the south side of the entry courtyard (42) were identified as stalls and *cellae vinariae*; on the east were a kitchen (76) and various other service rooms. A double row of small rooms on the west side had unplastered walls and earthen floors (or perhaps wood planked), ten of 3 × 3 metres and two 3 × 4 metres; the doors directly on the courtyard opened into the rooms.[30] The arrangement has been compared to an army barracks with its front and back rooms (*papilo* and *arma*), each housing eight men. Andrea Carandini offers two hypotheses of the numbers and occupants of this arrangement, each of which supposes the inhabitants included both ordinary male labourers and foremen (each with his own 'wife').

In the Trajanic and Antonine periods, the owners built a new courtyard to the southwest adjoining the old one, labelled the 'new slave quarters' by Carandini (107, fig. 4.1b). The courtyard created a corridor (58) between the older service courtyard (42) and the new one (107); off this hallway opened rooms that Carandini supposes were a kitchen (82), infirmary (83), dining room (78), storage rooms (86, 64), and *ergastulum* (65). Instead of the arrangement of double rooms that lined the west side of 42, single rooms (3 × 3.5 metres) with doors that opened outward surrounded the south, west, and north sides of the courtyard (107).[31] The number of slaves housed in these quarters increased, and, Carandini assumes, there was a change in their social composition, from men only in the first arrangement (except for the foremen) to slave families, each occupying one of the *cellae* in the second.[32]

The new courtyard (107) was removed from the entrances to both the *pars rustica* and the *pars urbana*, which could only be reached via 42 by circuitous route. To provide access to this older entry / service courtyard, the owners cut a doorway at the back of room 201. Thus, a slave walking from courtyard 107 to the *pars rustica* or *pars urbana* of the main core of the villa had to pass through hallway 192, then rooms 201 and 108, and finally across courtyard 42. The entrances / exits to the countryside were reduced to two (210 and 110), later to one (110 was closed off).

The identification of the rooms on the two courtyards, and most especially the rooms supposed to have been slave quarters, has been questioned, most recently and carefully by Annalisa Marzano.[33] She examines the general suppositions on which the identifications depends: the character of the agricultural system in various parts of Italy; the status and organization of agricultural labour; and the influence of the literature, especially Cato, Varro, and Columella, on the interpretation of archaeological material. In addition, she interrogates the assumptions about physical details that led to the conclusion that these rooms were for human habitation rather than stalls or storage, everything from the door widths of stalls to the appropriate floors and walls for storage.[34] In Marzano's view, Carandini et al. tended to find what they went looking for, that is, a large-scale slave estate. Without denying that slaves were present at Settefinestre, she argues that the rooms identified as *cellae familiae* probably had a variety of purposes, such as storage, stalls, and housing; she urges us to 'remember the possibility that various structures on rural estates, including slave dwellings, may have been built using perishable materials … [that] leave no trace in the archaeological record.'[35]

Yet, as Marzano herself points out, the use of rooms for storage, animals, and slaves, known from other villa sites, does not mean these are not slave quarters; rather, in fact, such 'manifold' use seems appropriate for all those 'things' that figure as *instrumenta*.[36] In effect, the fact that small, plainly decorated, or undecorated rooms housed goods, tools, and / or slaves is itself significant. The exchangeability in room usage that characterizes the archaeological record might represent ancient reality. At any rate, critical analyses must be careful not to make slaves disappear from the material record, especially where the Romans who wrote about farming for those who owned farms are so clear about the housing of slaves in the *villa rustica*.[37]

Rather than debate the details of Carandini's conclusions about the change of social arrangements and allowing for the varied use of *cellae familiae*, I want to enquire into a 'geography of containment' that might be mapped in the architecture from the early first century to the second century CE. It would seem that the architecture offers the structural potential for containment whose realization depended on locked doors and / or human surveillance. At Settefinestre, the architectural changes meant fewer ways for slaves to get out of the area in which they were housed, and the reduction and positioning of the entrances / exits made it easier for supervisors or foremen to patrol slaves' comings and goings out to the countryside or into the main block of the villa. This development seems to be complemented by the enlarged possibilities of surveillance within the quarters. In the first period, slaves had to enter or exit a *cella* through a single doorway (108, 112, 113, 114, 41, 40, 39, 38); however, the rooms in the back row (201, 200, 115, 47, 48, 37) were hidden from the view of a supervisor watching from the courtyard and its entrances / exits. Spatial arrangements, too, created corners in which slaves could escape supervisors' patrolling gaze. In the later period, however, ordinary slaves in the single cells that surround the north, west, and south sides of courtyard 107 would have found it difficult to escape the gaze of a foreman in the courtyard or at one of the entrances. Moreover, in the second period at Settefinestre, direct access to the kitchen and storage areas was cut off, which is interesting in terms of the constant complaints in the literary sources about slave thefts of food and stores. In either period, the greatest assurance of the control of slave movement, especially at night, was the locked door.[38]

The smaller villa at Gragnano, Villa 34 (fig. 4.2), in Campania allows us to explore a different though related aspect of a geography of containment.[39] Built perhaps in the first century BCE, the wide main entrance (A) to the villa opened to a large courtyard (B) flanked by animal stalls on the east (2) and a bakery (14–15) on the south; northwest and west of the main court-yard (and inaccessible from it) were a pressing room (28), a *cella vinaria* with *dolia* sunk into the ground (E), and an area for storing timber (27). Five small rooms of 3 × 2 metres with unplastered walls (25–26, 21–23 on the west side of the main courtyard may have been slave rooms; a staircase (24) led to a second storey and probably at least five more rooms. In courtyard D there were iron stocks with fourteen openings to chain one or both ankles of slaves, so at least one of the area's functions was the physical chaining of slaves. Another set of stairs led to an upper floor, used for habitation or storage.[40] Eleven small rooms surrounded the neighbouring courtyard (C). We can only guess at how these rooms were used, but if at least some of them housed slaves, it seems likely that occupants shared rooms and, per-haps, beds.[41]

Lacking information on doors and thresholds, we have difficulty tracing a geography of containment; however, we can observe how the owner's ar-rangement of space shaped the movements of his slaves. The terms used by Mark Grahame to analyse space in the House of the Faun at Pompeii help us to see how 'segmentation in architecture' structures 'relations between peo-ple by control over the body through its location and movement in space.' As Grahame observes, some spaces are 'more "open" in that they ... permit relatively free movement.' In open spaces, 'the probability that an encounter will occur is increased, because in such space one is more visible to others. In short, it involves *disclosure* of the body.' Closed spaces are cell-like spaces with a single entrance; within them walls act as an 'architectural barrier,' making individuals within them 'less visible.'[42] In these terms, courtyard B in the villa at Gragnano is the most open space with respect to 31–35, 21–26, and courtyards D and C. If, as Grahame suggests, 'privacy relates to the ability to enclose the body and remove oneself from the sight of others, then the individual rooms 31–35, 21–26, and courtyards D and C (at least with respect to B) offer their occupants some concealment, or rather some 'power to control the degree of knowledge which others may have about oneself.'

Yet, as Grahame notes, a space that allows the individual an escape from scrutiny may limit the privacy it provides, if he 'or she cannot move elsewhere 'without coming under surveillance.' That is, enclosure may become 'confinement.'[43] At Gragnano, the single entrance to C would have made it easy to patrol slaves leaving for and returning from the surrounding fields and pastures. The position of the main entrance, too, made it possible to observe the movement in and out of rooms 31–35 and 21–26, courtyards D and C, and the secondary entrance at 20. Within D and C, the entrances/exits, too, enabled a surveilling gaze. In D, 'confinement' was not merely a matter of location in space but of the physical restraint of fetters. It has been suggested that rooms 31–35 were the quarters of the manager and/or foremen, and the location of these rooms, too, would have enabled observation of movement in and out of the yard and within it.

The Rival Geography: The *Villa Rustica*

Our ignorance of the ancient landscape surrounding the *villa rustica* and the lack of slave testimony handicaps the search for slaves' rival geography. For the most part, as noted above, we rely on interpreting slave owners' warnings, complaints, and practices as a response to slave behaviour. If we set aside owners' pejorative terms, we can glimpse how rural slaves might have gained time, space, and extra resources for themselves, crossing or refiguring slaveholders' boundaries and altering their owners' attempts at choreographing their movements. Most of the complaints from which we patch together a possible rival geography involve timing, that is, seizing opportunities offered in particular circumstances.

The practice of chaining and use of the *ergastulum* suggest that some slaves tried to flee or rebelled against their owners' control of their bodies and time. Others engaged in daily, low-level resistance or actions that facilitated some autonomous movement within the constraining regime and choreography of slave owners. The latters' attempt to prevent laziness and to keep slave hands busy suggests that some slaves did in fact slow down the pace of work or took control of it themselves. Saserna's calculations of time and *iugera* for digging a field even included slaves' own rhythms, only he saw them as a matter idleness (*inertia*) and laxness (*indiligentia*).[44] In a similar moralistic tone, Columella complains (1.7.6) that, left to themselves, slaves hire out the farm's oxen, do not feed the animals adequately, plough carelessly, claim to plant more seed than they actually do, fail to tend crops they have planted, and steal grain from the threshing floor or lose some of it through their sloppiness. Other slaves feigned illness or damaged tools to give themselves some time off.[45] Behind or beyond slaveholders' moralism may lie slaves' own ways of doing things, whether they represented their own farming practices, timing, and appropriation of the products of their labour or actions calculated to irritate their owners.

Slaveholding writers, too, indicate that slaves moved around the farm out of the control of their owners, and their movements hint at an alternative geography to that mapped by the manuals and by the apparent order of rural architecture. In literature and law especially, we glimpse a 'rival geography' of paths, woodlands, and places of refuge. Slaves made their own ways around the estates following their own directions, hence Columella's injunction to the *vilicus* to allow no new footpaths.[46] Some hid out, whether as preparation for flight or as a temporary measure to avoid punishment or simply to take a break. In the legal sources, woodlands are specially named as a hiding place. Roman jurists, too, suggest that the countryside was a place to flee or hide out and charge that rural slaves, including the *vilicus*, sheltered runaways.[47]

The agricultural writers stress the integrity of the boundaries of the farm and repeatedly charge the *vilicus* to allow no slave to leave the estate and to limit his own trips to town, market, and neighbours.[48] The injunction, repeated in detailed permutations, especially around the *vilicus*'s activities in the market, calls attention to the slave manager's amblings, relations with outsiders, visits to the local town or weekly market, and carrying on business other than his owner's.[49] From the repeated and rephrased warnings, too, we must suspect that other slaves left the farm temporarily, with or without the permission of the *vilicus*, on some errand for the *vilicus* or for themselves. Some went into the local village, if there was one; others paid visits to relatives, perhaps on neighbouring farms.[50] Varro, for one, suggests that slaves had relations, friendly and hostile, with slaves on neighbouring estates.[51]

As noted above, both the geography of control mapped in villa architecture and the regime of containment spelled out in the manuals depended on the surveillance and command of slave foremen and overseers.[52] Columella's instructions on the required behaviour of the *vilicus* suggest that his control of the farm's slave workers depended on creating a gap between the *vilicus* and his charges by inhibiting the *vilicus*'s fraternization with ordinary slave labourers. [53] Yet the detail that he lavishes on this practice should make us wonder just how wide the gap was. Slaves on estates distant from their owners, Columella claims, did exactly as they pleased; the slaveholders' stereotype of the slave as greedy, careless, and dishonest undermined their faith in the *vilicus*'s loyalties.[54] Indeed, Roman jurists suspected *vilici* and *procuratores* of hiding slave fugitives on the farms that they managed. We might suspect that in some cases the slave *vilicus* and the slave labourers negotiated a regimen of work that satisfied their own needs and interests, at least within the conditions of their enslavement. Visits by the slaveholder, actual or promised, threatened the slaves' own arrangements. Columella himself notes that the purpose of the slaveholder's visits was to instil fear (*metus*) in both ordinary labourers and the *vilicus*.[55]

We might see two of slaveholders' frequent complaints – slave theft and slaves' trips to town or market – in relation to each other. From the accusations of Roman authors, it seems likely that slaves appropriated more than the rewards handed out by their owners. Columella's observations of grain that disappeared from the threshing room floor, fleeces that went missing at shearing time, and sheep's milk that did not make into the slaveholder's bucket all suggest that slaves took for themselves some of the products of their labour.[56] The *vilicus*, *vilica*, foremen, and provisioners had more opportunities to 'relocate' goods and foodstuffs.[57] Such thefts were put to daily use, like the livestock that Varro allowed rural slaves to raise for themselves, yet Columella's charge that slaves in general stole and his insistence that the *vilicus* was a farmer not a trader – that he should buy and sell only on his owner's orders – raise questions about what he sold. Slaveholders' anxiety about slaves leaving the estate and their restraint on the *vilicus*'s visits to marketplace and town might have been well founded. Certainly, the *vilicus* could have done business only for himself, but it is possible that he also traded in products on behalf of his fellow slaves.[58]

The Geography of Containment: The Urban House

Although work in the country was seen as harder and more rigorous, the investment in the control and choreography of slave movement did not vanish in the city.[59] Slaveholders display an awareness of the potential entertainments and diversions for slaves in the city and the greater possibilities of slave movement. Indeed, the occupational titles found in all the Roman sources suggest that certain slaves, such as *lecticarii*, bath attendants, *pedisequi*, various child attendants, administrators of various sorts, regularly moved out of the house into the city. Yet, at the same time, the literary and legal sources voice a concern about the comings and goings of slaves as well as flight. The evidence points to slaveholders' particular attention to the unscripted movement of urban slaves moving about the city and to the scripted motions of their domestic servants within the house.

An invisible net formed by owners and their agents, neighbours, and the law seems to have circumscribed slave mobility, and this net became particularly important in the urban setting, where slaves could and apparently did move about in the city outside their owners' houses and business establishments. Slave owners or their agents kept track of slaves who left the house.[60] In Petronius's satire of the vulgar freedman Trimalchio, for example, the novel's narrator observes a sign on the door of Trimalchio's house: 'Any slave who goes out without the master's permission will receive one hundred lashes.' Despite the problems with this evidence, the exaggeration here may not be the control of slaves' mobility but the way the Trimalchio practices it and shows off his power to visitors.[61] In addition, neighbours knew who belonged where, and the legal sources give us instances of third parties identifying fugitives or betraying their hiding places.[62] Last but not least, there were the state apparatuses for capturing runaways that could always be deployed for the slave who did not return.[63]

Inside the house, slaves laboured not only in service areas like the kitchen and stable yard; as George has pointed out, work also carried slaves to nearly every room. In effect, the Roman house was not divided by status or gender but by activity and time.[64] This does not mean, however, that there was no choreography of slave movement. The ubiquitous complaints of the slaveholders about the idleness of slaves make it unlikely that hanging around in the peristyle whenever slaves pleased was acceptable. Like the agricultural manuals, the sources that describe domestic urban slaves indicate slave owners' desire to locate them in a particular place and to keep slaves in motion at their jobs. Sometimes, place was defined by person served: nurses with their charges, *pedisequi* near their owners, maids or *cubicularii* at the foot of their owners' beds or on the threshold of their rooms. Sometimes, place was defined by room or area: the cook in his kitchen, the *ostiarius* at the *ostium*, the *atriensis* in the atrium. Some occupational titles located slaves by place – *atriensis, ostiarius, cubicularius*. The owner or guest who called a slave by his title identified him as a part of the house. Seneca indicates that a slave owner might not know his own slaves' names; still, he could command slaves by use of the job title assumed from their location.[65] The House of the Menander at Pompeii had a visual analogue for locating slaves in their places: a caricature of a macrophallic bath attendant holding the tools of his job, strigil and oil flask, faces the bather on the floor of the entrance to the caldarium.[66] Here, in representation, the *balneator* becomes part of the decoration of his place.

The movement of slave bodies in the house often depended on the desires, activities, and demands of owners.[67] Many domestic slaves served to display their owners' wealth and social importance; the choreography of their movements, therefore, was important.[68] At times, this meant making the attentions of servants visible; at other times, it required from them a kind of invisibility. Petronius ridicules Trimalchio for the excessive and inappropriate contortions of Trimalchio's slaves as they guide guests into the dining room and serve the meal. When, at their master's invitation, Trimalchio's slaves lie down with the guests, the novel's narrator, Encolpius, is disgusted: these slaves are out of place, moving in improper ways. In material terms, Petronius's cook brings the stink of the kitchen to the dining couch.[69] Seneca's observations on 'bad' mastery spell out the expectations of Roman slaveholders. In general, slaves should keep to their proper places; at dinner, they should stand around quietly, waiting – unseen and unobtrusive. Yet, at work, they should hustle to obey an order or to complete their assigned tasks; when their owners travel, they should keep pace with them.[70]

Roman mosaics, reliefs, and paintings that include servants represent in some small measure the choreography of slave movement, visible and invisible to owner and guest.[71] Dining and drinking scenes put slaves in motion serving the guests or stick them at the margins of the scene, waiting and watching. For example, in a painting from the House of the Triclinium at Pompeii (fig. 4.3) slaves bustle about: one removes the shoe of a guest; another hands the guest a cup of wine; and a third supports a much larger man as the latter vomits.[72] In a tomb relief from Trier, four young women (the one on the far right is damaged), probably slaves, cluster round their older, seated mistress, doing her hair, holding the mirror, and bringing the necessary items for her toilette.[73] Until the Late Roman Empire, paintings and reliefs most often depict one or two slaves, and most often, servants stand at the edges waiting, as in the famous paintings of intimate scenes in cubiculum D at the Villa della Farnesina in Rome.[74] The representations fix slaves in place or in the prescribed motions of service, mirroring for owners, guests, and themselves their proper relations to other bodies in a defined space.

The architecture of the house itself maps a varied physical complement to the practices evident in law and literature. Scholarship of the last ten years has enlarged our understanding of the architecture and decor of the Roman house, its functioning, and its use of space. Overwhelmingly, however, the position from which interpretation proceeds, and hence our knowledge, tends to be that of the male house owner, his guests, and clients. Although the work of scholars like Penelope Allison, Andrew Wallace-Hadrill, Keith Bradley, and Michele George has put women and slaves into the Roman house, the house continues to be seen as an expression of the owner's political and social position, or that of his family, his *romanitas*, his personality, identity, and tastes.[75]

As noted above, we can look at the architecture and decoration of Roman houses as the 'contexts of servitude' established by slaveholders, remembering, at the same time, that 'they did not control those contexts absolutely.'[76] George has demonstrated the difficulties of finding slaves in the archaeological remains of Roman houses, especially when we look for slave quarters.[77] My concern here is less with where slaves slept (with quarters) and more with how they moved out of the house and within it. I indicate where scholars have identified possible slave *cellae*; that some were or were also storerooms does not eliminate their use by slaves. I assume that slaves certainly occupied kitchens and stable yards.

The Houses of the Vettii and the Menander at Pompeii (VI.15.1 and I.10.4) serve as useful examples precisely because they are familiar and much discussed and because the presence of service areas is so clearly articulated on the ground. At the same time, the difference in their size and complexity offers a revealing contrast.[78] In the House of the Vettii (fig. 4.4), a door on the northwest side of the atrium near the fauces opened to a small atrium (v) surrounded by four small rooms (α, z, y, x) and the entrance to the kitchen (w, off which was a small room, x^1, with erotic paintings). On the southeast side of the atrium, a passageway (γ; fig. 4.5) led to the stable yard (β) and a latrine (in the southwest corner of β).[79] In the House of the Menander (fig. 4.6), a low door on the west side of the peristyle opened to a dog-legged corridor (M1) that ends in the kitchen (27) and a latrine (26); this corridor turned north into another hall (M2) that passed room 28 (which contains a horseshoe-shaped stove). Another dog-legged corridor off the southeast corner of the peristyle (P1 and P) passed the stable yard (34; fig. 4.7), turning north, continuing past four *cellae* (P2; fig. 4.8) and a latrine (39) into an interim space (40) and then into an older house absorbed by the owners of the Menander. Both the stable yard and corridor facing this older house opened on to two storeys of small rooms identified as slave quarters.

In both houses, the kitchen and stable yard areas were located at the periphery of what we think of as the main part of the houses, that is, of the atrium, triclinium, peristyle, and all those rooms whose use we cannot really pin down (but imagine as sites for the owners' activities due to their decoration, size, and other formal criteria). These service areas have no axial entrances, especially in terms of the flow of space and the sight lines mapped so carefully by art historians.[80] In the House of the Menander, this arrangement was highly articulated by the long dog-legged passageway (fig. 4.6, M) from the peristyle to the kitchen and by the long corridor off the southeast corner of the peristyle (P), probably a stairway down to the stable yard (34), that continued north past the four *cellae* (P2) and the latrine (39), into an interim space (40) and the absorbed older house (figs. 4.7 and 4.8). Both corridors seem too narrow to make them convenient spaces for hiding or hanging out, only for movement to and from.[81]

Spatial arrangements in these houses shaped the movement of slaves at work. For meals served in the Houses of the Vettii and of the Menander, servants had a long walk from kitchen to dining room. In the House of the Vettii, a slave carrying a tray walked fifty-three of my paces out of the kitchen through the kitchen atrium into the house's atrium, along the peristyle to triclinium q; in the House of the Menander, the slave walked out of the kitchen into M1, then M, around the peristyle to the huge triclinium /salon 18 (seventy-five of my paces).[82] Each of these long treks expressed the power of the slave's owner, and it does not matter that these hikes resulted simply from the marginalization of the service areas rather than a calculated mode of subjecting slaves.[83] That is, whatever the slaveholder's intentions, his power over the slave servant translated his ability to command into the slave's many steps from the kitchen to the dining room.

The architectural arrangements that marginalized or hid service areas produced the sight lines so carefully traced by art historians, from one room or position to another, through the atrium, tablinum, into the peristyle, from triclinium through the peristyle and its garden to another room (and / or painting), or from the dining couch to floor mosaics and wall paintings.[84] These sight lines belonged to the owner, his clients, and his guests, and they were most enjoyed when owner and guests strolled around the peristyle, stood still, or lay on their couches in the triclinium.

By contrast, slaves in these spaces were not supposed to stroll leisurely, although they often stood still; however, their standing still involved the work of waiting. When slaves were on call for owner and guests in the triclinium, cubiculum, or peristyle, where do we imagine that they stood? Art and literature locate them sitting at the feet of their owners, standing behind them, or simply standing around.[85] In their owners' line of vision, slaves could be commanded by a wave or an oral command. The positioning of lamps created shadows and dark areas in rooms, potentially places for lurking unseen or obscured until called out for some task.[86] It has been observed that slave owners accustomed to being surrounded by slaves ignored their presence or saw through them.[87] The same was not possible for slaves, who had to watch for the gesture or listen for the command. What might *their* sight lines trace? What configuration of space can we map if we begin with slaves' positions and points of view?

Again, the terms used by Mark Grahame to analyse space in the House of the Faun are useful for glimpsing the way architecture shapes human relations through the control of the location of bodies and their movements. In terms of open and closed spaces, the atria and peristyles of both houses were the most open spaces; with respect to them, the stable yards and kitchens, though not cell-like, were closed spaces. If, as Grahame suggests, the ability to 'enclose the body and remove oneself from the sight of others' constitutes privacy, then slaves in kitchen areas and stable yards were removed from the gaze of their owners – afforded 'privacy' – in Grahame's terms.[88]

Yet, as Grahame notes, we must also consider how 'escape from scrutiny' becomes 'confinement' when an individual cannot walk elsewhere 'without coming under surveillance.' The entrances and exits to kitchen area and stable yard in the House of the Vettii would have been easily patrolled, as would the main (VI.15.1) and secondary entrances (VI.15.27) to the house. A watchman or supervisor, positioned in or near d or k, could have observed movement in and out of the kitchen area, the front door, and g to the stable area. A substantial door at the main entrance (and presumably, too, at the stable yard entrance) most probably was locked at night.[89] In the larger House of the Menander, there were simply more doors and spaces to patrol. Beside the main door at I.10.4, there was the stable yard door at I.10.14 and a second entrance (to the older absorbed house) at I.10.16, and the presumed shop at I.10.17 (the door at I.10.15 was quite late). The evidence of thresholds, closure systems, and keys or lock pieces indicates that these doors could have been locked.[90] In the case of slave movement within the house, slaves passing through the non-service areas of the Menander or walking in and out of the kitchen area or stable yard (to and from the main body of the house) could have been tracked by an *ostiarius* or supervisor stationed in or at room 1.[91] Observations of slave movement in and round the stable yard required a guard at I.10.14, although he would not have been able to watch slaves in P2 or the older house at I.10.16, whose surveillance necessitated another observer.[92]

If the kitchen courtyard in the House of the Vettii (v; fig. 4.4) and the stable yard in the House of the Menander (34; figs. 4.6 and 4.7) were closed spaces in terms of atrium and peristyle, they were open spaces in terms the small rooms around or near them. In the House of the Vettii, courtyard v is an open space with respect to w, x, y, z, and a. In the House of the Menander, 34 is an open space with respect to 29, 31–33, and so, too, *cellae* 35–38. These small closed spaces offered their occupants some concealment.[93] Yet, they were not removed from the gaze of the owner's supervisors, stationed in or near v or 34. Moreover, in the kitchens or kitchen areas of each house were *lararia* that included a genius of the owner, in a sense, simulacra of masters in their absence.[94] In effect, the figure and gaze of masters looked on slave activities when slave owners themselves were elsewhere.

Whereas the architecture of both houses and the marginal positioning of the service areas allows for a geography of containment, its practice, as in the *villa rustica*, required human agency. Not surprisingly, the larger and more complex the house (and the more potentially porous in terms of external doorways), the larger the project of control for owners who wished to patrol slave movement. The choreography of slave movement was a necessity for any slaveholder with a desire for display or elite presentation; perhaps, too, it supplemented (or even substituted for) surveillance where slaves had more places to go inside the house and more exits to leave it.

The lavish, aristocratic maritime villa at Oplontis (Villa A) may show us what we must in some way recreate or imagine in other houses (fig. 4.9). Built around 50 BCE and enlarged and refurbished until some time before 79 CE, the villa had a central core with atrium, triclinia, oeci, baths, a kitchen, and a service court. A later eastern wing included elaborate suites and a large swimming pool; there was probably, too, a symmetrical western wing.[95] Like many of its neighbours on the Bay of Naples, the villa provided its owners with the pleasures of sun, sea, and lush gardens.[96] In Bettina Bergman's view, 'architecture, gardens, paintings, mosaics,' and the site itself all worked together to create 'an absorbing experience for inhabitants and visitors.' She traces out that experience by examining 'the key strategies to arrange space, orchestrate movement, and stimulate the eye ... by the correlation of different media, the framed visual axis, and the repetition, or echoing of motifs ... in different locations.'[97] Her wonderful analysis is predicated on two assumptions. First, it presumes the leisure to stroll or to contemplate gardens and paintings. Second, slaves hurrying on some task or simply wandering around would have disturbed the effects that she describes. The villa, I shall argue, included a visual system of choreography for its slave staff that avoided this sort of disturbance.

The service areas, a kitchen (7) and service court (32), as in other villas and houses, do not have axial entrances and exits. This lack, certain utilitarian features, and the zebra-striped painting in the service court (a striking contrast to the decoration of atrium, triclinia, and oeci) indicate that the court was not particularly designed for display like other parts of the villa. However, its location, unlike that of the kitchen, ended up at a central point for the core and both wings of the villa, and a practical, if not necessarily intended, location for effective service. Nonetheless, slaves had to wend their way around to perform their jobs, whether moving from the kitchen to the dining room in the central core of the villa or from the service court to either wing. A waiter carting food from the kitchen (7) to the triclinium (14), for example, had two choices: [1] he walked out the door on the west side of the kitchen through courtyard 16, all the way through salon 15, to the area before the dining room, or [2] his path took him out of the door on the south side of the kitchen into room 9 through 10bis to the front of the triclinium. A servant leaving the service court (32) for work in the eastern wing had a number of alternative routes, all of them requiring a long walk and all of them seemly complicated. So, for example:

[1] the slave walked out of the service court (32) through passage 39, along porticos 24 and 40 into the entrance to corridor 77 at the southeast corner of 40, and then north through 77 into the suite of rooms around 78, or he walked further north through 76 into corridor 46, and then along portico 60 into any of the suites that bordered the swimming pool, or he entered these suites through 63, and / or 67, and / or 71 and so forth;

[2] the slave left 32 through interim space 45 and took passageways 52 and 53, and then walked through 62 and 63 and so on; or

[3] the slave exited 32 through interim space 45 and continued on into corridor 46 from which he could turn south into 76 or north into portico 60 or the back way through 63, 64, 67, etc.

Such varied paths are particularly interesting in terms of the decoration of the service court and certain other spaces and passageways in the villa. The entire walls of the service courtyard (32; fig. 4.10) are painted in zebra stripes, a style known from Pompeii and other villas in the Vesuvian area; at Oplontis, the stripes continue in spaces and corridors throughout the villa, including 4, 32, 45, 46, 52, 53, 62, 63, 67, 71, 76, 83, 94, and 97 (figs. 4.9 and 4.11).[98] With few exceptions (the peristyle is the major one), the stripes cover the lower part of the walls, divided vertically into panels marked by yellow or red borders.[99] Compared to the fine paintings in the atrium, triclinium 14, and salon 15, to name only a few examples, the zebra stripes do not invite study, reflection, or pause. In fact, according to Lara Laken, they nurture movement: the stripes fit corridors and rooms that are the sites of activity. While the alternating directions of the stripes may add 'some variation in long corridors,' they may also denote 'speed' as the appropriate pace of those who walk through them.[100]

Laken argues that the zebra stripes indicated 'public' or 'common' space, as in a corridor in an apartment building that leads to different units.[101] We must, however, think a bit more carefully about the meanings of 'public' and 'common' in private houses and villas.[102] Laken includes owner, guests, and clients in the 'public,' and at Oplontis, in the tablinum (4) and corridor 46, for example, there would have been no reason to exclude guest or client.[103] Alternatively, I want to suggest that in the setting of Oplontis what we have are directional markers for slave servants, slave residents of the villa who would have known the villa's layout, slaves of its owners who were new to service or the villa, and slaves who belonged to and served guests. In a villa of this size and luxury, there was perhaps a need for markers: the villa was large and complex; its many paintings, mosaics, and gardens were carefully arranged to delight its owners and guests; its rooms for entertainment and repose were numerous; and the routes to reach these rooms varied. Navigating the villa in the service of its owners, guests, and upkeep, and at the same time contributing to, rather than detracting from, its orchestration of nature, art, and architecture, would seem to have required planning and attention. I suggest that the stripes signalled to slaves that this was an area or a corridor that they could enter without specific permission, orders, or directions from their owners. The stripes were visual traffic signs: no slave had to remember the villa's layout, had to read, or even be told where to go. It is striking that the corridors and space so marked took slaves to every part of the villa, and they marked paths that avoided the artfully designed views. Corridors 46 and 76, for example, provide a path around colonnade 40 and its garden (59); 76 (fig. 4.11) around the suite composed of rooms 66, 78, and 79; 53 around the colonnade and garden at 56.[104] In the case of salon 65 or 69, the doors at 63, 67, and 71, which give access to these elegant rooms, could have been closed to shut out even the zebra stripes from guest and owner. The point is not that owners or their guests had to keep out of the zebra-striped areas; rather, it is that slaves stayed within them without an express order or invitation to do otherwise. The zebra stripes define a geography of containment that did not halt motion as much as they nurtured it, constraining *and* choreographing slave mobility. Moreover, despite the huge gap of complexity and sophistication between the zebra stripes and the villa's other paintings, the former as much as the latter belong to an overall orchestration of experience described by Bettina Bergmann because they insured that owners and guests were served in a way that seamlessly integrated slaves and their labour into the villa's aesthetic program.

The Rival Geography: The Urban House

Slaveholders' observations and complaints themselves indicate that slaves did not always adhere to their owners' geography of containment. Through slaveholders' words and a critical look at the material environment, we glimpse what Camp calls 'alternative ways of using space.' The surveillance and control of slave comings and goings depended on the use of slave or freed supervisors and watchmen, and it is clear that, willingly or unwillingly, they did not exercise absolute control. Law and literature testify to slaves on the move in a 'bad' way. Some slaves fled or attempted to flee slavery; others took refuge at the statues of emperors to escape not slavery but a brutal master. More importantly, because such movements were more common, slaves visited mothers, lovers, and friends, apparently without the express permission of their owners.[105] Some, like Labeo's truant (*erro*), walked about the city for their own reasons, along their own routes, at their own tempos.[106]

The city offered various diversions, and slaveholders complain that slaves spent too much time enjoying them.[107] They attended games and public spectacles; they visited brothels and prostitutes and frequented taverns. We even hear of a slave obsessed with studying works of art. Others, charged slaveholders, joined up with religious fanatics (*fanaticos*) or celebrated the rites of Bacchus, 'cavorting around the shrines.' Although Columella disdains urban slaves, his charges about them neatly sum up the possibilities of slave movement throughout the city: 'This lazy and sleepy class of slaves, accustomed to leisure (time off from work), to the campus, the circus, and the theatres, to gambling, to taverns, to brothels, never ceases to dream of these follies.'[108]

The implication in this spiteful observation is interesting in terms of what slaveholders could glimpse of the 'rival geography': slaves moved about too much in pursuit of their own pleasures (purposes) and / or did not move enough on their owners' purposes; that is, they were idle. Seemingly universal, the charge came in many forms. Among a list of qualities of the bad slave, the jurist Gaius included: *desidiosus*, *somniculosus*, *piger*, and *tardus* (idle, sleepy, sluggish, slow). We should add here, too, slaveholders' suspicion that slaves feigned illness.[109] Other slaveholders complained about slaves' clumsiness, slow pace, and noise – talking at dinner, clanging metalware, shouting to each other, and banging doors.[110] In all of this, we should at least suspect slaves' low-level, daily resistance to their owners' geography of containment and attempts to script their motions.[111] Alternative interpretations of these complaints spell out slaves' own choreography that in small ways took control of their time and space, all of which depended on seizing particular moments and chance opportunities.[112] Some set their own pace at work or arranged for a needed break; others garnered time and space for social or family life; and still others simply achieved the goal of irritating their owners, sometimes at the cost of a slap or a whipping.

How slaves regarded various spaces in the house and how they used that space is nearly unrecoverable. Still, if we are not to leave the house to its owners, we can at least take Vlach's observation on the architecture of the plantation South into the Roman house. Although their archaeological remains reflect their owners' arrangements of space, 'an apparent order on the [ground] may not be the only order present.'[113] From our point of view, a point of view that we share with slave owners, stable yards, kitchens, and slave quarters are at the margins of the house – or at least, out of the flow of space that delighted owners and impressed visitors. Was, for example, the stable yard in the House of the Menander (figs. 6 and 7), with its surrounding or nearby slave *cellae*, peripheral to the slaves who worked, slept, and passed time there? The area included a water supply, a stove (though it was not in use at the time of the eruption in 79), and, perhaps, a dining room. Roger Ling speculates that a room on the second floor over 20 and 20a and b, lit by large windows and decorated in simple white-ground paintings in the fourth style, might have been a dining room for the staff.[114] We should note, too, the tavern at the corner of the insula (11.10.13) to the right of the wide entrance to stable yard (34).[115] Epitaphs testify to slave's' family and social relationships, and we must wonder whether the yard or the kitchen area of the House of the Menander, or the atrium outside the kitchen in the House of the Vettii, or the peristyle court (32) at Oplontis were hubs for slave communal life.[116] Slave owners certainly complained about one effect of slave gatherings: noise. Pliny the Younger, for example, was thankful for a room of his own that closed off the voices of his young slaves and, especially, during the Saturnalia, segregated him from the celebrations of his household.[117] That is, if we take into account the social life of slaves documented in their epitaphs, we might speculate that what was marginal for slave owners was central for the household's slaves.

These service areas and quarters offered their occupants varied conditions. Corridors were narrow and poorly lit; slave *cellae* and many kitchens, too, were dark. Latrines and their odours were often nearby, and in the case of stable yards, so, too, were animals that did not have latrines.[118] Yet, in some cases, there were certain physical advantages: the kitchen garden (R) off the kitchen in the House of the Menander, the huge tree, possibly a chestnut, that stood in the centre of the service court at Oplontis, and a lovely view of the sea off the service area near the kitchen at the Villa Arianna. Perhaps the most important advantage, ironically, lay in the slave owners' spatial arrangements. If the positioning of the kitchen areas and stable yards of the House of the Menander and of the Vettii restricted slave mobility and facilitated surveillance, they also enabled slaves to remove themselves from the gaze of their owners and offered them some power to limit what their owners knew of their lives.[119]

We must ask about the slaves' understanding and use of the rest of the house, especially since many houses lack slave quarters and since in the performance of their jobs, as George observes, slaves were everywhere. Instances of slaves hiding out in the house – Horace mentions a boy who shirked his work took refuge under a stairway – suggest that slaves knew nooks and crannies overlooked or ignored by the house owner (e.g., the space beneath stairwell and corridor g in the House of the Vettii; fig. 4.5).[120] The many graffiti in the corridor outside the kitchen in the House of the Menander suggest that slaves did 'hang out' here, rather than, or in addition to, striding along expeditiously at their tasks.[121] Poorly lit corners and storerooms, too, offered places to lurk, to be present and unseen. Penelope Allison has shown that the occupants of the atrium varied with the time of day, and we might imagine that the same would be true for peristyles, internal courtyards, or colonnades. When owners were elsewhere, either out of the house or villa, asleep in some other room, or occupied in some other area, slaves could and perhaps did occupy these spaces. At Oplontis, for example, a courtyard with a fountain and potted plants (16), adjoining salon 15 and bordering the bath complex, was easily accessed by the kitchen staff and convertible to their use when the villa's owners were elsewhere, strolling in the colonnade perhaps (and vice versa).

The question here is not simply slaves' use of space but their appropriation of parts of their owners' houses. Occupational titles like *atriensis*, *ostiarius*, and *cubicularius* raise the question acutely. As noted earlier, these titles defined the slave by place. Did slaves who identified themselves by these titles in their epitaphs, like owners or guests, view themselves as melded to parts of house? Elsewhere, I have argued that domestic job titles claim physicality and perhaps even a kind of awareness that slaves did for slaveholders what they could not do for themselves.[122] Now, in light of thinking about slave movement and use of space, I wonder whether such titles also represented a claim to space, a sort of appropriation of kitchen, atrium, cubiculum, etc. Unlike an owner or guest, who may have called 'hey, *ostiarius*' (if not, 'hey boy'), slaves on the epitaphs joined a name to a job title. In such a configuration, the slave becomes an agent distinguished from yet claiming a space, not an *instrumentum vocale* associated with a place. In these cases, we must talk about re-appropriation, for what slaves appropriated were their assigned places. In extant Roman houses and villas, we find few marks of such 'acts of appropriation,' yet at death, the claim to the master's space remained for those who would or could read it.[123]

NOTES

* I want to express my appreciation for the observations and criticisms of Michele George, Natalie Kampen, and the anonymous readers of the volume. John Clarke, Michael Thomas, and Lea Cline have added much to my understanding

of Villa A at Oplontis, and special thanks are owed Michael Thomas for his tours, insights, and analyses. Above all, I want to thank Margaret Laird for her invaluable suggestions, attentive reading, and acumen, and Lauren Hackworth Petersen for hours of tramping through and of discussions of Roman houses and villas.

1 Camp 2004: 12.

2 Camp 2004: 6–7. By using Camp's concepts, I do not intend to compare the two slave systems. On the grounds for comparing slave systems, see esp. Hall 2000; Webster 2008a and 2008b; Mullins 2008; Mattingly 2008.

3 E.g., Schumacher 2001; Scheidel 2002; Roth 2007; George 1997a and b; Webster 2008a; Marzano 2007.

4 'One of the most prevalent shortcomings in historical archaeology as a discipline has been the failure to marry words and things (Hall 2000: 16). Cf. Webster 2008a: 115.

5 Webster 2008a: 126; Webster 2008b: 140.

6 So observes Vlach (1993: 17) of the plantation South.

7 Not revolutionary because the Roman slave system, at least after 70 BCE, hardly allowed large-scale rebellion; see Glymph 2008: 94–6 for a critique of a gender-limited notion of revolutionary. For limitations of the 'idea of 'resistance,' see especially Sharpe 2003: xv–xvi.

8 See Isaac 1999: 52–3 for what he calls 'slave opportunism' and 'an alternative territorial system.' On the problem of slave agency, see Hartman 1997 and Sharpe 2003. Sharpe (2003: xiv) warns that we must account for the 'possibility of action without negating the unequal relations of power that restrict the ability to act.' Note especially her use of Michel de Certeau's concept of 'tactic' as the 'art of the weak' (Sharpe 2003: xxi, 1995: 45; de Certeau 1984: 36–7).

9 Ian Morris (1998) in Greek archaeology and Jane Webster (2001, 2003, 2005, and 2008) in Roman archaeology have developed various strategies for finding the material culture of slaves in ceramics, artefact assemblages, houses, and graffiti. Interesting and provocative, their work 'focuses primarily on objects and patterns that are associated with resistance and used in the interstices of power' (Mullins 2008: 127); however, it does not enable us to put slaves into the predominant archaeological landscape available to modern eyes: the material remains of houses, workshops, streets, and villas that seem to bear no trace of slaves' existence.

10 Vlach 1993: xi and 1.

11 Travels with owners: *Digest* 29.5.1.31; Sen. *Ira* 3.29.1; Col. 1.3.4. Errands: *Digest* 21.1.17.14. Running businesses: *Digest* 14.3. Slave agents in the provinces: *Digest* 21.17.16; 28.5.35.3 40.9.10; 4. *Insitores*: *Digest* 5.1.19.3.

12 Thompson 2003: 217–38. Cato *Agr.* 56; Col. Pref. 9, 1.6.3, 1.8.16; 1.9.4, 11.1.22; Plaut. *Capt.* 110–118; Apul. *Met.* 9.12; *Digest* 4.3.7.7; 13.6.5.6.

13 Bradley 1994: 117–22, 1989: 32–40; Daube 1952; Bellen 1971.

14 Aside from outright, large-scale slave rebellions, the individual's escape from slavery altogether was the most extreme quest for freedom of movement: as Roman jurists acknowledged, 'flight is a form of liberty in that the slave is for the present relieved of his master's power' (*Digest* 21.1.17.10). On slave catchers and agents, help of official and troops, and advertisements, see *Digest* 11.4, 12.5.4.4, 18.1.35.3, 19.5.18; Petr. *Sat.* 97; Apul. *Met.* 6.7–8 and n. 13 above.

15 Bradley 1994: 129–30.

16 I focus on Columella as the apex of the customs, ideals, and practices discussed or mentioned in Cato and Varro. On agricultural writers as evidence, see Roth 2007.

17 Troublesome slave: 1.9.4; chained slaves: 1.8.16; 1.9.4; 11.1.22; 1.6.3.

18 The *procurator* should have a place over the entrance to keep track of the *vilicus* (1.6.7); cf. Varro, *RR* 1.13.2.

19 Slaves forbidden to leave the farm: 1.8.12; regulated paths: 1.8.7.

20 *Vilicus* not to leave estate: 1.8.7; 1.8.12–13; limited contact with outsiders: 1.8.6; 11.1.13 and 23.

21 *Vilica*: Col.12.3.7–9. Vilicus: Col. 1.8.11; 11.1.17–18; 11.1.26; 12.1.4. On the *vilica*, see Roth 2005.

22 Col. 1.2.1, 1.8.13; 1.8.16–20; 12.1.22–25. The owner's supervision of the *vilicus* was undertaken in such a way that those under the authority of the *vilicus* would have seen it (1.8.16–17), thus limiting the *vilicus*'s authority.

23 On *Cato* see Plut. *Cato* 21.22–24; Cato, *Agr.* 2.2–4; Col. 1.8.9; 1.8.11; 1.9.7–8; 11.1.17–18; 11.1.26; 11.1.29; 11.2.

24 Calculations of time and tasks: Cato, *Agr.* 2.2; Varro, *RR* 1.18.1–7; Col. 2.12.1ff.

25 For example, Col. 2.2.22–26, 6.2.4–6, 7.3.26. Various other activities mandated control of the diet and sexual lives of slaves – beekeepers, bakers, cooks, and provisioners (Col. 9.14.3, 12.4.2–3). Limits on bathing: Col. 1.6.19. Control of the *vilicus*'s drinking, eating, and sexual activity: Col. 11.1.13.

26 See Rossiter 1981 and 1978; White 1970; Carrington 1931; Thompson 2003. On problems of interpretation, see Dyson 2003; Greene 1990: 67ff; Marzano 2007; Schumacher 2001; George 1997b. Slave rooms: Thompson 2003: 81ff; Marzano 2007: 129–48.

27 De Caro's excavation and publication of the Villa Regina at Boscoreale (1994) is an example. Slave rooms: Thompson 2003: 81ff; Marzano 2007: 129–48.

28 Thompson 2003: 83; Bradley 1994: 84–6.

29 Aside from the two *villae* discussed here, see the Villa of Tiberius Claudius Eutychus (*NS* 1922: 459–79), the Villa of the Volusii at Lucus Feroniae (Sgubini Moretti 1998), the Villa of Pisanella near Boscoreale (*Monumenti Antici* 7[1897]: 397–554), for examples. On Villa A at Oplontis, see n. 96, below. The bibliography on working villas is vast: beyond surveys of particular areas or sites, see, in general, Marzano 2007 (with extensive bibliography); Terrenato

2001; Lafon 2001; Purcell 1995; Métraux 1998; Ortalli 2006. For a critique of the interpretation of these areas as slave habitations, see Marzano 2007: 129–48 with references to earlier analyses.

30 Scrapings on the elevated thresholds and the holes for hinges suggest sturdy doors that opened inward (Carandini 1985: 2.154, 166, and 1.69). There is no evidence for their locks (and if they locked). Only the thresholds on 114, 39, 40, and 41 were examined.

31 On the doors in this area, see Carandini 1985: 1.73 and 2.173–5. Again, not every threshold was examined. Of the seven that were, four thresholds (105, 106, 16, 77) had no holes for the door hinges or evidence of how they closed, though they probably closed in a way similar to those with holes for door hinges and a *paletto* for locking (102, 103, 174).

32 Carandini 1985: 1.176–7. See also the discussions in Thompson 2003: 7–101; Greene 1990: 89–92; and Carandini and Settis 1979.

33 Marzano 2007: 129–38.

34 See also Schumacher 2001: 101; Purcell 1988.

35 Marzano 2007: 136. It does seem curious that the owners of Settefinestre who built a pigsty in stone would not have done the same for their human workers.

36 *Digest* 33.7.8 and 33.7.12.2; cf. Varro, *RR* 1.17.1.

37 The agricultural writers rarely give much detail, as they subordinate slave housing to the productive aspects of a farm or villa; however, all three are clear that slaves lived in the *villa rustica* per se.

38 See notes 30 and 31, above.

39 On Gragnano, villa 34, see Della Corte 1923: 275–80; Croza 1942: 70–5; Thompson 2003: 84–5; Rossiter 1978: 43; White 1970: 436–7.

40 Croza (1942: 72) suggests that this area was for storage of agricultural products.

41 The presence of a large caldron (*caldaio*) led Della Corte (1923: 277) and Croza (1942: 70) to speculate that the courtyard was a site for processing cheese. Cato (11) sets out the equipment for a vineyard of one hundred *iugera*. For a staff of sixteen, he suggests four beds, four mattresses, and four coverlets, not to mention one chamber pot. Clearly, then, slaves shared beds and, we should expect, rooms. Except for the objects in corridor 20, the collection of objects in other rooms represented a very mixed range of artefacts, which points to Marzano's suggestion about the manifold use of *cellae familiae* (Della Corte 1923: 276–80). There were three types of collections which indicate the activities of daily life (cooking, eating, lighting) or the storage of products: items of everyday use like tableware and cooking ware and lamps (rooms 6, 25, 32); storage amphora only (21); and a mixture of everyday items and storage amphora (8, 22, 32, 26, 33, 35, B). In 20 that led to the secondary entrance to the villa, in addition to tableware, kitchen vessels, lamps, there were objects and jewelry in gold, silver, and bronze. Perhaps some resident with some of his or her precious goods was

trying to flee or piled these things here; the identity of this person is of course unknown.

42 Grahame 1997: 145–6. It should be noted that this use of Grahame's observations on open and closed space is not an attempt at access analysis.

43 Grahame 1997: 146.

44 Varro, *RR* 1.18.2.

45 Cato, *Agr.* 2.2; Varro, *RR* 1.22.6; Col. 1.8.8, 12.3.7.

46 1.8.7; 11.1.23.

47 *Digest* 11.3.1.2; 11.3.5.3; 11.4.1.1–2; 11.4.3; 21.1.17.4 and 8.

48 Cato *Agr.*5.2; Varro, *RR* 1.16.5; Col. 1.8.6–7, 1.8.12–13; 11.1.13, 11.1.23–34.

49 Col. 1.8.6–7, 1.18.13, 11.1.23–24.

50 Col. 11.1.23; Cato, *Agr.* 2.2; *Digest* 21.1.17.5; cf. Petr. *Sat.* 61–2 where an urban slave sneaks off to the country after a girlfriend when his owner leaves town (*Nactus ergo occasionem*). We lack information that allows Kaye (2007) to construct neighbourhoods in the antebellum American South whose configurations were established by slaves.

51 Varro, *RR* 1.15.1.

52 Cato, *Agr.* 5; Varro, *RR* 1.16.5, 1.17.5–6; Col. 1.6.7–8, 1.8.3–12, 11.1.14–22, 12.1.1ff. Even herdsmen whose freedom of movement seems greatest had a foreman (Varro, *RR* 2.10.2–5) and their movements were to be dictated by the animals (Varro, *RR* 2.2.2ff).

53 Col. 1.8.5, 11.1.13, 11.1.17–19.

54 Col. 1.7.6, 1.8.20; Columella (1.8.2, 11.1.7) urges the slaveholder to raise the *vilicus* from boyhood and test his knowledge and loyalty.

55 Jurists on fugitives: *Digest* 11.4.1.1; fear: Col. 1.2.1.

56 Col. 1.7.6, 7.4.2, 12.3.9.

57 See Camp 2004: 69 on stealing as 'relocating' things.

58 Raising livestock: Col. 1.17.7. On slave higglering or petty trading in the Caribbean and southern United States, see Simmonds 1987; Berlin 1998: 33–8, 68–70, 136–8. On trading off plantation and the association with theft, see Morgan 1998: 366–73. For the possibility of *peculia* for rural slaves, see Roth 2005.

59 More arduous work in the country: Sen. *Ira.* 3.29.1; Col.1.8.1–2. Country and city were not separate worlds, and slaveholders and slaves moved between them: *Digest* 28.5.35.3; 33.7.19; Petr. *Sat.* 61–2; Col. 1.3.3.

60 Most often those watching who entered and exited were called *ostiarii* (Sen. *Ira* 3.37.2; Sen. *Constant.* 14.2; Petr. *Sat.* 28.8 and 29.1; Vitr. 6.7.1); *ianitores* (Sen. *Ep.* 43.4; Col. Pref. 9; Livy 7.5.3; Cic. *Planc.* 66; see esp.: Ov. *Fas.* 1.138: *ianitor egressus introitusque videt*); *custos* (Prop. 4.7.21).

61 Petr. *Sat.* 28.7. How to interpret this piece of evidence is difficult. First, such a sign presumes slave literacy, certainly the case for some slaves, but not all. Second,

since it was posted on the front door, its audience would seem to be guests and visitors, not the slaves inside, so it displays to outsiders the power of Trimalchio as slaveholder. Last but not least, one hundred lashes would break even the strongest back, if they did not kill the slave.

62 *Digest* 19.5.15.

63 Petr. *Sat.* 97; *Digest* 11.4. See n. 15, above.

64 Hales 2003: 127; George 1997b: 22–3; Laurence 1994: 127–9.

65 Sen. *De Vita Beata* 17.1–2. Petronius's Trimalchio (36.8) solves the problem of remembering a slave's name by dubbing him by his job: '*Itaque quotienscumque dicit "Carpe," eodem verbo et vocat et imperat*' (So, whenever he says 'Carve,' he calls and orders him with the same word).

66 See Clarke 1998: 120–36.

67 See Joshel 1992: 147–54.

68 On slaves as display, see Joshel 1992: 73–,6, George 1997b: 22.

69 Petr. *Sat.* 70.12: *muria condimentisque fetentem* (stinking of pickles and spices). Seneca (*Ep.* 47.15) makes clear that dining with your slaves was generally unacceptable to slaveholders; nor was it good taste for guests and slaves to pass out in the dining room all together (Petr. *Sat.* 22).

70 Sen. *Ep.* 47.2–3, 6, 8; 56.7, 95.24; 122.15–16; *Ira* 2.25.1, 3.29.1, 3.35.2–5. On the invisibility of domestic slaves at work to their owners, see Joshel 2011: 238.

71 In general, as Margaret Laird has pointed, 'the visual record emphasizes activity when showing people who might be identified as slaves: for example, on the frieze of the tomb of Eurysaces, the togate figures stand still, while the "human machines" are in constant motion' (private communication). The same is true for representations of agricultural labourers and landowners.

72 See Clarke 2003: 239–45.

73 Kampen 1981: cat. no. 32, fig. 50.

74 Clarke 1998: 99–107. On the numbers and activities of dining servants, see Dunbabin 2003a: 100–2, 120–2, 150–6.

75 Women and slaves in the house: Allison 1999; Wallace-Hadrill 1994; Bradley 1994, 1989; George 1997a and b. View of the Roman house: Hales 2003; Ellis 2002; Wallace-Hadrill 1994; Bergmann 2002, 1994; Leach 2004; Clarke 1991; Gazda 1991.

76 Vlach 1993: xi and 1.

77 George 1997b: 16–19. See nn. 27 and 28, above.

78 The House of the Vettii (1100 m2) has two entrances; the House of the Menander (1700 m2) three. For a concise summary of their rooms and amenities, see Wallace-Hadrill 1994: 193 and 213.

79 Some rooms in the upper story were possibly quarters and / or work areas. Sogliano 1898: 383–7.

80 On sight lines, see Drerup 1959; Bek 1980; Clarke 1991: 14–19 et passim; Wallace-Hadrill 1994: 38ff.

81 M is 1.10 m across; M2 widens to 1.40 m; southeast corridor is 1.5 m wide, and narrows to less than 1 m wide as it runs along *cellae* 35–38 (see fig. 6).

82 That is, of a female historian who stands five foot four. Allison's work (2004 and 2006) on the location of objects means we need to take into account cooking in the peristyle. Yet this practice, too, required the movement of equipment and foodstuff and with them slaves.

83 The idea was suggested by Phil Taylor (private communication).

84 See note 81, above.

85 Locations of slaves in literature and law: see, for example, Petr. *Sat.* 64; *Digest* 29.5.14 (at owner's feet); Sen. *Ep.* 47.2 (standing around).

86 See Ellis 2002: 179, 151, plates 21–2 on lighting, shadows, and servants.

87 Hales 2003: 125; Joshel 2011: 237–8.

88 Grahame 1997: 145. The presence and closure system of internal doors would be useful. For the House of the Vettii, lack of information and modern reconstruction inhibit analysis (Sogliano [1898: 236] describes only the front door). In the House of the Menander, in the service areas, we do not know about the entrances to M, 27–8, P1 or from P into the stable yard (34) (Ling 1997: 274, 277, 278, 309–10, 341); locks or parts and / or door keys were found near entrance to P1, near the entrance to 20, in P near second entrance to 34; in 35, 38, and 43 (Allison 2006: 72, 109, 115, 116, 122, 135). Of the room whose closures are clear, 36 and 32 locked from the outside; 42, 43, and 33 locked from the inside (Lesley Ling, Appendix E: Thresholds and Doorways in Ling 1997: fig. 22; on the difficulties of analysing the thresholds, see 339).

89 On locked doors, see, for example, *Digest* 21.1.17.15. On the front door, see Sogliano 1898: 236.

90 Ling 1997: 264, 318, 320, 337.

91 Room 2 seems unlikely to have been a 'porter's lodge.' It had a stairway on the east, north, and west wall; underneath were niches, which may have been shrines (Ling 1997: 136, 266; cf. Allison 2006: 300). For the considerable collection of objects found in this room, see Allison 2006: 59–62, 299–300.

92 The easternmost door to 34 was blocked (Ling 1997: 132).

93 Especially where doors were or could be closed. See above nn. 88 and 89. Rooms 35–8 had wooden thresholds (Ling 1997: 339).

94 For the *lararia*, in the Vettii and Menander, see Fröhlich 1991: 279–80 (cat. No. L71) and 255 (cat. No. L14). The *lararium* in the House of the Vettii is on the west wall of courtyard v; the *lararium* painting on the west wall of the kitchen in the House of the Menander is no longer visible (Ling 1997: 95, 278). On *lararia* in general, see Orr 1978, Foss 1997.

95 Thomas and Clarke 2007: 225.

96 Oplontis included an orchard and a vineyard, and agricultural tools and storage
facilities in rooms around the service area (32) have led to the suggestion that
the villa housed workers whose main activities were agricultural. Still, orchard,
vineyard, and the villa's extensive gardens would have required a fairly large
number of workers in themselves. For surveys of the villa, see Fergola and
Pagano 1998, Guzzo and Fergola 2000. On gardens, vineyard, and orchard at
Oplontis, see Jashemski 1987: 71–5 and 1993: 2.293–301; Thomas and Clarke
2007, 2008, 2009. See also http://www.oplontisproject.org.

97 Bergmann 1994: 90 and 96.

98 Laken 2003; Goulet 2000 and 2001–2; see Laken 2003 for their locations
(177–86).

99 See Laken (2003: 167–72) for permutations of stripes; see Cline 2012, forthcoming, for a more careful examination and for the chronology of the types of
zebra stripes.

100 Laken 2003: 172–3; cf. Goulet 2000: 366. Both Laken (2003: 173, 177) and
Goulet (2000: 367) note their practical value – dirt and scratches would have
been less visible, and dark areas in need of 'path illumination' were 'made
more vibrant.'

101 Laken 2003: 177.

102 On the meanings of private and public, see Wallace-Hadrill 1994; Hales 2003;
Grahame 1997.

103 Note that in the tablinum there are stripes on the very lowest section of the
wall. Interpretations of 46 have been shaped by the presence of red-painted
benches along both sides of the corridor. For some scholars, this immediately
evokes clients waiting for visits with a patron; however, it should be noticed
that while 46 give direct access to the eastern wing and pool from the core
of the villa or its western wing, it does so through the service court. More
scenic routes were available along 24 and 40. Others have suggested that these
benches could have been a waiting station for slaves called to service in any
part of the eastern wing.

104 The wall in 53 is a later addition; it is clear that stripes continued all along corridor without break (Michael Thomas, private communication).

105 *Digest* 21.1.17.5, 11.3.1.5; Petr. *Sat.* 61–2, 105.

106 *Digest* 21.1.17.14, cf. 21.1.4.1, 21.1.25.6.

107 For more holidays in the city, see Sen. *Ira* 3.29.1.

108 Col. 1.8.2. Games, entertainments, brothels, and prostitutes; Col. 1.8.2; *Digest*
11.3.5, 21.1.65 pr.; Petr. *Sat.* 95. On slaves, brothels, and taverns, see McGinn
2004. Art lover: *Digest* 21.1.65 pr. Religion: *Digest* 21.1.1.9–10.

109 Gaius *Digest* 21.1.18. Col. 12.3.7; Cato 2.2.

110 Sen. *Ira* 2.25.1; 3.29.1, 3.35.2 and 5; cf. Sen. *Ep.* 56.7, Plin. *Ep.* 2.17.22 and
24. Note also failures of service: Sen. *Ira* 2.25.1; Petr. *Sat.* 30.7–8, 47.13 and

49.5–6, 54.1; Apul. *Met*. 3.16.5; Mart. 2.66, 8.23, 3.94; Juv. 6.489–95; Ov. *Am*. 1.14.16–18, *Ars Am*. 3.239–40; Plin. *Ep*. 1.4. On slave failures and punishment in Plautus, see Parker 1989.

111 See nn. 7 and 8, above, on agency and resistance.

112 However, the slaveholder's script for slaves' performance of their work introduced a certain predictability to opportunities and allowed slaves to anticipate.

113 Vlach 1993: xi.

114 Ling 1997: 121.

115 Ling 1997: 105.

116 See Flory 1978, Joshel 1992.

117 Plin. *Ep*. 2.17.22–24. It strikes me that we might put together several of the slaveholders' complaints to speculate about the use of these areas: slave drinking, gluttony, missing or stolen food and wine stores, and slave noisiness. Added up, they constitute the motions of a party or social gathering.

118 As Hales (2003: 124) observes, 'these areas, often well separated from the main house, are the locus for the dirty or polluted activities of the house.'

119 Apuleius (*Met*. 10.13–14) tells a story of two brothers and fellow slaves, a pastry chef and a cook, who shared a room, which, though it is a fiction, describes how slaves occupied *cellae*.

120 Hor. *Ep*. 2.2; cf. *Digest* 21.1.17.4; note that some assume that to hide is to act like a slave (*Digest* 40.12.10). On slaves hiding out in a house, and the instance of slaves hiding fugitives, see *Digest* 11.3.5.3 and 11.4.1.1. The space seems to have been used to store bridles and harness for horses (http://www.stoa.org/projects/ph/rooms?houseid=18#372).

121 Mouritsen 2010: 20. There is no certain evidence slaves wrote them, but, given their location, Mouritsen notes, 'no other explanation seems plausible.'

122 Joshel 1992: 155–60.

123 As Vlach (1993: 17) observes for the plantation South, such 'acts of appropriation leave few physical marks.' One interesting, if problematic, source, as noted above, is graffiti: beside the graffiti outside the kitchen in the House of the Menander, there are, for example, the numbers scratched on the wall of the kitchen at the Villa San Marco (Barbet and P. Miniero 1999: 355–6).

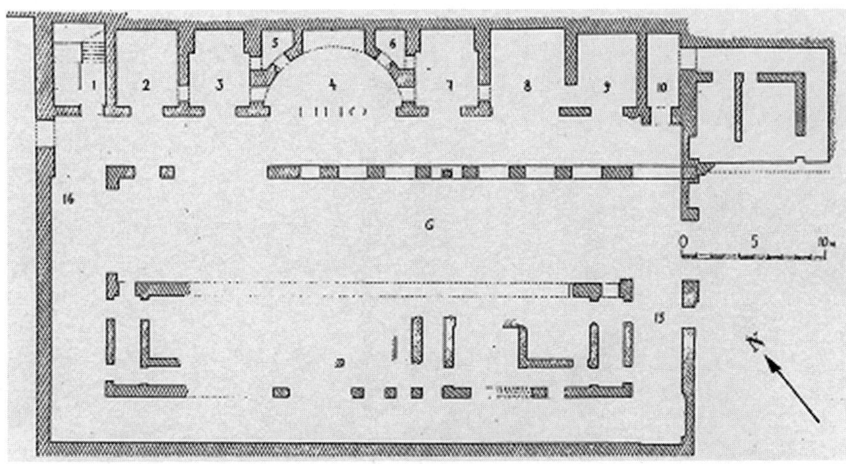

Fig. 3.1 Plan of the Palatine Paedagogium. From Solin and Itkonen-Kaila 1966: fig. 1.

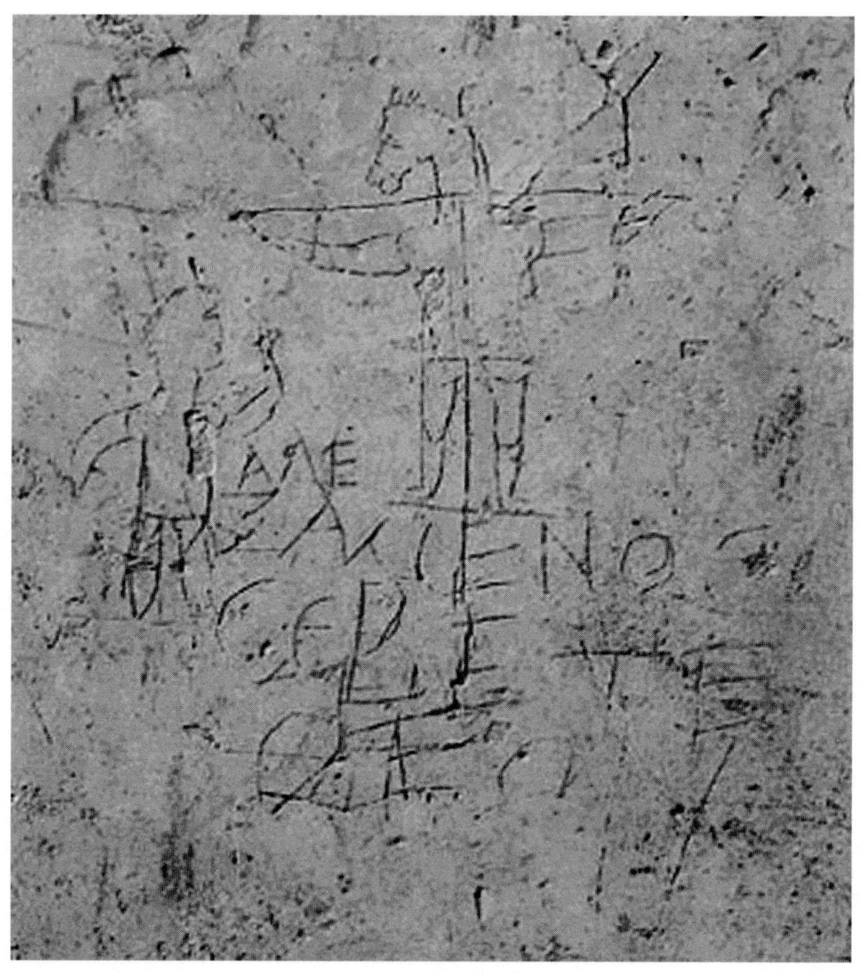

Fig. 3.2 Graffito of Alexamenos. From Solin. and Itkonen-Kaila 1966: 246.

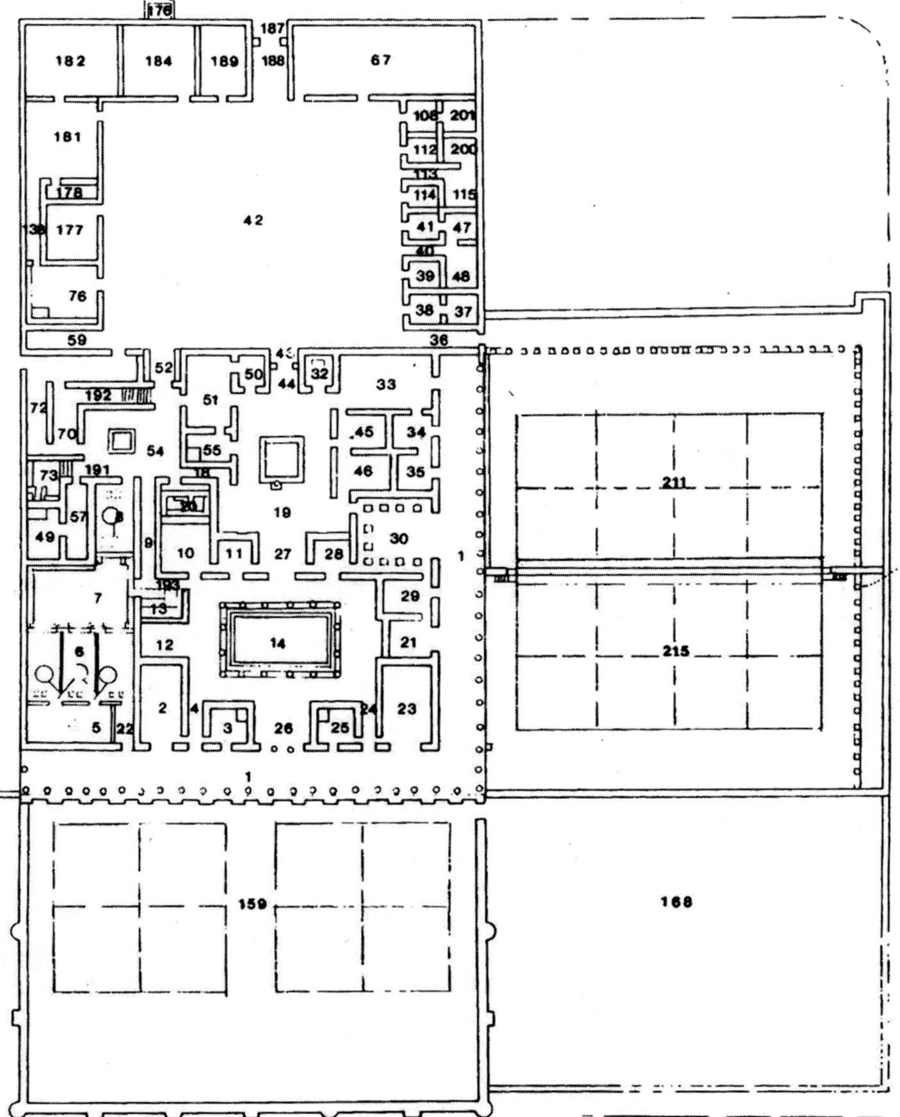

Fig. 4.1a Plan of slave quarters, first period, villa at Settefinestre. From Carandini 1985: 258.

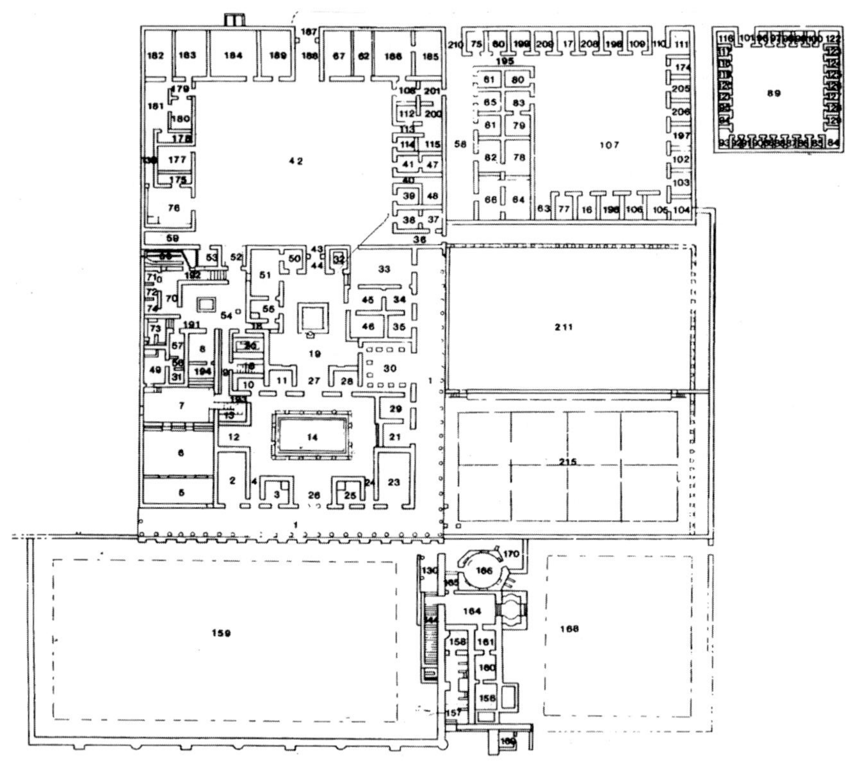

Fig. 4.1b Plan of slave quarters, second period, villa at Settefinestre. From
Carandini 1985: 259.

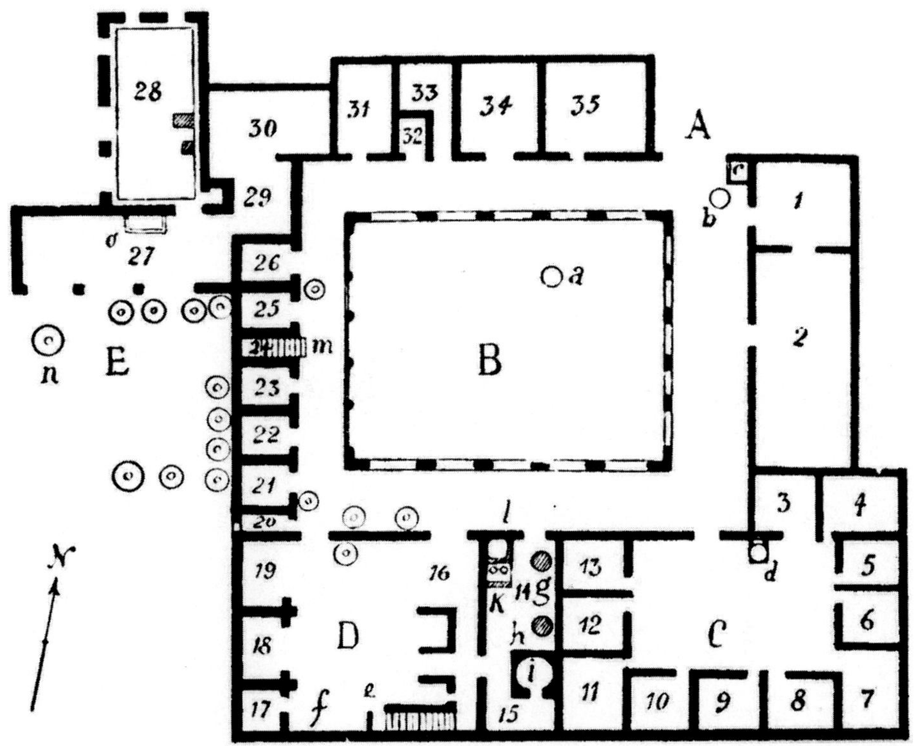

Fig. 4.2 Plan, Villa 34 at Gragnano. From Della Corte 1923: 276.

Fig. 4.3 Banquet scene, House of the Triclinium (V.2.4), Pompeii. Now in Naples, Museo. Archeologico Nazionale, inv. 120029. Photograph courtesy of Michael Larvey.

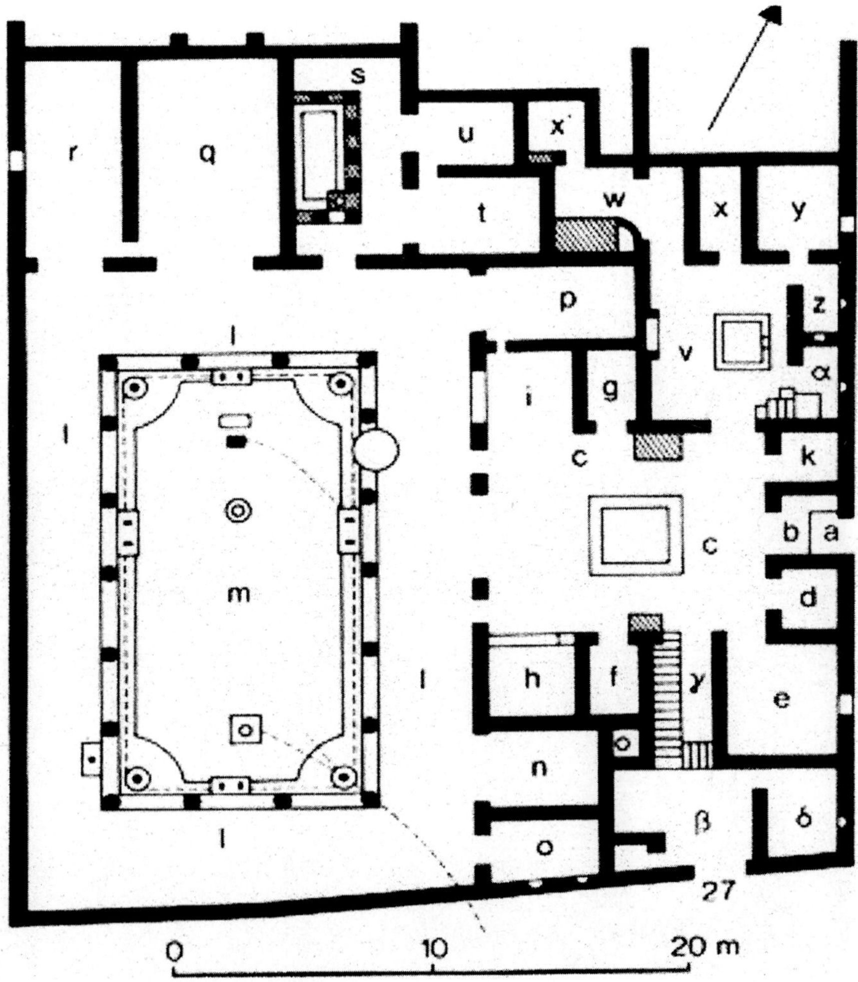

Fig. 4.4 Plan, House of the Vettii (VI.15.1), Pompeii. From http://www.indiana
.edu/~leach/c409/vplan.html.

Fig. 4.5 Stairway and corridor, House of the Vettii (VI.15.1), Pompeii. Photograph: Sandra R. Joshel.

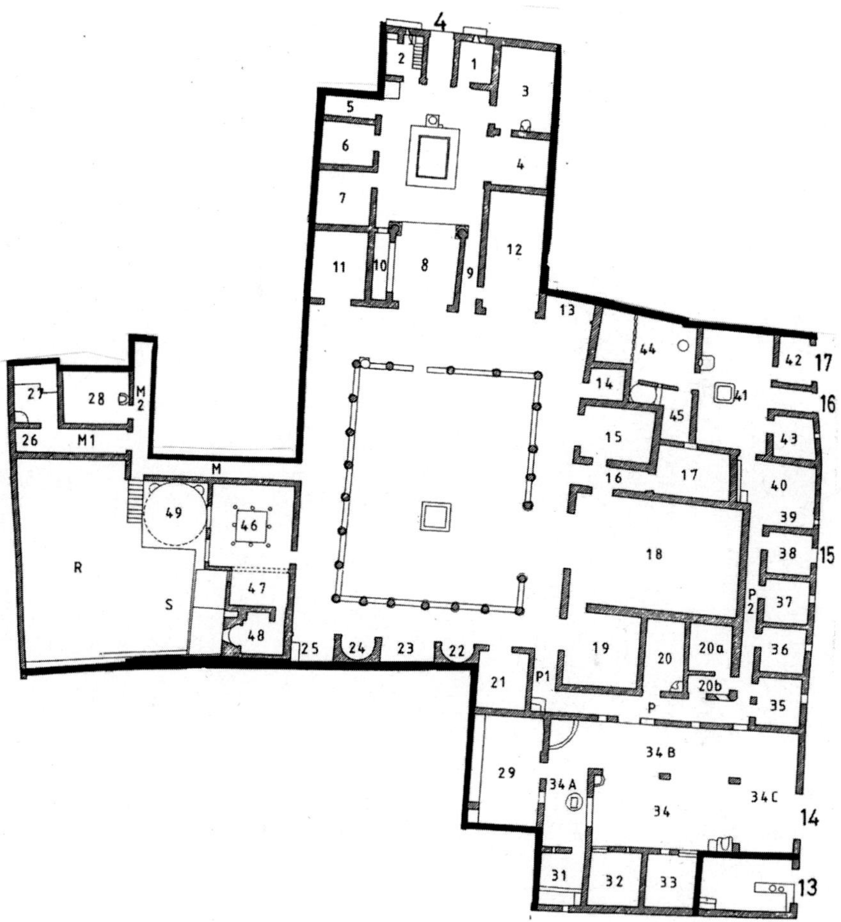

Fig. 4.6 Plan, House of the Menander (I.10.4), Pompeii. From Ling 1997: fig. 24.

Fig. 4.7 Stable yard (34), House of the Menander (I.10.4), Pompeii. Photograph:
Sandra R. Joshel.

Fig. 4.8 Corridor P2 past *cellae* 35–38, House of the Menander (I.10.4), Pompeii.
Photograph: Lauren Hackwoth Petersen.

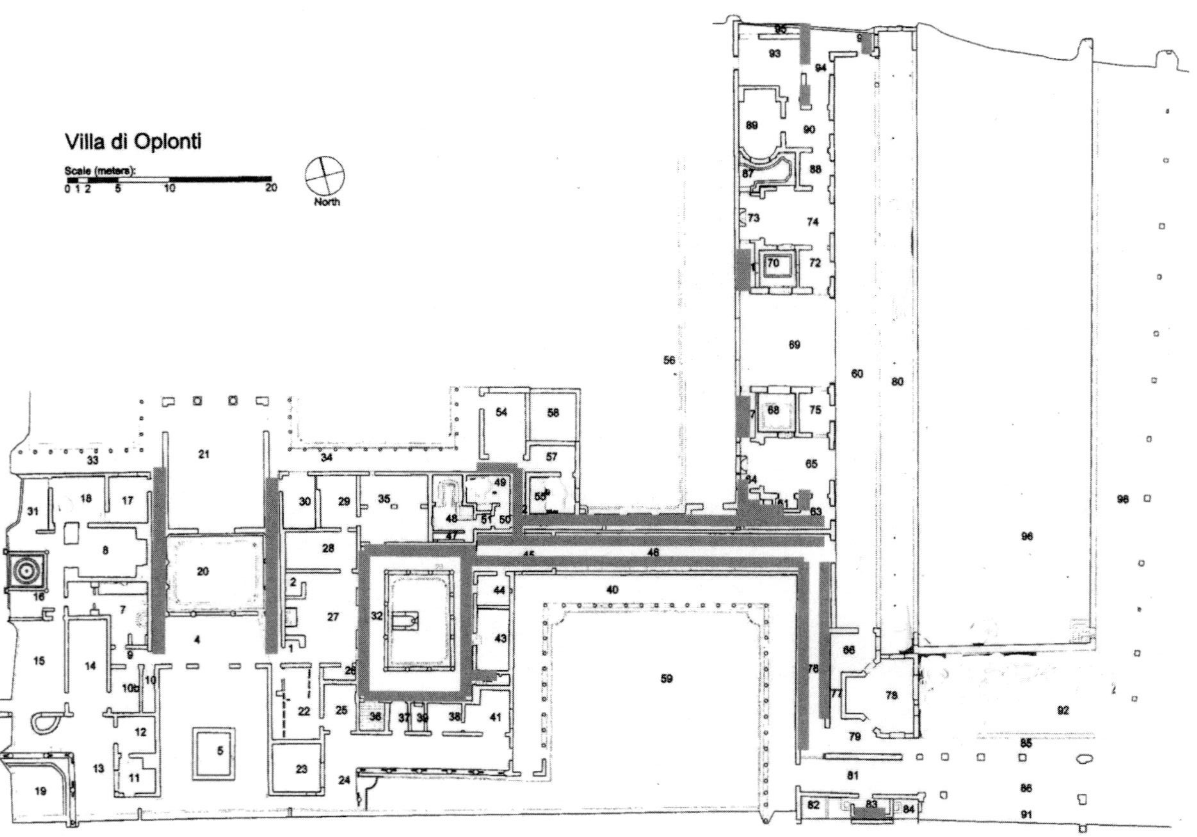

Fig. 4.9 Plan, Villa A, Oplontis. From Thomas and Clarke 2009: fig. 1.

Fig. 4.10 Service courtyard (32) with zebra stripes, Villa A, Oplontis. Photograph: Sandra R. Joshel.

Fig. 4.11 Zebra stripes on lower wall of corridor 76, Villa A, Oplontis. Photograph: Sandra R. Joshel.

Fig. 5.1 Thymiaterion. Now in Malibu, The J. Paul Getty Museum, Villa Collection, 87.AC.143.1.

Fig. 5.2 Terracotta lamp. Now in London, British Museum, EA 37561. © Trustees of the British Museum.

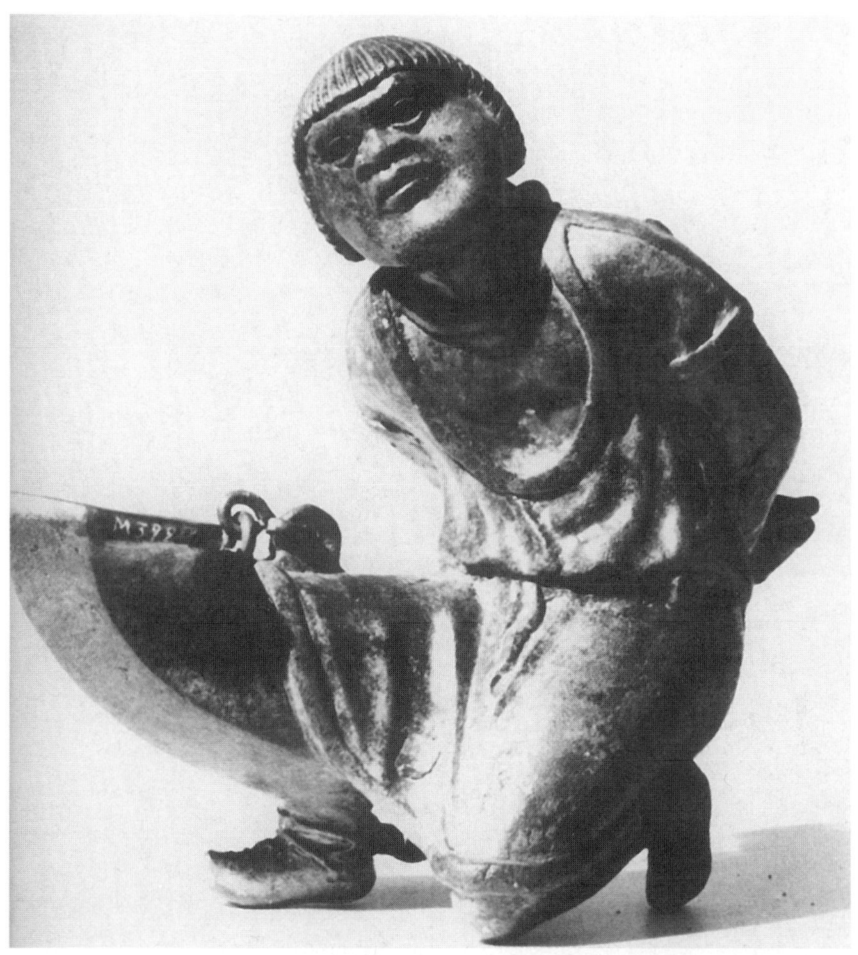

Fig. 5.3 Bronze lamp. Kavala, Archaeological Museum, M392. Photo: museum.

Fig. 5.4 Silver pepper caster. Now in London, British Museum, 145. Photo: museum.

Fig. 5.5 Uncle Mose and Aunt Jemima Salt and Pepper Shakers. Image from internet.

Fig. 5.6 Candelabrum (*lychnouchos*), Casa dell'Efebo (I.7.10–12) at Pompeii. Now in Naples, Museo Archeologico Nazionale, inv. 143753. Scala/Ministero per i Beni e le Attività culturali. Art Resource.

Fig. 5.7 Candelabrum (*lychnouchos*), Casa di M. Fabius Rufus (VII.16.22) at Pompeii. Now in Boscoreale, Antiquarium, inv. 13112. Photo: Soprintendenza Speciale per i Beni Archeologici di Napoli e Pompei.

Fig. 5.8 'Jocko' yard sculpture. Philadelphia, Charles L. Blockson Afro-American Collection, Temple University. Photo: collection.

Fig. 5.9 Banquet scene, Casa del Triclinio (V.2.4) at Pompeii. Now in Naples, Museo Archeologico Nazionale, inv. 120030, after drawing in Amelung, *JDAI* 42 (1927) 143 Abb. 7.

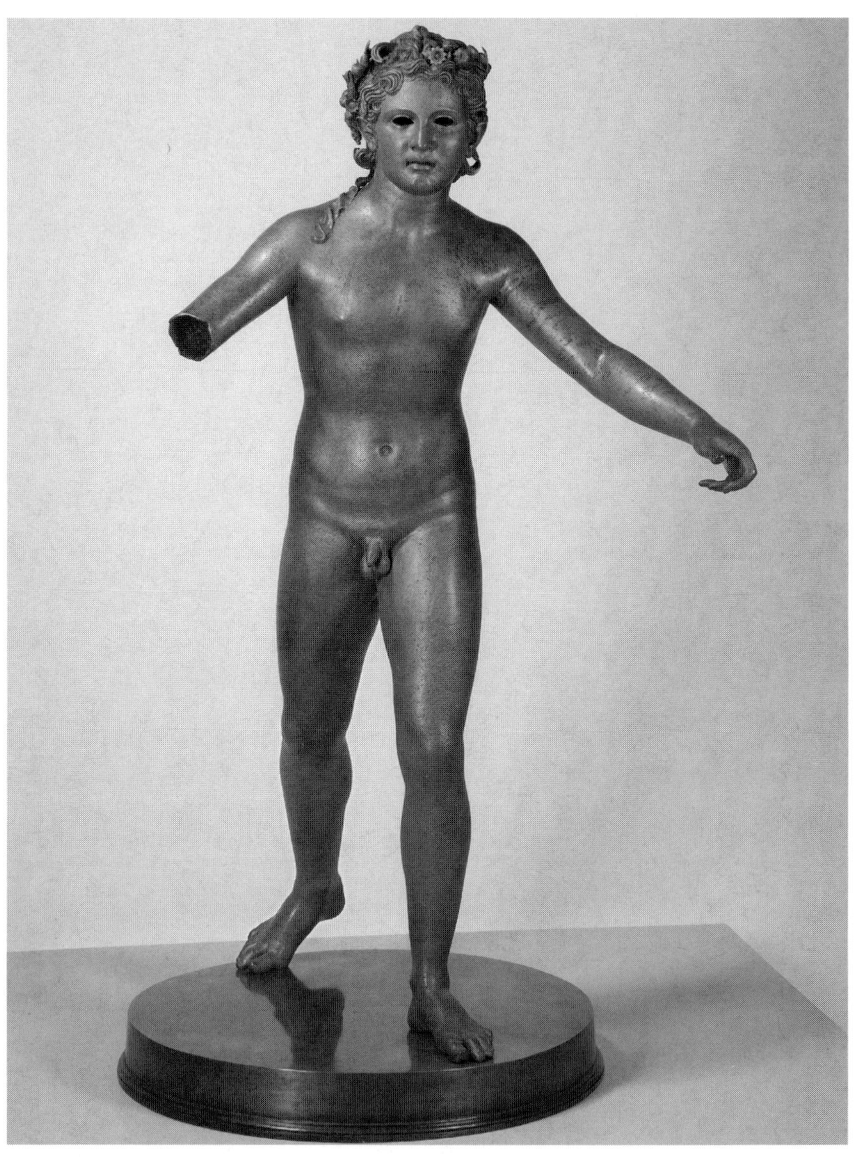

Fig. 5.10 Bronze traybearer from Xanten. Berlin, Staatliche Museen, Antikensammlung, Sk. 4. Bildarchiv Preussischer Kulturbesitz / Art Resource.

Fig. 5.11 Bronze traybearer from Tarragona. Tarragona, Museo Nacional
Arqueológico Provincial, no. 527. Photo: museum.

Fig. 5.12 Caylus figurine from at Chalon-sur-Saône. Paris, Bibliothèque Nationale, Collection Caylus, no. 1009. Photo: Reproductions Bibliothèque nationale de France.

Fig. 5.13 Traybearers (*placentarii*), Casa dell'Efebo (I.7.10–12) at Pompeii. Now in Naples, Museo Archeologico Nazionale, inv. 143760. Erich Lessing / Art Resource.

Fig. 5.14 'Blackamoor' statue. Denver, Molly Brown House Museum. With permission.

Fig. 6.1 Statue of Cupid Punished. Rome, Borghese Gallery, inv. 689. Anderson 4553, Art Resource.

Fig. 6.2 Statue of Cupid Punished. Florence, Pitti Palace. From Curtius 1930.

Fig. 6.3 Torso, Galleria dei Candelabri, Vatican Museum. Vat. XXI–14–9. DAI
Rome, inst. neg. 41.996.

Fig. 6.4 Fountain statue, House of the Vettii (VI 15, 1), Pompeii. Alinari 11349H, Art Resource.

Fig. 6.5 Painting of Cupid Punished, House of Cupid Punished (VII 2, 23), Pompeii. Art Resource 144631.

Fig. 6.6 Cast of gem (now lost), enchained Cupid with hoe. DAI Rome, inst. neg. 5225.

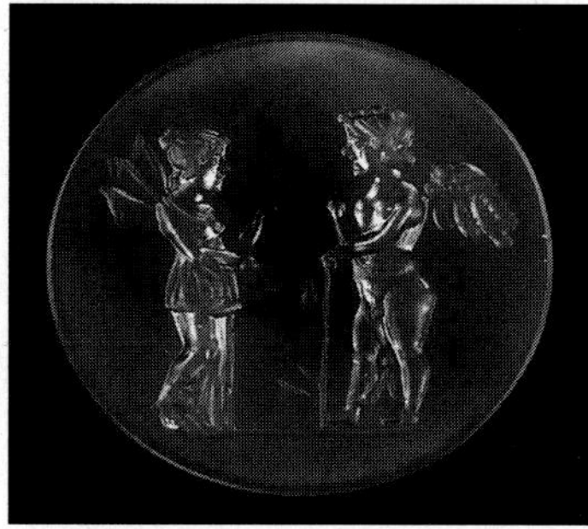

Fig. 6.7 Gem, enchained Cupid resting on a hoe with Psyche, Hannover, Kestner-Museum K 404. Photo: museum.

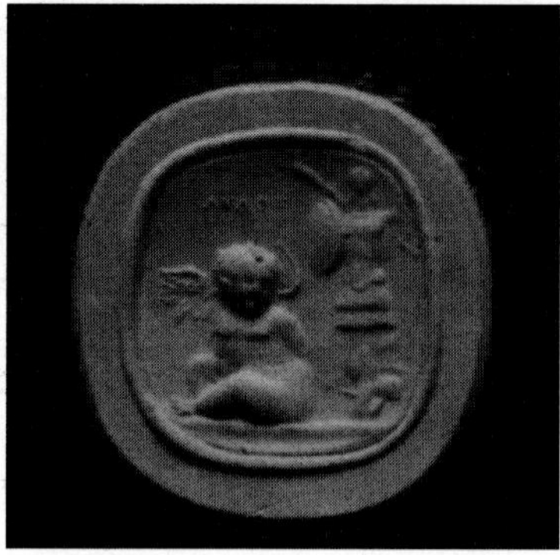

Fig. 6.8 Cast of gem with Cupid under trophy, British Museum, London. DAI Rome, inst. neg. 5225.

Fig. 6.9 Mosaic, Venus flogging Cupid, from Thina. Now in Sfax museum. DAI Rome, inst. neg. 64.555.

Fig. 6.10 Putti as goldsmiths, House of the Vettii (VI 15, 1), Pompeii. DAI Rome, inst. neg. 31.2736.

Fig. 6.11 Painting of the Cupid-seller, Villa Arianna, Stabia. Now in Naples, Museo Archeologico Nazionale inv. 9180. DAI Rome, inst. neg. 75.1481.

Fig. 6.12 The Cupid-Seller, Joseph-Marie Vien, Musée National du Château, Fontainebleau. Art Resource 156151.

Fig. 6.13 Drawing of painting of Cupid-Seller, House of the Coloured Capitals (VII 4, 31/51), Pompeii. From Birt 1919, taf. 19.

Fig. 6.14 Mosaic, House of the Peddler of Erotes, Antioch-on-the-Orontes, Baltimore museum.

Fig. 7.1 Stela of M. Caelius. Bonn, Landesmuseum. Photo: museum.

Fig. 7.2 Stela of Firmus, found at Andernach. Now in Bonn, Landesmuseum.
Photo: museum.

Fig. 7.3 Stela of Faltonius, found in Mainz. Now in Mainz, Römisch-Germanisches Zentralmuseum. Photo: museum.

Fig. 7.4 Stela of Maris, found in Mainz. Now in Mainz, Römisch-Germanisches Zentralmuseum. Photo: museum.

Fig. 7.5 Stela of Muranus, found in Wiesbaden. Now in Wiesbaden, Stadtmuseum. Photo: museum.

Fig. 7.6 Stela of Attucius, found in Klagenfurt. Private collection. Photo: Ortolf Harl.

Fig. 7.7 Stela of Exoratus, found at Carnuntum. Now in Bad Deutsch-Altenburg Museum Carnuntinum. Photo: Ortolf Harl, courtesy of museum.

5

Working Models: Functional Art and Roman Conceptions of Slavery

NOEL LENSKI

Introduction

When in CE 66 the emperor Nero ordered the execution of the renowned general and former governor of Britain Ostorius Scapula, the centurion sent to murder him offered his victim the chance to commit suicide. The courageous Scapula boldly obliged, but, Tacitus tells us, 'as his veins, though severed, allowed but a scanty flow of blood, he used the help of a slave, simply to hold up a dagger firmly, and then pressing the man's hand towards him, he met the point with his throat.'[1] The slave thus served, in the crudest sense, as a human tool, a knife holder upon which his master could impale himself. A less gruesome if equally disturbing example of the same phenomenon is provided by the sixth-century sophist Aeneas of Gaza, who describes a garden fountain cleverly designed to operate by the action of a slave running inside a sort of human hamster wheel. Art and artifice were thus combined, allowing the viewer to delight in the spectacle of jets of water driven by a human motor.[2] Descending to the banal, Encolpius, the hero of Petronius's *Satyricon*, first encountered his crass but fabulously wealthy host Trimalchio at the baths where Trimalchio was playing ball. When he had to urinate, Trimalchio snapped his fingers without interrupting his game, whereupon his eunuch brought a piss pot into which Trimalchio emptied his bladder. This accomplished, 'he demanded water for his hands, then dried his moistened fingers a bit on the head of the slave boy.'[3] Here the slave served as animate hand towel. In a highly satirical and thus not entirely trustworthy epigram, Martial even relates that the opulent fop Zoilus made his eunuch direct his member when he urinated.[4] This gratuitous exploitation of the slave as penis-prop strikes us as so extreme that we might question Martial's veracity, but the underlying situation it reflects does not: in some very real sense, the Romans regarded their slaves as implements. Indeed, this is stated explicitly in Varro's infamous discussion of tools in his treatise on the management of the Roman estate. As is well known, Varro argues that the working apparatus (*instrumentum*) of a farm is best divided into three categories: the speaking tools, the non-speaking, and the mute, with the first comprising slaves, the second beasts, and the third inanimate instruments.[5] These five texts offer only the tiniest sampling of testimonia to the fact that, at the most basic level, the ancient slave was regarded as an object whose very body could be employed by the master to accomplish tasks: committing suicide, powering a fountain, drying hands, urinating, tilling fields, etc.

This investigation explores the manner in which this same conception, that of the slave as tool, surfaced in ancient art. It is divided into three sections: the slave as tool, the slave as prop, and the slave as dumb waiter. The first explores anthropomorphic figurines designed to perform work for their owner: burning incense, lighting a room, raising a vessel, even serving as pepper shakers. The second examines anthropomorphic statuary used in banquet contexts to delight the eye but also to hold up lanterns. The third builds on the second with examples of anthropomorphic statuary, at times beautiful but at others exotic or grotesque, that was used to hold trays or tables.

In exploring these objects, we must keep in mind one fundamental principle: very few of them can be irrefutably argued to have represented slaves. Indeed, many related objects almost certainly do not portray humans in bondage. Since the archaic period, Greek and Etruscan art, as indeed Egyptian and Mesopotamian before it, displayed a pronounced and well-known affinity for the human form. Kantharoi in the shape of human heads, thymiateria supported by dazzling athletes, mirrors raised by beautiful maidens, paterae attached to muscular youths, the handles of hydriai and situlae formed into figurines, all recur in Greek, Etruscan, and Roman sculpture and the minor arts from the sixth century BCE onward.[6] It would be wrong to assume that the artists who crafted these objects always intended to represent slaves, just as it would also be wrong to assume that viewers interpreted these works in this way. Nevertheless, it is just as incorrect to assume that artist and viewer never understood such objects to represent slaves or captives. Indeed, this paper will show that, at least in some instances, there is good evidence to prove that they did.

This discussion thus proceeds from the assumption that the use of anthropomorphic objects to perform work was a constant in the calculus of ancient iconography. This was in part because of a prevailing aesthetic that valorized the human form as the supreme expression of beauty. Nevertheless, the obsession with anthropomorphism was also related to the fact that, in a pre-machine-age world, there was a prevailing conception that work was accomplished through the labours of the human body. Given this aesthetic of the human form and this preconception of labour as the province of the human animal, it took only a small step for artists and viewers to reinterpret these objects into slaves. In a world permeated with slavery, the artist would always have been tempted to cross the line from the portrayal of the working human to that of the working slave. So too his viewers had no trouble seeing his figures, bound as they were in clay or bronze, as bondsmen.[7] The ancient model of the working human was thus available as a working model, capable of being reworked in the hands of the artist or the mind of the viewer into a representation of the slave.

1. Human Tools

We begin with thymiateria, objects with a long history of figural representation in Greek, Etruscan, and Roman art. There is no question but that many of the human figures depicted on thymiateria were not thought by their creators or viewers to represent slaves. A famous mid-fifth-century BCE incense burner from Delphi, for example, forms its base as a female figure who balances a large crucible on her head and supports it at its sides with her upraised arms.[8] The figure thus performs work, lifting what would seem an unwieldy load, but there are no further indications that she is a slave, and her long Doric peplos indicates the contrary. Figural thymiateria are especially characteristic of Etruscan art. From this repertoire countless examples could be brought to bear and almost none could be shown with confidence to depict slaves performing work. Some do, however, come tantalizingly close to evoking this impression. To take just one example, a late-fourth-century BCE incense burner now in the Museo Gregoriano Etrusco bears a total of five figures.[9] Its tripod footing is fashioned in the shape of three females who – as often in Etruscan thymiateria – perform an acrobatic stunt, in this instance leaning backwards into the base of the shaft to support it with their heads. All seductively raise their skirts with their right hands to reveal their upper thighs, thus raising the suspicion they may represent courtesans, and thus possibly slaves. A male figurine who forms the lowest part of the shaft with his body is clearly depicted as a satyr, but the nude male figurine who forms the shaft's top is strictly humanoid. He works to raise above himself the incense crucible that has replaced his hand at the tip of his arm. We are thus seeing working figures whose interpretation is ambiguous: one is a mythical creature, but the rest could be free or slave and the artist has given indications that nudge us in the latter direction.

When we arrive at a first-century CE Roman thymiaterion from the Getty Museum (fig. 5.1), we are on much firmer ground in identifying the subject as a slave.[10] The figure is wearing a grotesque comic mask typical of the slave in New Comedy. Moreover, his pot belly, his clingy tights, his short, sleeveless tunic, and his short skimpy mantle (*pallium*) girt high around his waist are all telltale indicators that he is meant to represent a comic actor playing the role of a slave.[11] The figure sits upon a garlanded, circular altar the top of which is removable. Inside it is hollow and its bottom is penetrated with ten slots for ventilation. Through these air would have entered to feed the burning incense and smoke would have issued from the mouth of the mask. Further confirmation that this type of image represents a comic slave was first noticed by Margarete Bieber, who showed that the motif of the clever slave (the *servus calidus*, literally 'hot slave') taking refuge upon an altar was a topos of New Comedy. In Terence's *Self-Tormentor* the slave Syrus is told he need *not* seek refuge on an altar despite his machinations, while in Menander's *Perinthia* the servant Daos is smoked off an altar by his fellow slaves. Plautus's *Haunted House* features the *servus calidus* Tranio planting himself on an altar to avoid torture by his master Theopropides, who threatens, 'It's the fire and faggots for you now carrion!'[12] The comic master thus longed to put the tinder to his slave's backside, something the owner of these thymiateria could do literally, albeit in symbolic form.

Nor was this object unique. Further examples of the slave-on-altar bronze thymiaterion can also be found in a second instance in the Getty Collection (likely a pendant to the first),[13] and another in the Wadsworth Atheneum in Hartford,[14] and a less skilfully modelled version from the Princeton University Museum, all dating to the first century BCE or the early first century CE.[15] A terracotta variant on the slave-on-altar theme was moulded as a lantern with the wick hole projecting from the slave's upper back so that from a frontal perspective the slave would have seemed to be on fire.[16] Indeed, the slave-on-altar type shows up in non-functionalist figurines going all the way back to classical Athens,[17] but it seems to have been the choice of Roman artisans to transform the image into a 'working model' that actually performs the task of burning incense.[18] This allowed the owners of these objects to amuse themselves not just with their sarcastic portrayals of the big-talking 'hot slave' but also with the fact that the slave quite literally blew hot air from his mouth while occupying the hot seat. To be sure they represented the slaves of fiction, but in so doing they also represented a stock character type that an owner might often have associated with specific slaves truly present in his own *familia*. Using this object the master could not only burn his incense, he could also mock his troublesome blowhard of a slave while viewing his sculptural likeness fuming atop a smoking altar.

Turning from incense burners to lamps, we arrive at a curious hanging lamp now in the British Museum (fig. 5.2).[19] Dated to the second or first century BCE, it represents a young man wearing tunic and himation and an elaborate headdress fashioned from ivy leaves and large fruits (?), perhaps associated with bacchanalian feasting. The youth seems unsteady, likely from excessive drinking, and thus supports himself on a walking stick at his right hand and an African attendant at his left. Both the figure's relatively short stature and its clothing – almost identical with that of the previous figure – leave no doubt that the attendant is of servile status. The slave himself bears a lamp and thus stands in as a metonym for the object of which he forms a part. As we shall see, the role of lamp bearer played by ancient slaves was in turn played upon by artists in various figural types. With this object the slave is doing double duty, for he not only lights his master's way but also serves as a crutch or support for his master. This notion of the human 'prop' will form part of the basis for future discussion.

Even more curious is a bronze lamp found in 1961 in northern Greece, and now housed in the Kavala Museum (fig. 5.3).[20] The piece dates to the fourth century CE and was likely used in a small fortress near its reported find site. Given both of these facts, it can thus be safely termed Roman despite its Greek provenance. The figure represented has a flat, fleshy, prognathic face with a broad and flaring nose and prominent brow ridge. His longish straight hair falls low on his forehead and is coiffed awkwardly in a 'bowl cut.' The artist has thus taken pains to depict the figure with the characteristics associated with comic actors and, in this period, northern barbarians. The fact that he too wears only a short tunic with short sleeves further cements the link not just to the comic actor but to the comic slave. Lest there be any further doubt, he is made to genuflect humiliatingly, his neck is surrounded by a torque, and his hands are bound behind his back. The object was made to dangle from the ceiling on chains and its oil chamber was made to be refilled below its head, which pivots back on a hinge. To put this barbarian to good use, then, the owner literally knocked its head off, filled and lighted it, and then hung it on chains. In this sense, the lamp is a symbolic depiction of the violence wished upon barbarian captives by the late Romans, who would have been interested in acquiring and displaying such an object.[21] Man is made object, just like a slave, but man is also made instrument. The barbarian becomes a working model that works for its *dominus* even as it works its way into the mind of the beholder – *dominus* and *servus* – as the *ideon* of servitude.

A similar shift in the semantics of anthropomorphic iconography on functional objects can be found in handles. Female figurines serve as handles for ancient mirrors and males as handles for paterae with such frequency that they seem banal.[22] So, too, the handles on various storage vessels are regularly portrayed in human form. In most classical Greek and Etruscan instances there is no indication whatsoever that the figure depicted was a slave. In some instances, however, the situation becomes more complicated, as for example on a second- or first-century BCE situla from Pompeii, now in the Naples Museum, each of whose handles are formed in the shape of two gladiators whose interlocking shields the user can grasp to lift the vessel.[23] While it must remain speculative, one can assume given the dating of the piece that the gladiators portrayed would likely have been captives or slaves. We cannot of course know whether artist or viewer consciously thought of the implications of this fact, but it remains a reality that the figures whose arms and shields support the work of lifting the vessel were likely to have been enslaved. As such, slaves not only support the artistic program of this container's decoration, they also supported its owner in the practical employment of his bucket.

We are on even firmer ground with a second-century CE bronze handle housed in the Louvre.[24] Although now detached from the vessel it originally served, its size and shape indicate that this was a jug. The handle is elaborately fashioned and shows traces of silver inlay, indicating it likely belonged to a prize piece. At its top and facing upward, it depicts a long-haired female figure, likely meant to represent one of the northern provinces, who sits behind a fortification wall that protects a bearded male and a female. Below her and facing downward three figures are attached to the handle. In the centre a bearded barbarian, nude but for his mantle, carries a bundle over his shoulder as he moves right in the act of fleeing. Below him are two pantalooned barbarian males, one bearded and one youthfully smooth-faced. Their bodies curve awkwardly in conformity with the crescent attachment of the handle to which they appear to be bound. These were clearly intended by the artist to represent captives bonded to the vessel, which they help lift with their bodies. He was thus playing on the convention of figural handles to depict captive men performing work for the vessel's *dominus*.

The slave as tool can also be seen in an object with close parallels to modern functionalist art, a silver pepper caster found with the Chaource Treasure in 1883 near Montcornet in France (fig. 5.4).[25] This *piperatorium* formed part of a complete *ministerium* (table service), which was probably produced in the third century CE and was later wrapped in cloth and buried, apparently in the turbulent times of the third century. It depicts a slave lamp bearer of African descent. He wears a sleeveless tunic and mantle (*paenula*) with a hood (*cucullus*), no doubt to protect against the cold of his night-time outings. His lantern, which rests between his legs, is attached to his left hand by a chain. The slave squats on his haunches and rests his head on his right hand as if catching up on the rest he has lost from accompanying his master during late-night excursions.[26] The lamp bearer's task was not without strain nor even peril, both because of the long hours of night-time walking out in the elements and because of the dangers one could expect along a dark roadway. Augustus actually lost a lamp-bearing slave (*servus praelucens*) who was struck by lightning while leading the emperor's entourage on a stormy night.[27] This African, of course, brings to mind the slave bearer of the terracotta lamp discussed earlier. Two further African lamp bearers are reproduced as lanterns in one example from Alexandria, where the figure is naked, and another from Athens, where he wears a *cucullus*, as in the Chaource pepper castor.[28] Both date to the Roman period. It seems to have been fashionable to have had a black man to light one's way in the dark, a suspicion that is confirmed by a passage in Athenaeus which reports that Cleopatra offered Aethiopian lamp bearers as special gifts to all her guests to accompany them home at the end of a lavish feast.[29] The same penchant for visual pun made it equally fashionable to possess an object that portrayed a slave figure performing the work actually assigned to that object, for instance, lamp bearers who were lanterns. Even if the Chaource *piperatorium* is not quite in the same category – lantern bearers do not cast pepper – it did offer its owner a way literally to take a slave in hand and put him to work for his benefit.

In this respect it was related to the widely collected Aunt Jemima and Uncle Mose salt and pepper shakers produced and sold in the United States from the 1920s into the 1950s (fig. 5.5).[30] This sort of object, of which we will see several further examples, became particularly popular in the post-Reconstruction American South, where, from about 1890 onward, white Americans nostalgic for their slaveholding past acquired a dizzying variety of demeaning Negro figurines on a mass-consumption level.[31] At this point in American history, of course, blacks no longer worked as slaves for their white owners, but the whole point of representing them in this fashion was to reinforce the message that the African as racial type could still be compelled to 'do work' for the white man, even if only as a pepper shaker, and the Negro as object could still be owned by the white man, even if only as a trinket.[32] These figurines crystallized stereotypes rooted in an idealized re-imagining of the idyllic plantation past into easily ownable and easily serviceable icons. While this sort of black memorabilia fed a mass consumer market made up of primarily middle- and lower-class Americans, Roman functionalist art objects – produced as they were for a pre-consumer society – were aimed more at the upper class, often of real-life slaveholders. There is no overt racism in the Roman objects, but like the happy Negro figurines, they too serve to normalize the control and even violence arrogated by the master class over the slave. In both contexts such objects naturalize slavery into social praxis by repackaging the human form into plastic symbols of the slave *qua* ever-ready and ever-willing servant of the master's / owner's (*dominus*) needs.

2. Human Props

The terracotta hanging lamp depicting the inebriated young master leaning on his lamp-bearing slave, mentioned above, introduced the theme of the slave as prop. In that instance the emphasis was on the force of the word 'prop' in the sense of a support for something that, in the absence of the prop, would topple. This same role can be detected in a number of other iconographic contexts. A famous wall painting from the House of the Triclinium (V.2.4) in Pompeii (see fig. 4.3), for example, depicts a slave on its lower right literally propping up a guest at a *convivium* who has become so intoxicated that he is doubled over in paroxysms of vomiting.[33] The slave is thus called upon to serve literally as a physical support in the course of the banquet. Yet this very practical function, one no doubt often performed by slave attendants, is complemented by an artistic one as well, for in the instance of both the fresco from the House of the Triclinium and the terracotta hanging lamp, the artist chose openly to portray slaves performing these parts. Both art objects thus proudly display human 'props,' now in the sense of 'stage properties,' playing a 'supporting role' amidst the goings-on around them. Their purpose was in this sense partly functional – holding things up – and partly aesthetic – being seen holding things up.

There is perhaps no better instance of this dual function than the sculptural type first rediscovered in the legendary statue known as the Idolino, now in the Archaeological Museum of Florence.[34] In 1530 the statue was found broken into fragments near Pesaro at a site occupied in Roman times by the villa of the *gens Aufidia*. It was reconstructed and furnished with its elaborate bronze base, replete with a laudatory verse inscription by Pietro Bembo. The care and expense that went into the base are indicative of the honour accorded the work, which was praised as an unparalleled example of classical Greek artistry. To be sure, the Idolino has strongly classicizing elements, particularly its head, which is clearly modelled on that of Polycleitus's Doryphorus. The body, however, seems more late classical or early Hellenistic with its lithe and youthful limbs, its studied avoidance of heavy modelling of the musculature, its languid bearing, and above all its slouching contrapposto – created by planting both of the figure's heels on the ground, making for an awkward and uncoordinated stance. These incongruities led to considerable confusion over the identity of the work's artist. Much of this could have been resolved earlier if the accoutrements found with the statue had been kept in association with it from the time of its discovery. Indeed, though the Idolino as displayed would appear to be, so to speak, idle, a closer examination of its history reveals quite the opposite. Among the fragments originally found with it were two traces of bronze vines fitted with hooks, obviously racks for holding some object. Although knowledge of these racks led to some passing speculation about their role in its original composition, most preferred to ignore the function of these accessories, which were detached from the statue and stored separately from it.[35] Nevertheless, when a number of closely related, near life-sized bronze ephebes began to surface in the early twentieth century, all replete with similar racks or fittings for them, it became clear that the Idolino would have to come down from its pedestal and resume its original job.

The first two such rack-bearing ephebes to be identified were both found in Pompeii, the first outside the north wall at the Porta Vesuvio in 1900[36] and the second in what is now called the House of the Ephebe (I.7.10–12) on the Via dell'Abbondanza in 1925 (fig. 5.6).[37] With the first was found a single floral rack that fitted into a slot in its right hand and with the second were two acanthus racks whose handles also passed perfectly into slots in each hand. Initially the discoverers of both statues, Antonio Sogliano and Amadeo Maiuri, respectively, saw in them classical originals, and Maiuri went so far as to describe the second as emerging miraculously from the ashes of the ruined city like a 'divine apparition.'[38] Both were of course fine archaeologists and made no effort to expunge the vine racks from the record, but both argued that these original 'classical' bronzes had been altered to hold such devices in some *officina* in Pompeii, thereby ruining their splendour.[39] Already in 1926, however, Carlo Anti and Arnold Schober reached a different conclusion in two articles written independently of one another. First, neither statue represented a classical original; indeed, both were pastiches of variant – even contradictory – classical forms. Secondly, the racks originally held by both were outfitted with small hooks that were clearly meant to hold lanterns. Both were, they rightly argued, glorified candelabra, *lychnouchoi* (lamp bearers) as they would have been called in Greek.[40]

Soon further examples began to turn up elsewhere and yet others were rediscovered from bronzes that were already part of the archaeological record but had not yet been identified as representative of the type. In 1932 an example was uncovered at Volubilis in North Africa with no vine rack but with its right hand fashioned to hold one.[41] In 1934 yet another surfaced from the excavations at Sakha on the Egyptian delta, again with no vine rack but with a fitting hole for one in its left hand.[42] By 1939 Andreas Rumpf demonstrated that the Idolino had also been a *lychnouchos* and dated it to the Augustan period.[43] In 1960 a *lychnouchos* emerged in excavations at the house of M. Fabius Rufus (VII.16.22) in Pompeii with a rather more elaborate rack that will be discussed in what follows (fig. 5.7).[44] Further examples have been identified from as far afield as Zifteh in the Egyptian Delta,[45] (possibly) Achaean Salamis,[46] and (possibly) Samsun on the Turkish coast of the Black Sea.[47] Finally, in 1977, a fourth example from Pompeii was unearthed from the House of Julius Polybius (IX.13.1–3) in the winter triclinium with its two lamp racks still in its hands.[48]

Today there is no question but that these images represented a common type: bronze rack-holding lantern bearers fashioned in near life size to look like youths, often on quadripedal square bronze pedestals, and always portrayed as if in early pubescence – with small genitals and no pubic hair. The consistency in functional type and general composition is matched by considerable consistency in height, indicating that they conformed to a uniform standard designed to fill a certain market niche for a familiar product (see table 1). Nevertheless, although uniform in type, they were by no means uniform in artistry, for as discussed, each figure represents a pastiche of styles, and no two are alike in their selection of forms for recombination. Some display archaic elements (the head, hair, and pose of the ephebe from the House of Julius Polybius), others distinctly classical (the Idolino's head), and still others late Hellenistic (like the head and hair of the pudgy nude from the house of M. Fabius Rufus). All also self-consciously intermingle elements from both genders, a feature especially notable in the ephebe from the House of the Ephebe which borrows a female portrait type for the head. Furthermore, there is no uniformity in composition, for while all are outfitted to carry racks, some have one and others two; some do so in only one hand, others in both; and some raise one hand while others keep both arms down. Furthermore, even if all stand in contrapposto, this pose varies in presentation and with it the angle from which they were to be viewed. These were thus not collectors' copies of some famous classical original, but functionalist objects created by a variety of workshops to meet demand for a common type (ephebic *lychnouchoi*) that could be produced according to a variety of stylistic standards.[49]

Nevertheless, their aesthetic value was hardly secondary. In addition to providing light, they were obviously also meant as stand-ins for the beautiful mellephebe every Roman host aspired to own for serving drinks at his banquets.[50] The bronze ivy wreath worn by the figure from Volubilis (and the one from Antequera discussed below), the horn-like pigtails of the Sakha statue, and the grape-vine shape of the racks born by the Idolino and the *lychnouchos* from the house of M. Fabius Rufus make it clear that they were heavily imbued with Bacchic symbolism. In this sense they recall

Table 1

Provenance	Height (including base)	Date of Find
Villa of the gens Aufidia, Pesaro (Idolino)	148 cm	1530
Zifteh, Egyptian delta	160 cm	before 1840
Salamis (Sabouroff Ephebe)	(missing head)	1878
Porta Vesuvio, Pompeii	124 cm	1900
House of the Ephebe, Pompeii	149 cm	1925
Volubilis	140 cm	1932
Sakha, Egyptian delta	130 cm	1934
House of M. Fabius Rufus, Pompeii	139 cm	1960
House of Julius Polybius, Pompeii	130 cm	1977
Samsun, Turkey	141 cm	1979

Trimalchio's youthful slave boy described with envy in Petronius: 'while we were discussing this, a beautiful boy, garlanded with grape and ivy vines, first pretending to be Bacchus the Reveller, then Bacchus the Deliverer, then Bacchus the Inspirer, brought grapes round in a basket and gave a rendering of the poems of his master in a most shrill voice.'[51] Never one for subtlety, Trimalchio had driven home the point by naming the boy Dionysus.

Similarly ephebic table servants are described with varying measures of envy, pity, and scorn in Apuleius, Juvenal, Martial, and Seneca.[52] These refer to such boys as *criniti*, *capillati*, or *comati*, emphasizing the importance of their beautiful hair, and Philo stresses the same in his critique of the Roman fashion for ephebic wine stewards: 'they have long, thick hair which is not cut at all or else the forelocks only are cut at the tips to make them level and take exactly the figure of a circular line.'[53] Their designations with substantives denoting 'big hair' are well matched by the attention paid to the coiffure of all the *lychnouchoi*, and Philo's description fits particularly well with the coiffure of the *lychnouchoi* from the house of M. Fabius Rufus, Sakha, and Zifteh.[54] To their advantage, these sculptural boys provided their *dominus* with the added advantage of remaining eternally youthful. In his forty-seventh letter, Seneca puzzles over the paradox of the ephebic slave: purchased for his boyish beauty, he is quickly forced to wrestle with the force of age to maintain his lithe figure and delicately smooth skin.[55] These bronze beauties, by contrast, never aged a day nor showed a trace of body hair on face, chest, or genitals. Finally a passage in Lucretius describes just such figural lamp holders in the shape of youths, gilded – as indeed was the figure from the Casa dell'Efebo[56] – adding lustre, literally and metaphorically, to the parties of wealthy Romans.[57]

In her article 'Greek Masterpieces and Roman Recreative Fictions,' Bettina Bergmann has shown how the Romans regularly redeployed classical Greek artistic models to new effect in order to suit their own tastes and needs.[58] That the *lychnouchoi* offer a case in point is beyond doubt. First of all, the type is definitely Roman: all datable exemplars trace to the Roman period (first century BCE – second century CE), and six of the ten known examples are from western contexts. Though they borrowed from Greek ideals and standards, the original types were reassembled by contemporary bronze casters in order to suit Roman tastes for the serving mellephebe who could 'adorn' the banquet in a Bacchic guise. Just as important, however, the Greek types were refashioned to make them suitable to perform actual work through the very practical task of holding up the lights. Like the images seen in the first section, then, the *lychnouchoi* were 'working models.' They worked as 'human props' in both senses of the word: supports and adornments, part of the structure and part of the scenery.

A brief comparison with related figures from modern art and architecture is instructive. Anthropomorphic lamp bearers have not disappeared even up to the present. Among the most famous are the semi-nude gilt-wood female lamp bearers fashioned for the Galérie des Glaces in the Palais de Versailles by Pierre-Edme Babel in the late eighteenth century.[59] The connections with the ancient *lychnouchoi* are readily apparent: individual human forms, exposed to the viewer as objects of beauty, perform the menial task of holding elaborate light fixtures in the shape of cornucopias. The eighteenth-century examples are clothed from the waist down – to suit the waning modesty of a nominally Christian court – and re-gendered feminine – to suit contemporary early-modern sexual preferences. But like the ancient *lychnouchoi*, their work was both physical and aesthetic. It would be impossible to contend that Babel or his viewers conceived of the Versailles lamp bearers as slaves. On the contrary, while the eighteenth-century Frenchman was more than comfortable with slavery – at least in the colonies – the features of the Versailles lampbearers make it clear that these were beauties of European stock and thus unsuitable for servile subjection. Contrast this with another common form of functionalist anthropomorphic statue, the cast-iron yard sculptures of late nineteenth- and twentieth-century America often sold with the trade name 'Jocko' (fig. 5.8). Generally also figured as lampholders (though also as faux hitching posts),[60] these outdoor statuettes harked back to the same idealized slaveholding past advertised with the Mose and Jemima salt and pepper shakers. Like Mose and Jemima, 'Jocko' was usually portrayed with exaggerated African features to emphasize his 'otherness' and thus create distance between the viewer subject and the African object. The obvious reference to racial difference in the context of early twentieth-century America as well as the perpetual service into which the subject is locked are surely meant to symbolize slavery. Such statues were intended in part, even in large part, to keep the Negro down in a post-emancipation world.

Between these two poles – colonial France and post-Reconstruction America – the ancient *lychnouchoi* take their place. They clearly do not portray freeborn male youths. Quite apart from the evidence we have seen from contemporary texts describing boyish table slaves who match perfectly the physique, features, and bearing of the *lychnouchoi*, the posture and function of these objects speaks the visual language of servility. The fact that they *stand* in the midst of reclining banqueters, that they *wait* during private feasts, that they are *exposed* to the leering eyes of guests, and that they *'serve'* by holding lamps proves that the *lychnouchoi* were surely understood by artist and viewer as slaves. Yet their physiognomic resemblance to the ethnicity of the ancient Mediterranean diner and the glorification of their beauty set them apart from the American yard jockeys by removing a level of alterity and thus inviting the diners to a greater sense of intimacy with the slaves they portray. So, too, the choice of males and of nudity sets the Roman *lychnouchoi* apart from the Versailles lampbearers in ways that also reveal much about the respective cultural practices at play. The Romans idealized Mediterranean boys, on the cusp of puberty, to serve their wine, to port their lamps, to arouse their passions, and to represent the human tools in whose ownership and control they prided themselves.

3. Dumb-Waiters

Well-off Romans took delight in portrayals of themselves dining in good company with their slaves on hand to attend them.[61] In many of these images the slaves bear trays heaped with an abundance of food. Examples of this are found in many of the feasting scenes that became commonplace on wall paintings, mosaics, and tomb and sarcophagus reliefs.[62] In wall paintings from Pompeii, for example, male servants are deployed as tray bearers who stand among reclining guests ready to supply them with the treats of their choice. The servant depicted in the dining panel (P3) from the House of the Smith (Casa del Fabbro, I.10.7) is shown standing near a group of reclining diners and offering a large rectangular platter that he holds in both hands.[63] His bronzed body, poised in contrapposto, is nude but for a loincloth and his head appears to be garlanded with ivy. He is, in other words, very much modelled in the manner of the *lychnouchoi* except that he holds a tray rather than a lamp. In her recent work on the Roman banquet, Katherine

Dunbabin has shown that the taste for portrayals of solicitous servants offering food and drink was widely diffused in Roman art beginning in the first century BCE and that it grew even more prominent in late antiquity, even if the serving boys came to be fully clothed to suit the more prudish tastes of the age.[64] Roman artistic patrons thus treasured portrayals not just of themselves at table but of themselves being served at table by male slaves.

This fascination also carried over into the plastic arts. That the living, breathing tray-bearing servant was at times replaced by working statues like the *lychnouchoi* would only stand to reason. The existence of such tray-bearing statuary is in fact confirmed in a wall painting from the House of the Triclinium (V.2.4) in Pompeii (fig. 5.9).[65] This painting – from the same dining room as the painting described earlier with the servant supporting a vomiting partygoer – portrays a figure on the lower right who is of a uniformly dark colour, clearly meant to represent bronze, and the round base at its feet leaves no room for doubt that we are viewing a representation of a statue rather than an actual male servant. Like the *lychnouchoi*, the figure appears to be nude, and like the traybearer portrayed in the House of the Smith, his tray is rectangular and his head garlanded. Even more compelling, we have several bronze candidates for this type, sometimes referred to as the *trapezophoros*. One has been identified in a statue from Antequera in southern Spain.[66] Discovered about 1963, it stands 154 cm tall – roughly equivalent to the *lychnouchoi*. Its pose, features, and accoutrements, including an ivy wreath, also resemble those of the *lychnouchoi*, but only its right hand is formed to hold an object, and, given its shape, this could only have been considerably smaller than a lamp rack. This may have been some small tray or large cup.[67] Furthermore, the *lychnouchos* already discussed from the House of M. Fabius Rufus in Pompeii has a vine rack that not only bears attachment hooks for lanterns but also two horizontal bars with pegs that were clearly used to secure a large tray. Its raised right hand would appear to have held some other object – perhaps a cup or bowl – as well. It was thus capable of 'multitasking,' serving both as lampholder and traybearer.[68]

A different type of bronze traybearer is best known from a first-century CE bronze youth recovered from the Rhine near Xanten in 1858. This ephebe has a similar stature (154 cm) to the *lychnouchoi* as well as similarly supple skin, a similarly youthful body, similar facial features, and a similarly long, curly coiffure graced with a garland of fruits and flowers (fig. 5.10).[69] Its pose, however, differs in that the Xanten statue strides forward eagerly while extending both arms towards the viewer. Though the right arm is now broken above the elbow, the hand of the left is clearly fashioned so as to bear a large horizontal object. It is widely agreed that this must have been a tray.[70] Hilde Hiller has identified a similarly striding ephebic traybearer with arms forward and palms up (in miniature, 22 cm), now in Autun, as well as two related traybearers in the shape of hermaphrodites with arms outstretched and hands fashioned to bear horizontal trays, precisely like the Xanten statue.[71] Although these last two, also in miniature (84 and 60 cm, respectively), are now in separate locations, they bear so many similarities that they appear to derive from the same workshop, which must have been western and must have been operating in the first century CE. In addition to bronze ephebic lampbearers, then, there also appears to have been a class of bronze ephebic 'dumb waiters,' some life-size, others miniature. In contrast with the modern dumb waiter, which emphasizes the mechanical and kinetic as it moves food up and down or round and round on pulleys or bearings, these ancient versions emphasized the anthropomorphic and the aesthetic. They were unable to move whatsoever, but glorified the food they served and the master serving it through their youthful male beauty. Obsequious and silent, they were as useful for their striking appearance as for their un-flinching reliability.[72]

This same emphasis on the aesthetic lies at the heart of a different type of ancient dumb waiter, one that highlighted variation from the aesthetic ideals of the northern Mediterranean rather than conformity with them. These objects portray nude African youths as tray bearers. As with the *lych-nouchoi*, these statues have not always been recognized as conforming to a type. In his comprehensive study entitled 'Iconographical Evidence on the Black Populations in Greco-Roman Antiquity,' for example, Frank Snowden features a number of such figures without identifying their original purpose. He describes a bronze African child found in Tarragona (fig. 5.11) in neutral terms as extending 'his hands in front of him, palms up.'[73] By these terms the Tarragona boy, like the Idolino, has lost his job, for he was originally discovered with an angular serving tray that he held in his flat, outstretched hands. On this he could have offered small items of food to diners.[74] Standing 82 cm tall, the figure was just under life size (for a child of approximately five), much like the *lychnouchoi*.

Most African male figures, however, seem to have been rendered in min-iature. A Hellenistic figurine now in the Metropolitan Museum in New York also depicts an African youth, nude but for a bizarre loincloth, with out-stretched arms.[75] Here again, Snowden sees the image in neutral or posi-tive terms, as a young athlete, a dancer, or a charioteer, an interpretation he believes is confirmed by the strangely revealing drapery.[76] But the globular shape of the left hand – the right is damaged – makes it clear that it was fashioned to attach some object being borne by the boy. His stooping pos-ture and buckling knees would indicate that this burden was meant to seem heavy. Gisela Richter, who first published the piece in 1921, argued rightly that it represented a slave bearing something to his master.[77] As to the thong, it was clearly designed not to gird up the subject's loins but to expose them. Standing only 18 cm tall, the figurine cannot have carried much, but this was also likely to have been some small platter with which it offered a tiny treat from its crouching posture. Another figurine of a nude African boy now in the National Museum of Antiquities in Reims stands in a more comfortable, if exaggerated, contrapposto.[78] Unfortunately, it lacks a right arm, but its left hand held up with a flat open palm would seem to indicate that this statuette also bore some object, most likely a tray or bowl. Like the figurines from both Tarragona and the Metropolitan Museum, the Reims statuette is small, standing only 16 cm. From Budapest, a bronze statuette of a nude African boy with a similarly exaggerated contrapposto also has upraised arms with one flat palm – as if to support a tray – while his other fist clasps at what must have been some sort of handle.[79] This figurine, dated to the second century CE, stands 15 cm and has long been understood to be a tray bearer. Another youthful nude African found in Perugia but now in the British Museum has a similarly jaunty pose, almost as if walking, but differs from the others in holding his right arm akimbo and his left raised above his head. The left hand is held out flat, palm upwards, and clearly held some object. F.H. Marshall, the object's original publisher, notes: 'A small portion of the object remains, however, between the thumb and forefinger, and the shape suggests that it was a shallow bowl.'[80] It stands 23 cm without its base (36 with it).

These African traybearers, all of a known provenance that derives from the Roman west, indicate that, as of the *lychnouchoi*, such fundamentally Hellenistic forms were adapted by the Romans to serve as functionalist objects. Here again, the development of an African dumb-waiter type in a Roman context is not surprising, for Juvenal in the same satire where he focuses on the idealized ephebic servant – the 'flower of Asia' (*flos Asiae*), as he terms it – also features African servants whose description fits the waif-like examples we have in bronze. With characteristic disgruntlement, he complains that skinny Africans were fobbed off on inferior guests like himself because they were distinctly déclassé compared with the waiters whose features matched those of the *lychnouchoi*.[81]

Petronius also attests to African waiters (*Aethiopes capillati*) as banquet slaves during Trimalchio's feast. These entered the scene carrying small skin bags to clean up the mess after a dish was dropped, 'just like the ones you are used to seeing in the arena when they sprinkle sand,' but instead sprinkled wine on the hands of the diners.[82] One wonders if perhaps this was not the function performed by the famous Caylus figurine found at Chalon-sur-Saône in 1763 and now in the Bibliothèque Nationale de Paris (fig. 5.12).[83] At 20 cm it stands at about the same height as the other African figurines but is more finely modelled and carefully finished. Its hands are clearly fashioned to grasp some round object that had long been assumed to be a string instrument, but the recent arguments of Michèle Daumas have laid this misunderstanding to rest.[84] Its exaggerated pose, like that of the Reims figurine, indicates that this boy was also meant to be labouring to support some burden under his spindly frame. Daumas speculates he may have held an ivory tusk, but it seems just as likely that he carried a small wineskin.[85] How he might have functioned is again hinted at in a vignette from the *Cena Trimalchionis*, which describes a platter on whose corners were posed four figurines of Marsyas carrying wineskins (*utriculi*) that drizzled fish sauce onto the fish dish below.[86]

Moving from the exotic to the grotesque, we also have a series of tray-bearing figures once used in a banqueting context in four statuettes from the House of the Ephebe on the Via dell'Abbondanza, that is, from the same house as the *lychnouchos* discovered in 1925 (fig. 5.13).[87] They form two identical pairs, two of which bear their trays in their right hands and two in their left. All had been carefully stored away in a purpose-built wooden box. Each stands 25 cm including its base, slightly larger than the African tray bearers. They have traces of gilding on their bodies and the trays they bear were elaborately engraved and plated in silver, as were their bases. Maiuri, their discoverer, wanted to see in them 'honey-cake salesmen' (*placentarii*), whom he likened to the pizza sellers of 1920s Naples wandering the streets and hawking their wares. He also wished to think of them as Jews, marred with the taint of acquisitiveness. One look at their obviously uncircumcised members belies this speculation, but his designation *placentarius* has stuck despite its obvious weakness. Their nudity would have been unthinkable for street vendors and their elaborately chased trays out of character for the huckster. Much more likely is that these are grotesque representations of household servants, worthy of admiration not for their youthful beauty nor even their African exoticism but for other, noticeable qualities. The fact that they are portrayed as singing strengthens the case if we recall the ephebic steward of Trimalchio mentioned earlier who sang his master's hymns as he distributed grapes from a *calathiscus*.

Again, parallels can be drawn to related images from the modern world. African servants were regularly depicted supporting tables or offering trays in the context of colonial Europe and America. The type was popularized in Venice late in the baroque period and from there spread throughout Europe. In the early eighteenth century, for example, the master German carver Balthasar Permoser fashioned a variety of such images in Dresden, now housed in the renowned treasure room known at the Grünes Gewölbe.[88] His renderings emphasize the exotic nature of the subjects, who tend to be naked, shiny black, and bedizened with jewels. By the nineteenth century, classicizing trends had given rise to an emphasis on starker realism. For example, a set of French table leg supports in bronze from Houston's Menil Collection depict four muscular Africans, each bearing one leg of a table on disks that they hold behind their backs in both hands.[89] Their powerful bodies, draped scantily in work clothes, were thus harnessed to the service of the owner, a way of objectifying them, taming them, controlling them. In the United States and Great Britain, the mid- to late nineteenth century witnessed a proliferation of so-called 'blackamoor' statues, usually near life-size, which generally served as dumb waiters holding lamps or trays. Like Roman *lychnouchoi* and *trapezophoroi*, their subjects were youthful and androgynous, though they differed from the ancient parallels in tending to be heavily draped to suit Victorian tastes. An example (fig. 5.14), from the Molly Brown House in Denver, holds a lamp in one hand and a tray in the other, the latter of which was used to display calling cards for guests. The blackamoor, clad in lurid, orientalizing vestments and thus self-consciously redolent of the East, could create distance between its post-abolition owner and his or her latent claims to slaveholding. By evoking harems in remote parts of the globe, it foisted the pretence to the enslavement of the black subject onto another culture, however wistfully.

Each of these forms thus conveys a clear but slightly different message. Permoser's eighteenth-century figures emphasized the exotic beauty of the African slave, the French table-leg supports his physical effort, and the nineteenth-century blackamoor his cross-cultural otherworldliness. As such, each highlighted aspects of servility and subjugation evident in the various Roman examplars. These too ranged from the lithe and beautiful *trapezophoroi* like that from Xanten, to the wiry African miniatures straining under their loads, to the otherworldly bizarrerie of the so-called *placentarii* of Pompeii. Like the *lychnouchoi*, all the Roman *trapezophoroi* were part of the structure and part of the scenery in the houses they adorned. Unlike the *lychnouchoi*, however, they came in a greater variety of types. Some were youthful and beautiful, while others livened up a banquet with appeals to different registers of interest: the erotic, the exotic, and the grotesque.

Conclusion

We have seen a number of ways in which the ancients, and particularly the Romans, glorified the labour of their slave subjects in art. Just as owning a human to perform work constituted a desirable commodity in ancient culture, so too did owning an image of a human performing work. This fetishization of human labour led to the adaptation of various anthropomorphic forms to the accomplishment of certain very concrete tasks, be it burning incense, lighting rooms, shaking pepper, holding lamps, or serving food on dinner trays. The ancient fascination with the human form left room for the creation of anthropomorphic images unrelated to enslaved humans. It was thus probably common for ancients to interpret many of the working figures with which they surrounded themselves without reference to slavery. Indeed, prior to the Roman period this seems to have been the norm. Nevertheless, this same fascination with anthropomorphism, coupled with the predominance of slave culture in antiquity and particularly in Roman antiquity, opened a window onto the creation and interpretation of related forms with explicit connections to servitude. Just as slaves were tools, tools could be made to look like slaves; just as slaves were props (in both senses of the word), props could be made to look like slaves; and just as slaves were table waiters, dumb waiters could be made to look like slaves.

In this sense, both slaves and the institution of slavery could be trapped in clay or above all bronze, whose tensile strength rendered it the most useful medium for the manufacture of tools and thus for most of the working figures we have seen. The master class revelled in both the ingenuity and the beauty (or at least curiosity) of these useful objects. The generally sympathetic treatments the artists offer their subjects rendered them relatively innocuous, indeed quite pleasing to look at. As such, they normalized the labour of slaves as something right and good, even pleasing to the eye. Slaves themselves, who worked in the presence of these images, could see in them models of servile ideals, ideals of beauty, of hard work, of obedience, of silence.[90] By viewing these slave replicas and the steely permanence they represented, slaves could also be locked more tightly into their role as bondsmen. This aesthetic of service, this objectification of servile labour as an expression of beauty, allowed for the recreation of an ideal world where artistic forms could be adapted as working models for the ongoing subjugation of a class of menials by the owners of art – and slaves.

NOTES

1 Tac. *An*. 16.15: 'manu servi usus ut immotum pugionem extolleret, adpressit dextram eius iuguloque occurrit.' Slaves were commonly called on to effect the death of a master whose execution had been ordered. See Bradley 1984: 135 for further examples. I should like to thank both Beth Dusinberre and Erika Doss for their helpful discussion of the themes of this paper, and also Michele George and Grey Gundaker for their useful comments.

2 Aen. Gaz. *Ep.* 25: ἐπὶ δὲ τῷ καταστρώματι παιδίον ἔνδοθεν ἐκτρέχει περὶ τὸν αὐτὸν τόπον μακρόν τινα δρόμον· ὁ δὲ κύκλος συμπαραθεῖ καὶ τοσοῦτον ἀκολουθεῖ ὅσον τὸ παιδίον βούλεται (Above the superstructure a slave boy runs inside in a long course, keeping in the same place. The wheel moves along with him and goes as fast as the slave boy wishes).

3 Petr. *Sat.* 27: *Trimalchio digitos concrepuit, ad quod signum matellam spado ludenti subiecit. Exonerata ille vesica aquam poposcit ad manus, digitosque paululum adspersos in capite pueri tersit.*

4 Mart. *Epig.* 3.82.15–17: *digiti crepantis signa nouit / eunuchus et delicatae sciscitator urinae / domini bibentis ebrium regit penem* (The eunuch knows well the signal of his snapping fingers and coaxes out the delicate urine as he manages the tipsy penis of his drunken master). Note that a snap of the fingers sufficed for both Trimalchio and Zoilus to set their urination rituals in motion.

5 Varro *DRR* 1.17: *alii [dividunt] in tres partes, instrumenti genus vocale et semivocale et mutum, vocale, in quo sunt servi, semivocale, in quo sunt boves, mutum, in quo sunt plaustra* (Others divide them into three categories: the articulate sort of tool, the inarticulate, and the mute; the articulate includes slaves, the inarticulate cattle, and the mute wagons). For discussion see Bradley 1984: 21–30. The description of slaves as living tools can be found as early as Arist. *Pol.* 1.4.1253b–1254a: οὕτω καὶ τὸ κτῆμα ὄργανον πρὸς ζωήν ἐστι, καὶ ἡ κτῆσις πλῆθος ὀργάνων ἐστί, καὶ ὁ δοῦλος κτῆμά τι ἔμψυχον, καὶ ὥσπερ ὄργανον πρὸ ὀργάνων πᾶς ὑπηρέτης (Thus any sort of possession is a tool for supporting life, and one's property is a collection of tools; the slave is a living possession, and every servant is like a tool in charge of tools). Another striking example of the use of the slave body as tool comes from Lact. *DMP* 5.3, which describes how the Sasanian Shapur I used the captive emperor Valerian as his footstool, forcing him to stoop on hands and knees whenever the Shahanshah needed to mount his horse. On the slave as tool in Greek literature, see DuBois (2003), esp. ch. 4.

6 For use of the human form in these types, see especially Jantzen 1958; Keene Congden 1981; Mertens 1990; Barr-Sharrar 1996; Stibbe 2000: 21–56.

7 This paper will focus on free-standing objects, but I hope to make a similar argument regarding anthropomorphic architectural sculpture in another publication. There caryatids and atlantes, in the broadest sense 'figural supports,' will also be shown to have been interpreted, at least in Roman times, as slaves. On these figures see especially the studies of Schmidt-Colinet 1977; Schmidt 1982; Schneider 1986.

8 Delphi, Archaeological Museum, inv. 7723; see Rolley 1986: 121, no. 250; Barr-Sharrar 1996: 107, fig. 6.

9 Vatican, Museo Gregoriano Etrusco, inv. 12650; see Haynes 1985: 309, fig. 169.

10 Malibu, Getty Museum, 87.AC.143.1; see Kozloff and Mitten 1988: 299–302, no. 54; Webster 1995: II.334 4XB11f; *The J. Paul Getty Museum Handbook of the Antiquities Collection* 2002: 178.

11 On the distinctive costume of the comic slave, see Duckworth 1952: 90–1. I
    should like to thank Ariana Traill for her help with issues related to ancient
    comedy.
12 Ter. *Haut.* 975–6; Plaut. *Mos.* 1041–1180, esp. 1114: *iam iubebo ignem et
    sarmenta, carnufex, circumdari.* See Marshall 2006: 54 on the scene from the
    Perinthia (P.Oxy. 855). On the iconographic type, see Bieber 1961a: 150, 162.
13 Malibu, Getty Museum, 87.AB.144. This figurine wears the clothing of a comic
    slave but ports no mask and carries a sistrum in his right hand. See Kozloff
    and Mitten 1988: 303 no. 55; *The J. Paul Getty Museum Handbook of the
    Antiquities Collection* 2002: 179.
14 Hartford, Wadsworth Athenaeum, 1917.886. Bieber 1961a: 105, fig. 412; Oliver
    1993; Webster 1995: II.332 (4XB8a) (illustrated at vol. I, pl. 46), which dates the
    figurine to 50 BCE – CE 50.
15 Princeton, University Art Museum, 48–68. Bieber 1961a: 105 fig. 410; Bieber
    1961b: 96, figs. 378–9; Sams 1976: no. 37; Webster 1995: II.257 (3XB1), which
    dates the figurine to 150–50 BCE. Controversy remains as to whether this piece
    was an incense burner.
16 Harris and Fleischman 1994: 234–5, no. 118; Webster 1995: II.288 (4EL1).
17 Webster 1995: II.4–5 (1AT3–5); 10 (1AT16); 52 (1KT3); 112 (2BT2); 139 (2NV4–
    7); 155 (2TT2); 171 (3AT2); 203 (3DT 35); 227–8 (3ET8); 239–40 (3NV2–6);
    257 (3XB2); 262 (3XT4–5); 272 (4BS1); 277 (4DT 9–10); 293 (4ET2–3); 297
    (4HT2); 332 (4XB8a–d); 334 (4XB11a–f); 374 (4XS4a–g); 447 (5XB7); 511 (6XI2).
    Cf. Bieber 1961a: 104–5, 150, 162, figs. 406, 410–13, 556–8, 587; to which add
    Rahms 1994: 391–2.
18 Cf. Kozloff and Mitten 1988: 302: 'The adaptation of the composition as a prac-
    tical device (an incense burner) is a decidedly Roman approach.'
19 London, British Museum, EA 37561. Published in Snowden 1970: fig. 114;
    Walker and Higgs 2001: 90, no. 98.
20 Kavala, Archaeological Museum, M392. First published at Rhomiopoulou 2002,
    who believes the object was used by Roman military personnel. On the theme
    of kneeling barbarian prisoner-slaves, see Schneider 1986: 22–39.
21 On barbarian captivity in late antiquity, see Lenski 2011. See also Bradley 2004
    and Gaca 2010 on captivity more generally.
22 For overviews see Jantzen 1958; Keene Congdon 1981.
23 Naples, Museo Archeologico Nazionale, inv. 73146; see de Caro and Pedicini
    1996: 225. This handle recalls earlier Etruscan handles constituted from two
    warriors with interlocking arms or two vertical warriors bearing the horizontal
    body of a fallen comrade. It thus played on a pre-existing motif, but did so using
    a type of combatant who, in the second century BCE, would have been a captive
    or slave. On Republican-era gladiators as captives or slaves see Schumacher
    2001: 226–9.

24 Paris, Louvre, BR2825; see Lamb 1929: 235–6, pl. X; Mitten and Doeringer 1967: 306, no. 307.

25 London, British Museum, Silver 145; see Walters 1921: 38–9, no. 145, pl. XXIII; Snowden 1970: 82, no. 57, 1976: 236, fig. 325.

26 A bronze unguentarium now in Berlin (Staatliche Museen, Antikensammlung, inv. 30242) also features a lamp-bearing slave, bearing Germanic features, in nearly the same position, Neugebauer 1924: 98, taf. 71.

27 Suet. *Aug.* 29.3: *Tonanti Iovi aedem consecravit liberatus periculo, cum expedtione Cantabrica per nocturnum iter lecticam eius fulgur praestrinxisset servumque praelucentem exanimasset* (He dedicated a temple to Jupiter the Thunderer after escaping from danger when lightning struck his litter on a night-time journey during his Cantabrian expedition and killed his slave lampbearer). See also George 2003: 170 on African *cursores* who preceded their master on journeys.

28 Alexandria, Graeco-Roman Museum, inv. 23100; see Snowden 1970: 248, fig. 113. Athens, Agora Museum, L3457; see Grandjouan 1961: 80 no. 1062–4 and pl. 30; Snowden 1976: 236, fig. 324. Cf. Snowden 1976: 164–6, 206, figs. 194–5, 223, 262–3 for the iconographic type of the squatting African taking a nap.

29 Athen. *Deip.* 4.29 (148b): καὶ κατὰ τὴν ἄφοδον τοῖς μὲν ἐν ἀξιώμασι φορεῖα σὺν τοῖς κομίζουσι, τοῖς πλείοσι δὲ καταργύροις σκευαῖς κεκοσμημένους ἵππους, πᾶσι δὲ λαμπτηροφόρους παῖδας Αἰθίοπας παρέστησε (And for their journey home she gave to the dignitaries litters along with litter bearers, to the majority horses bedizened with silver trappings, and to everyone she gave African slave lamp bearers). Athenaeus derived his testimony from Socrates of Rhodes, *Civil War, FrGH* 2B.192 fr.1. Note that Snowden (1970: 187, cf. 325 n. 115) catalogues lamp bearers among other professions as if this were a trade for free men. What little evidence we have indicates otherwise. All epigraphic attestations of *lampadarii* from Rome identify these as imperial slaves: *CIL* VI.8867: *Aprilis lampadar(ius) Titi Caesaris ser(vus)*; 8868 = *ILS* 1780: *Falanx … Araps Caesar(is) n(ostri) ser(vus) ex peculiaris lampadari(i)s*; 8869: *Flaviae Hygiae Araps Caes(aris) n(ostri) ser(vus) / peculiaris lampadar(ius)*. It is interesting that the last two are identified ethnically as Arabs. Note that 'lampadarius' appears in a number of North African inscriptions, but always as a cognomen, cf. *CIL* VIII.827, 1239, 12355 = *ILTun* 744, 16608 *ILAlg* I.3291, 25972, 26040 = *ILTun* 1347; *ILAfr* 603; *ILAlg* I.2389.

30 Goings 1994: 67–72; Turner 1994: ch. 3; Harris 2003: ch. 3.

31 For a broader history of these demeaning images, see Goings 1994; cf. Schildgen 2000. For a sociological interpretation, see Dubin 1987. Among the most uncanny parallels is a type not treated here: African boys being attacked by alligators or crocodiles. These were modelled into rhyta by the Greeks (see Snowden 1976: 176, figs. 213–4, cf. fig. 299) and also appear regularly in greeting cards

and figurines in Jim Crow images produced in the United States (see Goings 1991: figs. 26–7, 55–6, pl. 27; Dubin 1987: 127; Turner 1994: ch. 2). In a private email Steven Dubin informs me that very similar objects were produced in apartheid-era South Africa.

32 Parallels can also be seen between an ancient bronze coin bank (found in Rome, now in Malibu, Getty Museum, 72.AB.99) – which does not, however, represent an African nor in any obvious way a slave – and the 'jolly nigger' coin banks of the late nineteenth and early twentieth centuries. Both depict grotesque children with outstreched hands begging for money, though the modern banks offer the – typically modern – feature of mechanically operating arms that snatch the coin and feed it to the child. For the first, see Kozloff and Mitten 1988: 353–6, no. 70. For the second, see Goings 1994: 19–20, pl. 4.

33 Naples, Museo Archeologico Nazionale, inv. 120029; see Pugliese Caratelli 1990–2003: III.815, fig. 41; Schumacher 2001: 200, Abb. 96; Dunbabin 2003a: 59, fig. 28; Ritter 2005: 316, Abb. 6; Roller 2006: pl. V. For a related image of a what is likely a slave propping up a drunken female guest in the House of the Chaste Lovers (IX.12.6–7), triclinium, west wall (P4), see Dunbabin 2003a: pl. I; Roller 2006: pl. II. Also see the sculptural image, in relief, of a comic scene with a slave propping up a drunken youth at Bieber 1961a: 92 fig. 324; Schumacher 2001: 202, Abb. 98.

34 Florence, Museo Archeologico, inv. n. 1637. On the Idolino and its history, see Iozzo 1999; Beschi 2000; cf. Zanker 1974: 30–2, no. 28, taf. 33.2–3, 34.4.

35 Descriptions and drawings of two exist, but only a fragment of one survives to the present, Florence, Museo del Bargello, inv. 1879 n. 525; cf. Iozzo 1999: 32–3; Beschi 2000: 13–15.

36 Naples, Museo Archeologico Nazionale, inv. 125348; see Sogliano 1901; Anti 1926: 80; Rumpf 1939: tav. X, fig. 3, tav. XI, fig. 6; Jashemski 1979: I.113, fig. 184; Pedicini et al. 1989: 146, no. 251; Heilmeyer 1996: taf. 36–8; cf. Zanker 1974: 37, no. 34.

37 Naples, Museo Archeologico Nazionale, inv. 143753; see Maiuri 1925a, 1927: 63–6; Amelung 1927; Jashemski 1979–1993: I.93, fig. 148; Pedicini et al. 1989: 146, no. 252; Maderna-Lauter 1991: 361, Abb. 226; Heilmeyer 1996: Taf. 67; Iozzo 1999: 36–8, tav. XVII; Zanker 1998: 179, fig. 102.

38 Maiuri 1925a: 337: quasi una divina apparizione, una bellezza viva e palpitante miracolosamente risorta dalla morta città (Like a divine apparition, a living and quivering beauty miraculously resurrected from the dead city).

39 Sogliano 1901: 651–2; Maiuri 1925a: 348: L'effetto che ne risulta, per il nostro giudizio estetico, è sgradevolissimo … sono insomma un'aggiunta illogica, irrazionale e, nella loro pretenziosità decorativa, sfacciatamente inestetica che falsa e deturpa la spirituale e formale bellezza dell'opera d'arte (The resultant effect is, to my aesthetic judgment, most unpleasant … ultimately they constitute an

addition that is illogical, irrational, and – in its decorative pretensions – brazenly unaesthetic, which adulterates and sullies the spiritual and formal beauty of the work of art).

40 Anti 1926; Schober 1926; cf. Amelung 1927: 141; Zanker 1974: 76–7.

41 Rabat, Musée Archéologique, inv. vol. 62; see Michon 1933; Zanker 1974: 34–5, no. 31, Taf. 33.1, 35.2, 4, 36.3, 6; Maderna-Lauter 1991: 360, Abb. 224–5; Riposati 1991: 56–7, no. 3.

42 Chamoux 1950.

43 Rumpf 1939.

44 Boscoreale, Antiquarium, inv. n. 13112; see Iozzo 1999: 39–41, tav. 85; *Rediscovering Pompeii* 1990: 257, no. 180; Mattusch 2008: 137 fig. 44.

45 The Zifteh statue, acquired by the British Museum in 1840, was not recognized as a representative of the type until Chamoux 1950: 77; cf. Walters 1915: pl. XLI.

46 The statue is missing the head and its hands are not drilled for attachments but were clearly made to hold something, cf. Furtwängler 1883–7: vol. I, pl. 8–11; Neugebauer 1924: 18, taf. 39; Heilmeyer 1996: passim; Knittlmayer and Heilmeyer 1998: 210, no. 126. It was first identified as a possible *lychnouchos* by Anti 1926: 84, but Heilmeyer 1996: 40–5 doubts it corresponds to this type.

47 On the Samsun statue, which is missing its arms and thus is by no means certain to have been a *lychnouchos*, see Işkan 1998.

48 Pompeii, inv. P22924. Published at Zevi 1996: no. 229 fig. 23, tav. 17; Mattusch 1996: pl. 5, 2008: 143 fig. 48; Ridgway 2002: pl. 59; Salskov Roberts 2002: fig. 10. Maiuri 1927: 65 n. 1 points out that the National Museum in Naples possesses two further sets of vine racks with handles (inv. 125180, 110991–2), which were not found with statues. This indicates that there were at least six *lychnouchoi* in Pompeii.

49 The exception appears to be the the example from the House of Julius Polybius, which very closely resembles the Piombino Apollo in the Louvre and was thus representative of an archaizing fashion in the first century BCE that did not so much recreate originals as create anew types with archaic features, cf. Mattusch 1996: 139–40; Ridgway 2002: 148, 152–3. The statue was not apparently originally designed as a *lychnouchos* but was retooled to perform this function by having its hands mortised. For this reason, the right hand is extended flat and upright, forcing it to balance one of its racks awkwardly on its palm.

50 On Roman banqueting, see Roller 2006. On the Roman fashion for ephebic slaves, see Williams 1999: 30–8. That the *lychnouchoi* were indeed placed in dining halls is confirmed by the example from the House of Julius Polybius, which was found in a winter triclinium together with a whole set of banqueting apparatus (Zevi 1996: 78–9) and by that from the House of the Ephebe, whose base was found positioned to light up a summer triclinium (Maiuri 1925a: 338, 1927: 64; Jashemski 1979–93: I.92–4, II.38–40); cf. Stemmer 1995: 450–1.

51 Petr. *Sat.* 41.6: *Dum haec loquimur, puer speciosus, vitibus hederisque redimitus, modo Bromium, interdum Lyaeum Euhiumque confessus, calathisco uvas circumtulit et poemata domini sui acutissima voce traduxit.*

52 Apul. *Met.* 2.19; Juv. *Sat.* 5.56–66; 11.146–8; Sen. *Ep.* 47 passim; 95.24; 119.14; Mart. *Epig.* 8.51.19. For the ephebic *crinitus* not in a banquet context see also Sen. *Ep.* 123.7; Plin. *NH* 7.56. On table servants in literary texts, see D'Arms 1991.

53 Philo *De vit. cont.* 50: βαθυχαῖται γάρ εἰσιν ἢ μὴ κειρόμενοι τὸ παράπαν ἢ τὰς προμετωπιδίους αὐτὸ μόνον ἐξ ἄκρων εἰς ἐπανίσωσιν καὶ γραμμῆς κυκλοτεροῦς ἠκριβωμένον σχῆμα. It must be noted that, in contrast with the *lychnouchoi*, Philo's ganymedes are clothed in chitons, albeit mini-cut; cf. Hor. *S.* 2.8.69–70 on clothed male table servants. Further textual and iconographic references on long-haired serving boys at Pollini 2002: 53–8.

54 Although the ephebe from Salamis in Berlin is now headless, traces of its long locks still grace its shoulders.

55 Sen. *Ep.* 47.7: *Alius vini minister in muliebrem modum ornatus cum aetate luctatur: non potest effugere pueritiam, retrahitur, iamque militari habitu glaber retritis pilis aut penitus evulsis tota nocte pervigilat, quam inter ebrietatem domini ac libidinem dividit et in cubiculo vir, in convivio puer est* (Another acting as wine servant, all gussied up like a woman, struggles with his age: he is unable to escape boyhood, to which he is dragged back, and now with his military bearing he stays smooth skinned from having shaved his hairs or plucked them out altogether. He remains awake the whole night, which he must divide between his master's drunkenness and lust, for he is a man in the bedroom but a boy in the banquet hall). On the importance of hairless table servants (*glabri*), see Sen. *Brev. Vit.* 12.5; *CIL* VI.8817, 8956. On efforts to retard or disguise the onset of puberty, see Bradley 1984: 115–6.

56 Maiuri 1925a: 340. Traces of silver-plating were originally reported on the ephebe from the Porta Vesuvio (Sogliano 1901: 642), but technical analysis has proven this claim unfounded, Heilmeyer 1996: 50.

57 Lucr. 2.24–6: *gratius interdum neque natura ipsa requirit, / si non aurea sunt iuvenum simulacra per aedes / lampadas igniferas manibus retinentia dextris / lumina nocturnis epulis ut suppeditentur* (It is more pleasant, meanwhile, nor does nature herself require it, if there are no gilded statues of boys bearing fiery lamps in their right hands spread across the house in order to provide light for nightly feasts). As Bailey 1947: II.802 points out, Lucretius's image traces to Hom. *Od.* 7.100–1, but Homer's elaborates a fantastical setting while Lucretius is describing a real type of candelabra to be seen in the wealthy houses of his own time. Maiuri 1927: 64 first made the connection with this text, on the suggestion of F.W. Kelsey. See also Athen. *Deip.* 4.130a.

58 Bergmann 1995: esp. 79–81 and 100–1 on *lychnouchoi*.

59 Kemp 1978: 66–70; Baulez 2007: 85–8.

60 A legend even arose that these statues were meant to represent a famous lamp bearer from George Washington's Continental Army who froze to death in the line of duty, Goings 1994: 52; cf. Turner 1994: 9–11.

61 Schumacher 2001: 195–203; Dunbabin 2003a: 52–63, 108–32, 150–6.

62 Dunbabin 2003a: figs. 64, 68, 90, pl. X, 2003b: figs. 1–2, 5, 8, 11–13, 16; Roller 2006: fig. 18.

63 Pugliese Carratelli 1990–2003: II.402–3, fig. 5; Roller 2006: pl. I. The exact same scene with the same figure appears in panel P15 of the House of Giuseppe II (VIII.2.38–39, now in Naples, Museo Archeologico Nazionale, inv. 8968), see Pugliese Carratelli 1990–2003: VIII.354–6, fig. 92; Roller 2006: fig. 8.

64 Dunbabin 2003b.

65 Now in Naples, Museo Archeologico Nazionale, inv. 120030; see Amelung 1927: Abb. 6–7; Garcia y Bellido 1969: abb. 6; Pugliese Carratelli 1990–2003: III.818, fig. 47; Ritter 2005: 309 abb. 4. For a classic example of actual bronze statuary serving as the model for a wall painting, see the paintings of nymphs holding shell-fountains from the House of the Epigrams, House of the Vestals, House of Romulus and Remus, and the Stabian baths and the bronze type on which they are modelled from the House of the Ephebe, Bieber 1961b: 150, figs. 636–7; Moorman 1988: 45, nos. 185 / 1, 198 / 3, 231 / 1, 251. These too were functional objects, serving as fountains.

66 Antequera, Museo Municipal. Garcia y Bellido 1969.

67 Garcia y Bellido 1969: 76–7 suggests a cup, a tray, or even simply garlands for guests to use to adorn themselves. A miniature version of the same type found on the island of Funen (Danish National Museum, inv. C 1077) has also been identified as a cup, tray, or garland bearer, see Salskov Roberts 2002. The statue is only 16 cm tall, thus equivalent in size with the miniature African tray bearers to be reviewed below. Two Pompeian wall paintings from the same triclinium in IX.5.6–17 depict statues of a male and a female, draped, who hold, respectively, wreaths and garlands, see Pugliese Carratelli 1990–2003: IX.446–8, figs. 81, 83, 85–6.

68 Beschi 2000 believes the Idolino itself may actually have been a traybearer rather than a lampbearer; cf. Iozzo 1999: 17, 25.

69 Staatliche Museen zu Berlin, Antikensammlung, Sk. 4. Neugebauer 1924: 19 taf. 74; Kunze 1992: 238, no. 123; Hiller 1994, who dates to the mid-first century CE; Knittlmayer and Heilmayer 1998: 208, no. 125.

70 Compare the striding hermaphroditic torch bearers of the Mahdia horde: Fuchs 1963: 14, no. 2, Taf. 12–13.

71 Hiller 1994: 207–9, Abb. 12–14, referring to the striding youth in Autun (Musée Rolin, inv. B 3005) and the standing hermaphrodites in the Palazzo dei Conservatori and the Château Beaurepaire (originally found in Pont-Sainte-Maxence).

72 There may have been a classical Greek precedent for these miniature food-
bearing slaves. Numerous examples of even smaller figurines (ca 7–9 cm high)
from classical Greek contexts depict comic actors bearing bowls in each hand
which – it has been asserted – may have been meant to hold small portions
of food: 1) Olynthus, Robinson 1941: 1–6, no. 1 pl. I; Barr-Sharrar 1996: 108,
fig. 10; 2) Saint-Germain-en-Laye, Reinach 1884: III.157, no. 7; 3) Mahdia,
Fuchs 1963: 21, no. 13 pl. 21; 4) Toronto, Mitten and Doeringer 1967: 120, nos.
118–19a–b.

73 Tarragona, Museo Nacional Arqueológico, no. 527. Poulsen 1933: 58, no. 17,
pl. LVIII, figs. 90–2; Garcia y Bellido 1949: I.442–3, no. 467, II pl. 325; Snowden
1976: 224, figs. 290, 303. Snowden has done a tremendous service both in collecting this material and in demonstrating the often positive interpretations
given it by ancient artists. At times, however, he does not attend adequately
to indications that many of the subjects portrayed were clearly enslaved. On
Africans in ancient art, see Ako-Adounvo 1999 and esp. Bolender 2000 and
George 2003, which correct for this problem. On Africans in ancient texts, see
Johnson 2006.

74 The figure was also found with a four-armed candelabra, though I have been
unable to find a published image of this and a description of how it was integrated into the work.

75 New York, Metropolitan Museum, inv. 18.145.10. Richter 1921: 33–4, fig. 3,
1953: 125 pl. 104f; Rolley 1986: 248, no. 301.

76 Snowden 1976: 204, no. 260, cf. 1970: 74 no. 44. The drapery would never have
done for a charioteer nor an athlete.

77 Richter 1921: 33.

78 Saint-Germain-en-Laye, Musée des Antiquités Nationales, no. 818. Snowden
1970: 247, no. 112, 1976: 224, figs. 295–6.

79 Budapest, Aquincumi Múzeum, no. 51344. Published at Szilágy 1956: 111,
pl. LIII; Snowden 1970: 247, no. 111.

80 London, British Museum, 1908.5–15.1. Marshall 1909: 163, fig. 16; Walters
1915: pl. LXVIII, dated to the first century BCE or the first century CE. Cf.
Snowden 1970: 90, fig. 66, 1976: 224.

81 Juv. *Sat.* 5.52–60: *tibi pocula cursor / Gaetulus dabit aut nigri manus ossea
Mauri / et cui per mediam nolis occurrere noctem, / cliuosae ueheris dum per
monumenta Latinae. / flos Asiae ante ipsum, pretio maiore paratus / quam
fuit et Tulli census pugnacis et Anci / et, ne te teneam, Romanorum omnia
regum / friuola. quod cum ita sit, tu Gaetulum Ganymedem / respice, cum
sities* (A Gaetulian boy will bring your cups or the bony hand of a black Moor,
the sort of guy you would not want to meet at midnight while you are riding
past the tombstones along the hilly via Latina. Meanwhile, the flower of Asia
stands before that guy, acquired for a larger price than the entire fortune of

Tullus or warlike Ancus and, in sum, all the trifles of the Roman kings. Not to put too fine a point on it, but you must look to your Gaetulian Ganymede every time you want a drink). Note that the African's hand – and thus the African by synecdoche – is described as 'bony,' much like these emaciated African figurines. Note too the frisson provoked by a nocturnal encounter with an African on the road, which also helps explain the thrill of owning an African lamp bearer intimated earlier in this article. More on African wine stewards in Roman art at Ako-Adounvo 1999: 120–31.

82 Petr. *Sat.* 34: *Subinde intraverunt duo Aethiopes capillati cum pusillis utribus, quales solent esse qui harenam in amphitheatro spargunt, vinumque dederunt in manus; aquam enim nemo porrexit* (Then two long-haired Africans entered with little bags, like the ones who sprinkle sand in the amphitheatre, and they poured wine into our hands; no one, of course, offered water).

83 Paris, Bibliothèque Nationale, Collection Caylus, no. BB 1009; see Babelon and Blanchet 1895: no. 1009, 1928: 55–6, pls. XXIII–XXIV; Bieber 1961b: 96, fig. 381; Snowden 1970: 84, no. 60, 1976: 199, figs. 253–5; Rolley 1986: 230, fig. 200; Daumas 1993; Bollender 2000: 95–6, Abb. 5–6; Schumacher 2001: 75, Abb. 24; Bol 2007: III.2, abb. 173a-d.

84 Daumas 1993.

85 Bolender 2000: 99 also suggests a 'Weinschlauch' and offers three examples of African figures depicted with them (n. 83). She eventually supports Daumas's suggestion of a tusk even as she herself points out (n. 84) that the holes in the hands are oriented perpendicular to one another and spaced so close together that any tusk would have to have been bent rather than curved.

86 Petr. *Sat.* 36: *circa angulos repositorii Marsyas quattuor, ex quorum utriculis garum piperatum currebat super pisces, qui tanquam in euripo natabant* (Around the corners of the vessel there were four figures of Marsyas from whose wineskins peppered fish sauce ran out over the fish, which were swimming as if they were in the Euripus).

87 Naples, Museo Archeologico Nazionale, inv. 143760; see Maiuri 1925b, 1927: 66–8; Jashemski 1979–93: I.92–4, fig. 149; de Caro and Pedicini 1996: 244. Zanker 1998: 174–80 offers an evocative portrayal of the House of the Ephebe and its likely owner, the wealthy freedman trader Cornelius Tages, about whom much is known from the accounting tablets found in Pompeii.

88 Dresden, Staatliche Kunstsammlungen, available on ARTstor under keyword 'Permoser'; see also Asche 1978: 109–10, taf. III, abb. 311–15. Permoser worked with the goldsmith Johannes Melchior Dinglinger on these figures, which were generally used as a vehicle for displaying jewels, artfully arranged on the trays presented by their eager African subjects. For similar images and the European fascination with collecting such exotica in the eighteenth century, see Kopplin 1987. Late baroque furniture design often heightened its fascination with the

sculptural human form with a heavy dose of racism against colonial ethnicities and particularly Africans, who were fashioned to labour, often in impossibly contorted poses, under the weight of some burden, cf. Morley 1999: 141–3.

89 Houston, Menil Foundation Collection, ID 15740–3, available on ARTstor.

90 McCarthy 2000: 21–2 and passim points out the paradox inherent in the objectification of the slave, who is most useful as an object only when he can operate as subject, using his rationality and understanding of self-interest to perform work for the master. This is of course where these inanimate objects fell short of their human counterparts. Like the Negro collectibles discussed above, however, they expressed a desire for a reality that never truly could or did exist, making them all the more revealing of the Roman imaginary.

6

Cupid Punished: Reflections on a Roman Genre Scene

MICHELE GEORGE

Introduction

Amidst the marmoreal splendour of the Borghese Gallery in Rome stands a small statue of Cupid, carved from Luna marble and dated stylistically to the Antonine period (fig. 6.1). The small, chubby boy weeps, rubbing one eye with his right hand while the other hand grasps his cloak, which is wrapped about the tree stump on which he leans, his weight on the left leg in a contrapposto stance. Clearly visible and rendered in realistic detail is a chain, attached to a band around his waist, which extends down his left leg and ends in a fetter around his ankle. This shackle and the child-god's remorse are a visual shorthand signalling that he has committed some mischief and must endure his punishment. The statue belongs to a minor genre scene in Roman art called 'Cupid Punished' that occupied a small corner in the broad repertoire of Roman decoration that abounds with a multitude of gods, goddesses, and other inhabitants of the mythological landscape. Combining the painful pleasures of erotic love with the idealized delights of childhood, the whimsical theme is compatible with the domestic sphere in which it is most often found. The 'Cupid Punished' motif offers an interesting case study of the role visual culture can play in enriching our understanding of the slave culture of ancient Rome, for behind its anodyne charm lie attitudes to physical punishment and suffering that are tied to Roman slavery.[1]

To the modern eye, the sight of chains on the softly modelled body of a small child is disturbing; even when we make the imaginative leap into the realm of mythology and identify the child as Cupid, a sense of incongruity lingers. Since this is a Roman statue, it is the ancient perspective on 'Cupid Punished' that must be re-imagined: how might this imagery have been understood within its contemporary milieu? In the last three decades there has emerged a sharper appreciation of the profound power of visual culture in the ancient world and the ways in which it expressed and influenced social and cultural values. Imperial monuments and elite art have benefited most from this approach, but it has much to offer slavery studies, for embedded in Roman art are traces of the slave society to which it belonged. A consideration of the Roman context, conditioned as it was by the reality of institutionalized slavery in ways now difficult to apprehend, permits an exploration of the appeal of this imagery.

The Motif of 'Cupid Punished'

A survey of this minor genre scene in Roman art, its appearance through the centuries, across the empire, and in different media, reveals its persistent relevance for a contemporary audience and the diverse ways it was tailored to the Roman setting. Precedents for 'Cupid Punished' in Greek and Hellenistic art appear in sculpture, terracotta, and carved gems that depict Eros pursued threateningly by other erotes, being beaten with a sandal by his mother Aphrodite, or, most frequently, simply with his hands tied behind his back. The theme was most commonly found on Hellenistic seals, which feature Eros seated on the ground or on an altar, hands tied behind his back, or standing with his hands bound and attached to a column or tree, in some cases visibly weeping. The motif's representation in Hellenistic art reflects the popularity of Eros as a figure in contemporary epigram, which features a mischievous, but powerful, Eros, alternately friend and foe to the poet / lover beleaguered by desire. Moschus (ca 150 BCE) furnishes the fullest treatment in his bucolic poem *Eros drapetes* (Fugitive Love), in which Aphrodite herself issues a description of her wayward son and his destructive habit of carelessly inflaming mortal passions together with a plea for his return and promise of a reward. Statues of Eros as disarmed and helpless, his hands bound, his own weapons of torch and arrow turned against him, are described with satisfaction by the epigrammatists as just vengeance for the god's role in the poet's suffering. There is, however, nothing from the Greek or Hellenistic eras that resembles the Borghese statue, nor is there the same quantity or variety of examples of the motif as there are from the Roman imperial period, suggesting that the imagery enjoyed more favour with a Roman than a Greek audience.[2]

The multiplication of figures of Eros that began in the Hellenistic era became a characteristic element of Roman art, where they are depicted as generic, childlike, nude, frequently (albeit inconsistently) winged figures, shown individually or more often in groups. Referred to commonly in the scholarship by the Renaissance term 'putto' (pl. 'putti'), they bear a range of artistic functions from the purely decorative to the symbolic. Out of the affiliation with love emerged more general associations with pleasure, fertility, and prosperity, leading to a connection with divinities beyond Venus such as Dionysus, as well as to more philosophical and allegorical concepts such as death and apotheosis. As an artistic device, putti were especially popular in the depiction of genre scenes, and scenes of putti engaged in human activities, from winemaking to metalworking to chariot racing, form a distinct corpus in Roman art, their childish form and mythological character lending an otherworldly allure to the commonplace. The 'Cupid Punished' motif is part of this artistic tradition, in which aspects of human experience are represented through the filter of mythological fancy and embodied in the form of a small child. In contrast to the Greek antecedents, in its Roman iteration the concept of punishment is given greater emphasis and is conveyed by shackles or by other means of physical discipline easily recognized by a Roman viewer as most typical of slavery.[3]

In the Pitti Palace in Florence there is another version of the Borghese statue (fig. 6.2), identical in size and in composition; he too rubs his eyes regretfully and is burdened with a shackle on his leg. Instead of a tree stump, he leans on a pilaster that is decorated at the front with a pair of ears, a bucranium, and ribbons, with a garland of fruit on the side, items which have been construed either as symbols of romantic attachment or as cultic in nature, and associated with the divine Cupid himself or with the goddess Nemesis. Despite the occasional presence of Nemesis, other artistic versions of 'Cupid Punished' lack these elements, which suggests that the motif was a genre scene representing an idealized moment from domestic life.[4] Although not yet widely acknowledged, several less complete statues with compositional variations on the theme can be identified with this genre. In the Terme Museum in Rome, where there is one example, and in the Vatican Museum, where there are two (one shown in fig. 6.3), all three headless, armless, and extant only to the knee, the torso retains the same unmistakable arrangement of chains, running down the left leg and attached to a band around the waist.[5] Rather than the childlike body for Cupid that comes to dominate Roman depictions of the god, these statues were possibly inspired by the adolescent statue type established by the influential but no longer extant cult statues of Eros at Thespiae in Pentelic marble and at Parion in bronze by the fourth-century BCE Greek artist Praxiteles. According to Pausanias (9.27.1–4), the Thespian statue was known at Rome, having been brought to Rome first by Caligula, then returned by Claudius, only to be carried off a second time by Nero, before being destroyed by fire while Titus was emperor. The absence of wings on these statues has led to their tentative identification as young boys rather than Cupids; only one extant statue (from Baia, now in the Naples Museum) has both shackles and wings. Statues of young boys without wings, whether depicted as children or adolescents, are commonly identified as Cupid, however, if the context or the presence of appropriate attributes such as bow, arrow, or torch recommend it. The chains on these torsos match exactly those of the childlike statues of 'Cupid Punished' in the Borghese Gallery and the Pitti Palace, as well as on the motif in other media, such as gems and in painting. Given this, and in the absence of an alternative explanation for the chains, it seems probable that these statues should also be identified as 'Cupid Punished.'[6]

The statue type found on Hellenistic gems, with hands bound, continued in use into the Roman era, as a third, more intact, statue in the Vatican demonstrates. Dated stylistically to the Antonine era, this version does have wings, but no shackles, and the body type falls somewhere between the plump child and the willowy adolescent; his hands are tied behind his back, and his head hangs down in contrition. Among the typical garden statuary in the portico of the peristyle in the House of the Vettii (VI.15.1) at Pompeii are two more examples (one illustrated in fig. 6.4) that are thus far also not associated with the 'Cupid Punished' statue type, but which probably belong to this category. Two matching fountain statues, *fistulae* tucked beneath their arms, were found set on opposing pedestals in intercolumniations on the west portico of the peristyle; they have the childlike form and elaborate hairstyle of the Borghese statue, but lack the shackles. Instead, punishment is signalled by their chastened demeanour and by their hands, which are held behind their backs by their cloaks.[7]

The example of the 'Cupid Punished' motif most familiar to the modern viewer occurs in the medium of painting in a Third-style wall panel from the house of the same name at Pompeii (fig. 6.5). In a pastoral landscape, on the left the goddess Nemesis, who is identified by her typical gesture of holding her hand to her face, leads by the hand the penitent Cupid to his mother Venus, who sits to the right on a rock, holding in her lap his quiver, which is presumably the means of his mischief. Behind her shoulder hovers another putto, who might be Cupid's brother Anteros enjoying a moment of *Schadenfreude* at his sibling's expense. The panel, which occupied the north wall of the *tablinum*, is a thematic pendant to the well-known painting of Venus and Mars on the south wall of the same room. Despite being a rear view, the band around Cupid's waist can be clearly seen picked out in red paint, and the shackles, rendered in paint as metallic, are visible extending down both his legs; in his left hand he holds a hoe, while he raises his right hand to his eyes in remorse. The inclusion of the hoe is a sign of additional punishment, indicating that not only has he been chained and fettered around the ankle for his transgressions, but that he has also been condemned to hard labour in the fields.[8]

The theme is most frequently met on carved gems of the Roman era, which sometimes reproduce the version common on Greek seals depicting Cupid sitting with hands tied behind his back, or hands pulled back and tied to a tree or pillar.[9] Another glyptic design recalls the Borghese and Florence statues as well as the Pompeian wall painting in the inclusion of shackles, with chains showing on both of his legs, rather than on just the one leg, while holding a hoe, alone (fig. 6.6), or with Psyche (fig. 6.7).[10] A final subset of the motif on gems presents Cupid punished with his arms tied behind his back as a captive of war (fig. 6.8): he sits at the foot of a trophy, hands tied behind his back, an empty cuirass, helmet, spear, and shield completing the standard imagery. Even in the shorthand of gem carving, on this amethyst signed by the gemcutter Aulos, an effort is made to indicate the chain at the waist.[11]

Two other forms of punishing Cupid survive only in a few examples but introduce a new medium, mosaic, and two new punishments, flogging, and condemnation to death in the amphitheatre; all come from North Africa and are dated to the end of the second to the mid-third centuries AD. From the House of Venus at Volubilis are two panels that flanked a large central scene of the myth of Hylas and feature Cupid punished in two different ways. In one panel, hands tied behind his back, Cupid is tied at the waist with a band that is held on both sides by two putti, their arms raised to flog him; a dove dead at his feet reveals his crime. In the other panel, Cupid receives comic punishment in the amphitheatre in the form of an absurd *damnatio ad bestias*: arms tied behind his back, he is propelled by one putto, who whips him in the direction of a tortoise (rather than a fierce tiger or other vicious animal) that is released from a cage by another putto. In two more mosaics Cupid is also flogged. In one, from Thina (fig. 6.9), Venus beats him with a tree branch while two other putti lift him by hands and feet, his back bared to receive the blows. In another, from Utica, Venus points as if giving instructions, while Cupid, kneeling with his hands tied behind his back, is flogged by two other putti.[12]

Establishing precise dates for much of this material is generally not possible. The Pompeian wall painting is classified as Third style and falls in the middle of the first century CE; in some cases the gems can be dated more narrowly within a specific century, but they often cannot be fixed more definitely in time. With the exception of the fountain statues in the House of the Vettii (which have an obvious *terminus ante quem* of CE 79), most of the statuary is without provenance and is dated stylistically to the mid-second century CE or has not been assigned a date beyond falling within the Roman imperial period. This diffuse chronological spread, however, and the appearance of the motif in North African mosaic in the third century CE in an innovative form indicate some degree of enduring popularity and recognition. The Gallo-Roman poet Ausonius, writing in the fourth century CE, describes a wall painting, which he claims to have seen in the *triclinium* of a man named Zoilos in Trier, of Cupid being crucified by angry women whom he has wronged in love; the image so impressed him that he wrote a poem about it (*Cupido cruciatur*). In the poetic version a weeping Cupid is hung up on a myrtle tree, his hands bound behind his back and his feet tied (l. 59–62); his mother Venus flogs him herself with a golden wreathe (l. 88–9); but in the end, as ever, he is pardoned (l. 97–8). It is impossible to ascertain whether the Trier painting was real or merely a fanciful justification for the poem, although the specificity of the allusion lends some credence to its existence. At the very least, it demonstrates the possibility that such a scene might have existed, and been understood, in a fourth-century provincial context.[13] It remains now to consider the motif as an artefact of Roman culture, in the broadest sense, and to suggest ways in which the reality of slavery informed its representation and meaning.

Cupid's Punishments

'Cupid Punished' appears in domestic decoration, where the punishments of the child-god were probably intended as gentle amusement, and on gems, which possibly functioned as amulets, love charms, or keepsakes exchanged between lovers. What is notable is the elaborated and diverse nature of the imagery of punishment in the Roman versions compared to the simpler, more one-dimensional Greek models. The Hellenistic Eros is punished by temporary helplessness: his hands are tied behind his back and he is deprived of his weapons of bow, arrow, and torch. In the Roman incarnation, however, the idea of punishment is exploited in greater detail. Not only is Cupid powerless, but he must also bear a set of additional, culturally specific punishments that were closely associated with Roman slavery: he is whipped, he is fettered at the ankle, or he carries a hoe, signalling his banishment to agricultural toil, all penalties which were identified above all with slaves. Bound and seated beneath a military trophy, Cupid is portrayed as a captive of war with imagery recognizable from imperial monuments and also closely tied to the beginning of enslavement, or he is condemned to die in the arena, another fate commonly suffered by slaves.

The various ways in which punishment is communicated in this imagery reflect both the brutal realities of institutionalized slavery and the degree to which they informed and even defined the Roman conception of punishment. Punishment was integral to slavery, an essential if unpleasant feature of the slave / master relationship that preserved social control. According to the Greek idea of natural slavery, which was fundamental to Roman slavery, slaves were criminal by nature, disobedient, dishonest, and lazy; proper slave management therefore required regular discipline to correct their many native perfidies. Corporal punishment, applied in Stoic good measure, was acknowledged as the appropriate action of a slave owner striving to maintain a peaceable household and to prevent domestic turmoil, and any master who wished to avoid the disagreeable task could hire a team of specialists to do it on his behalf. The intimate connection between slavery and punishment is verified in the technical language of punishment in Roman law and in its hierarchical application to different status groups along the social spectrum. Juridical texts refer to beatings as *servilia verbera* (servile lashings), and a free man condemned to the mines was referred to in law as a *servus poenae* (slave of the penalty); reduced to the virtual status of a slave, he was stripped of the right to inherit or make a will, in addition to being beaten and chained. The association was literal, in that slaves endured physical punishment as a matter of course at the hands of slave owners exercising their legitimate authority, as well as symbolic, since the connection with slaves, the lowest-status group in Roman society, made corporal punishment profoundly demeaning. The socially sanctioned treatment of slaves set a standard for debasement and humiliation against which the punishment of *ingenui* might be measured, and any free man who suffered similar punishments endured the pain of social degradation in addition to bodily suffering.[14]

Chains and whips above all were identified as instruments of slave punishment: being kept in chains while they worked was a common form of extended punishment for slaves, while prisoners of free status were normally shackled only on a temporary basis, and free men were forbidden by law from being kept permanently in chains. Shackles were associated specifically with agricultural slaves, although slaves in any work setting might be forced to wear them.[15] By law slaves received harsher treatment than other status groups: they were flogged with whips (*flagella*) rather than the rods (*fustes*) used on the free man, and punishment was often carried out in public as an example for other slaves as well as to demonstrate the slave owner's complete control over his household. Both chains and whips injured social status precisely because of their close association with slavery, making the momentary physical pain far less significant than the lasting burden of public disgrace.[16] Slaves were also punished by being condemned to the arena, initially entirely at the master's discretion, while in the Tiberian era the *Lex Petronia* restricted his power by requiring justification for such condemnation before a judge, presumably a condition that could readily enough be met. Moreover, although slaves were not the only unfortunates to suffer this fate, the convicts and prisoners of war who accompanied them into the arena were designated *servi poenae* under Roman law.[17]

The association between physical punishment and slavery, and by exten-sion between slavery and suffering, is found throughout Latin literature but is concentrated in Roman comedy and elegy. The interplay between behav-iour and punishment is directly explored in the comic plays of Plautus, where the 'threat-of-punishment' motif, as Erich Segal calls it, is constantly reiter-ated on stage as a possibility, but, unlike in real life, is rarely enacted. In the *Asinaria* a list of typical slave punishments, rendered with alliterative gusto in the Latin, includes burning with hot metal plates, crucifixion, strappadoes, chains, imprisonment, the stocks, fetters, and whipping. Roman comedy's role reversal, wherein the clever slave (*servus callidus*) always outsmarts his master and escapes the lash, is defined by a litany of physical abuse that plays an essential part in creating comic tension and eliciting laughter, but in the repeated invocation of slave punishments is also reflected the entrenched nature of physical violence in slavery at Rome.[18]

The punishments of slavery are associated with love in a rather different way in the literary *topos* of *servitium amoris* (slavery of love), a feature of the Augustan elegiac poets Tibullus, Propertius, and Ovid in which the suffering of erotic attachment is compared to the whips, chains, and other humiliations routinely endured by slaves.[19] While the Hellenistic epigram-matist relishes the punishment of Eros for the frequent cruelties he inflicts on the lover, the Roman elegists make a different connection between the pains of love and the pains of slavery, as the poet / lover casts himself in the role of slave to his mistress. By equating the emotional torments of separa-tion and jealousy with the frequent painful discipline endured by the slave, *servitium amoris* represents a parallel, literary strand to the artistic motif of 'Cupid Punished' in its expression of cultural assumptions about slavery and its profound connection to physical suffering. *Servitium amoris* was an innovation of Roman elegy, rather than merely another trope borrowed from Hellenistic poetry, and in a number of ways it is aspects of institution-alized slavery that give the poetic conceit its particularly Roman character. In Hellenistic epigram Cupid is punished through application of the very weapons he uses against the lover, while in Roman elegy, it is the punish-ments of real slavery – chains, the whip, the torturer's flame – to which the lover is figuratively subjected. Roman elegists introduced the idea of chains as part of love's punishment, and include servile punishments in their love poetry repeatedly and in vivid detail. Like the slave, the elegiac lover has lost his free will, performs typically servile tasks, and above all suffers the physical punishments and social humiliations of the slave. Tibullus, for ex-ample, presents himself as a slave to his *domina* Nemesis, willingly wield-ing the hoe as she orders him and offering up his body to shackles and the whip: 'Here see I slavery and mistress waiting for me. Now, ancient freedom of my fathers, fare thee well. Yea, harsh slavery is my lot – chains to hold me and Love that never slackens the wretched prisoner's bonds, and burns me whether I have deserved to suffer or have done no wrong. Ah, how I burn! Take the torch away, thou cruel girl' (Tib. 2.4.1–5).[20] Slavery as a metaphor for the experience of love in the Roman era draws on the reality of its slave society to explore ideas of passion and possession, giving the poet a prism through which to portray the powerlessness of an asymmetrical erotic attachment. For its poetic power the literary device relies on an awareness of the suffering of slaves as well as the humiliations of the institution as they were viewed from the perspective of the free man. Slavery and its punishments provided a readily understood frame of reference for expressing the suffering of love, the humiliation of complete submission to another, and the despair that can accompany such helplessness.

In attempting to explain the genesis of *servitium amoris*, literary critics have stressed its independence from Greek literary models, citing exclusively linguistic sources such as colloquial Latin, political rhetoric, or simply Roman poetic ingenuity, without giving much consideration to the reality of Rome's slave culture. Emulation by the elegiac poets, however, must have been inspired by the punitive nature of slavery itself, and by an appreciation of the physical, emotional, and psychological damage of the slave condition. The conceit depends upon the reader's willingness to enter into the imaginative realm of literature, ignoring the acknowledged harshness of slavery in order to be entertained by the harmless literary equivalent; without this mental stratagem, the poetic image has no force. In this respect, *servitium amoris* shares common ground with the 'Cupid Punished' motif, as artist and poet drew on the connection between punishment and slavery for their own diverse purposes, one in an exploration of erotic love, the other in a gentle parody of domestic life. In both language and image, slavery emerges as a cultural *koine* for suffering, which underlines the endemic nature of violence in Roman slavery and the acquiescence that permitted it.

Cupid's Appeal, or the Appeal of Cupids

The iconography of punishment in the 'Cupid Punished' imagery demonstrates what an ancient artist could expect of his audience in his effort to communicate notions of suffering. The appeal of the imagery, however, lies not in its realism but in its escapism, and in the ironic and playful rendering of punishment it delivered. As subject matter, 'Cupid Punished' belongs as much if not more to the domestic realm than to the mythological, and to the generic representations of putti that became a hallmark of Roman art. Best known from the painted miniatures from a reception room in the

House of the Vettii at Pompeii (e.g., fig. 6.10), putti are found in all artistic media and in contexts as diverse as marginal ornamentation on household objects to funerary commemoration on finely carved sarcophagi. Whether it is goldsmithing (fig. 6.10), perfume or cloth production, vintaging in the fields, chariot racing with birds instead of horses, or even gladiatorial combat, human affairs, and labour above all, become light entertainment when performed by putti. As Helmut Sichtermann has argued, the popularity of the genre has little to do with myth but rather reflects an interest in children, and with the representation of the adult world through children. While the putto's divine pedigree sets the scenes in a supernatural context, it is the incongruity of childlike figures engaged in adult pastimes that elicits a comic response and gives the imagery its winsomeness. Domestic life is explored indirectly, with putti as surrogates performing actions that have no relationship either to myth or to childhood. In this parallel universe populated with creatures simultaneously childlike and divine who mimic human endeavours, mundane or disagreeable activities are suffused with a rosy glow that enlivens the drabness of daily life or blunts the dangers of the arena.[21]

It is in this imaginative context, where the dull and familiar are rendered exotic and playful and where irony and parody flourish, that lies much of the appeal of the 'Cupid Punished' motif. Its charm depends upon the unexpected and the contradictory, where the punishments of slavery (an aspect of the quotidian, after all) are transformed into droll amusement. There is the incongruity of the image – the soft child's body burdened with chains (as if the god were a slave!), lying only loosely on his tender form, unlike real bonds (as if fetters could really bind him!); his ornate coiffure so different from the shaven heads characteristic of the chain gang; his demure, somewhat feigned contrition a far cry from real suffering. Underpinning the playful tone of the chastisement is the assumption that the boy is incorrigible, that he will err again, and that his mother Venus will once more be forced to play disciplinarian; such is the nature of his impish disposition. In this sentimentalized version of slave punishment can be heard echoes of conventional attitudes to the predictable misbehaviour of real slaves and the appropriate punitive response of their masters.[22] A positive version of the negative slave stereotype, the persona of 'Cupid Punished' is errant by nature, driven to aim his arrows hither, thither, and yon in a perpetual cycle of transgression and momentary penance. Much like a slave, deemed criminous by nature in Roman thought, Cupid is never properly rehabilitated, and much like a slave he needs repeated discipline to correct his inborn tendencies to bad behaviour. In the representation of 'Cupid Punished' we can also see the conflation of Roman attitudes towards children and slaves; to the latter were attributed many of the negative characteristics of childhood – mischief, deceit, wilfulness – even as adults. In the mosaics from Utica and Thina, Venus supervises the flogging of Cupid much as any *domina* might have punished a slave, even wielding a tree branch as a weapon herself; yet the mythological setting softens the pain of a real beating.[23] In the Pompeian fresco, Cupid's contrition is met with benign maternal disapproval, suggesting only a benevolent reprimand, and on the Borghese and Pitti statues he rubs tears from one eye while watching with the other for his mother's response, as if measuring the success of his pretence of remorse. Comically enchained, guilefully penitent and subdued, 'Cupid Punished' represents a transmutation of the suffering inflicted on slaves, which here is reduced and turned into a piece of visual whimsy.

The phenomenon of *deliciae,* favoured slave children who held a special place among slaves in the Roman household, emerges as another potentially relevant element in the backdrop to this imagery.[24] *Deliciae* were a form of luxury goods, specially selected child slaves often from Alexandria (or advertised as such) who were bought and kept by the elite as a kind of pet.[25] Chosen for their beauty and trained by slave dealers in a precocious talkativeness, *deliciae* were brought out at banquets, perhaps occasionally naked as the sources assert, to shock and titillate guests with their saucy chatter.[26] Resembling medieval court jesters, they broke social codes with their impertinence in a controlled manner, only with their master's indulgence, and to serve his purposes. As Seneca explains, permission to speak so boldly was not a sign of social power, but of social inferiority: 'The waggery of slaves, insulting to their masters, amuses us, and their boldness at the expense of guests has license only because they begin with their master himself; … For this purpose some people buy young slaves because they are pert, and they whet their impudence and keep them under an instructor in order that they may become practised in pouring forth streams of abuse; and yet we call this smartness, not insult' (Sen. *De Constantia* 11.2–3).[27] It is possible that the elite predilection for *deliciae* was part of the appeal of 'Cupid Punished,' and that the imagery embodied the positive associations of wealth and power that accompanied the possession of amusing child slaves.[28] We might therefore see in the enchained Cupids of the Borghese and Pitti palaces (figs. 6.1 and 6.2), as well as in the fountain statues of bound and penitent boys in Vettii peristyle at Pompeii (fig. 6.4), allusions in sculptural form to the real *deliciae* of elite households. On Roman sarcophagi with banqueting scenes putti are commonly used as ornamentation, bearing garlands, frolicking around the dining couch, or even seated on it alongside the deceased. Generic depictions of carefree, naked young children, winged or not, in some cases seem to have been interchangeable, for the inconsistent appearance of wings on such decoration blurs the boundary between putto and *deliciae*, between the idealized mythological associations of erotes and the more aspirational and status-conscious message typical of funerary commemoration.[29]

Given the sexual undertone that suffuses much of the textual evidence for *deliciae*, carnal pleasures must be acknowledged as a possible aspect of the appeal of representations of young children. Sexual abuse by masters of slaves, including slave children, was not only permissible but regarded as normal in the Roman era, and while political invective might explain the most outrageous anecdotes involving emperors, the frequency with which *deliciae* are referred to in amatory terms in the sources reflects the commonplace nature of the sexual exploitation of slave children if it suited the master's tastes.[30] The term *deliciae* is elastic enough to refer both to very young children (*infantes*) as well as to adolescents (*pueri*). Glaucias, the male favourite of Atedius Melior, whom Statius laments in *Silvae* 2.1 in highly erotic terms, died at the age of twelve; Martial's female *deliciae* Erotion, who was five years old at the time of her death, is gently mourned in 5.34, but in 5.37 her beauty is described at length in the same terms as any *puella* of love elegy. The poem turns on a humorous comparison between Martial's grief for his *deliciae*, expressed in mock-epic and somewhat detached terms, and Paetus's grief for his well-born, wealthy wife, whose death has made him rich. As Patricia Watson argues, the amatory literary allusions, however parodic in context, reflect the normalcy of sexual relations between master and slave, even a very young slave.[31] The sexual abuse of freeborn children was denounced, but when it came to slaves, social taboos were regularly broken: just as *deliciae* were encouraged to break the rules of proper behaviour with clever chatter in ways that were censured in freeborn offspring, slavery enabled the breaking of social norms and made slave children potential targets for abuse.

Homoerotic relationships between master and pubescent male *deliciae*, such as those commemorated in Statius and Martial, are well documented, and attest to the potential advantages of willing submission to a slave owner's sexual advances.[32] The age range of the body types covered by the 'Cupid Punished' genre fit the profile of *deliciae*, from the young child of the complete statues in Rome and Florence (figs. 6.1 and 6.2) to the idealized adolescent form exemplified by the Vatican torsos (fig. 6.3). Moreover, in the elaborate hairstyles sported by the 'Cupid Punished' statues in particular there is the potential resonance of the ornate locks worn by *deliciae*. John Pollini recognizes the typical hairstyle of the *puer delicatus* in shoulder-length locks that lie on the neck, conspicuous spit curls by the ears, and a bouffant at the front with stylized curls at the brow. In apparent contrast, the hairstyles of the young putti in the 'Cupid Punished' statuary include both the

'Melonenfrisur,' a crimped style bound back with a hairband (figs. 6.1 and 6.2), and the 'Scheitelzopffrisur,' a style characterized by a double braid fixed at the top of the head that is commonly found on putti and portraits of real children in the Hellenistic and Roman periods. The iconographic type identified by Pollini fits the adolescent *delicati* who were featured slaves at Roman *convivia*, but Philo's detailed description of banquet slaves suggests that, in real life, a wider range of coiffures was met, including hair that was 'plaited and bound up,' perhaps reflecting distinctions in hairstyle that were dictated by age difference.[33] It is possible, therefore, that there was an erotic dimension to the genre of 'Cupid Punished,' an element that was overt in the case of the beautiful youths who follow the Greek sculptural tradition but was perhaps also implicit in the younger versions because of the association with slavery for which I am arguing. This is not to imply that images of young naked children were intended to be viewed in the first instance as erotic (although they might have been so viewed by an individual viewer). Rather, I am suggesting that, in itself, the very potential for sexual satisfaction that *deliciae* represented was part of the social power conferred by slavery on the slave owner; consequently, imagery that can be related to *deliciae*, such as 'Cupid Punished,' carried with it culturally ingrained connotations of self-indulgence and an enviable hedonism. Slave ownership bestowed the licence, whether exercised or not, to satisfy every unbridled appetite; *deliciae*, like all luxury goods, were reflections of that power and the forbidden pleasures it afforded the slave owner, by opportunity and by law.[34]

Winged Love: The Cupid-Seller

A final connection between Cupid and slavery is derived from comparisons of the winged god with a bird, and then, by extension, a fugitive slave. The advantages of flight are a frequent theme in Hellenistic epigrams, but the idea was explored in its fullest literary form in two epigrams of Meleager (first century BCE). In epigram 5.177, Meleager reworks Moschus's conceit of Eros as winged escapee, while in its companion piece (5.178) the poet describes Eros as an evil changeling who deserves to be sold to the next trader who comes along.[35] Much like 'Cupid Punished,' in the Roman version of this conceit the Hellenistic model is adopted, then adapted for the Roman context. In visual terms, the portrayal of Cupids as creatures who could be bought and sold, and who might escape if care was not taken to control them, is explored in the genre scene known as the Cupid-seller. While winged Eros in Hellenistic epigrams escapes with ease, in the Roman construction the winged fugitive is granted much less liberty and is portrayed as securely domesticated, although requiring supervision. Of little advantage to him, his wings are reduced to ironic appendages useful as much for capture as for flight. In a painting from a *cubiculum* in the Villa Arianna at Stabia (fig. 6.11), a female peddler holds out by the wings a putto she has pulled out from a cage, offering it to two potential female buyers, one seated, one standing. A second putto waits in the cage, crouched in discomfort, while a third stands by the knee of the seated figure, looking up at her expectantly. The scene presents an ironic allegory of romanticized feminine desire, as the buyers contemplate which of the putti to purchase and which love suits their tastes. In reality a matter beyond human control, love is portrayed in idealized terms as readily available for sale as a slave, with as much choice open to the buyer as a slave dealer in the slave market might offer. In the irony that lies behind the scene, we glimpse the wry realization that love is not so simple, nor are suitable slaves, so tractable and subjugated, so easily found.[36]

The motif of the Cupid-seller from Stabia was taken up in the eighteenth and nineteenth centuries, where it appeared in paintings, on decorative porcelain, and as ornamentation on domestic objects used by women such as fans.[37] The most famous adaptation of the scene is the painting called 'The Cupid-Seller,' painted by Joseph-Marie Vien in 1763 (fig. 6.12), another neoclassical homage to an idealized ancient Rome.[38] As was customary in reworked versions of ancient art, Vien updated the background, furnishings, and garments, but several other seemingly minor departures from the original were presumably made to suit contemporary social sensibilities. In addition to making the middle-aged peddler a comely young girl, Vien has changed the receptacle in which the putti are carried from the cage of the Stabian scene into a basket. Moreover, in the Campanian original the putto who waits in the cage sits in discomfort, his arms tied behind his back, while in Vien's rendering the other putti nap contentedly in the basket, unguarded and unthreatening. The modifications in this version put into sharp relief the differences between the ancient and the modern artists' expectations of their viewers. In both periods, this is a fantasy genre scene, a flight of imagination designed to delight and amuse. But Vien's decision to change the cage to a basket in 'The Cupid Seller' indicates an attempt to soften the ancient image in order to create an atmosphere of cozy domesticity for the eighteenth-century viewer, with the putti portrayed as something akin to sleepy, nestling kittens, rather than unwilling captives who must be contained lest they escape.

Vien, however, did recognize the power of the cage as a symbol of captivity. In another painting of his, a mock romance entitled 'Love escaping slavery,' a putto flies away from a circular cage of the same type as shown on the Stabian original; the idea of love unbound is heightened by the presence of the cage, which signals his imprisonment and the potential chaos of passions his freedom brings.[39] The basket of Vien's Cupid-seller would have made little sense to a Roman viewer, however, for whom bound and caged putti were closer to the reality of the slave market than a basket of happily sleeping creatures. Unlike the eighteenth-century interpretation, in the Roman allegory the caging of the putti does not violate at all the playful tone of the scene but in fact gives the scene its meaning.

Another ancient version of this motif exists now only in an nineteenth-century drawing of a lost wall painting from the House of the Coloured Capitals (VII.4.31/51) at Pompeii (fig. 6.13), in which a bearded male vendor pulls a Cupid out of a rectangular cage, having removed the lid, while two other putti crouch together inside in cramped confinement. A woman standing nearby dreamily gazes at a flying putto bearing garlands, while to her lower left, another putto, apparently a fugitive from the Cupid-seller, hides behind her robe. The small colonnade indicates that this is the home of the buyer, who is depicted as a refined, well-dressed *matrona*, perhaps to whom the peddler has come by arrangement. A scene of Venus and Adonis accompanied by two winged putti was found in the same room (an exedra off the peristyle), perhaps reflecting a romantic decorative theme similar to that in the House of Cupid Punished.[40] In the Stabian panel the buyer is accompanied by her sister (or perhaps her personal servile maid), and the setting might be either her own residence or, as suggested by the drapery, a discreet stall in a public slave market that has been closed off to give privacy for such special purchases. Both scenes present an idealized, genteel portrayal of the transaction, the putti on offer controlled by their handler, who advises on the selection.

The motif occurs again in a mosaic in the House of the Peddler of Erotes at Antioch-on-the-Orontes (fig. 6.14), dated to the late second or early third century AD, where, however, it is inserted into a different point in the plot. Rather than showing the point of sale, the Antioch mosaic depicts an earlier moment in the commerce of Cupids, that is, the harvesting of putti by the peddler. A collage of staple imagery set in an exotic landscape portrays a group of happy-go-lucky putti fishing, cheering on a cockfight, sleeping, and wielding a bow, juxtaposed with the motif of the aged Cupid-seller, the threatening interloper in their paradise. The elements of the scene are the same as in the Campanian examples – the peddler, the cage, one putto held, another imprisoned – but in this configuration the Cupid-seller has become the Cupid-catcher, seizing putti from their native free state and caging them for sale; one Cupid caught in the Cupid-catcher's grasp is destined to join his comrade, who sits in the cage, already apprehended and subdued.[41] Relying upon the viewer's knowledge of the capture and transport of real slaves to give coherence and meaning to the fragmented motives, the fictive narrative of 'Love for Sale' in the Antioch pavement presents a playful rendering of the moment of enslavement itself. In evoking a blissful, carefree existence for the Cupids before captivity, the scene implies a recognition of the misery of servitude and the arbitrary reversal of fortune it represented, while simultaneously portraying that definitive moment in comic terms. Through the Cupid-seller and Cupid-catcher motives the conceit of the purchase of Love was easily conveyed to an audience for whom the sale of human beings was an utterly normal part of daily life and therefore easy fodder for fanciful artistic parody.

Conclusion

Slavery furnished a universally understood framework through which to examine and to express ideas of punishment and subjugation and the feelings of power and powerlessness, captivity and liberation that accompany love, in the form of a mischievous, wild child. In domesticating slavery's atrocities, both the 'Cupid Punished' and the Cupid-seller imagery also mitigates them, offering up a version of the institution that reflects the values of the dominant, slave-owning culture. Roman literature provides its own version of the intimate connection between slavery and suffering in the elegiac topos of *servitium amoris* and the punitive discourse that permeates Roman comedy. Representations of slavery's hardships in artistic and literary form reveal the profound influence the institution had on the Roman imagination, but they are also indicative of the ways in which even the most brutal aspects of slavery were commonplace. Moreover, the adoption of slavery in Roman art and literature to express the concept of punishment and to convey emotional distress reveals an acknowledgment of the slave's suffering, while the light-hearted nature of that treatment in text and image suggests a mentality inured to this suffering through long-standing social conditioning. In this appropriation of the cruelties of slave punishment, we can glimpse yet again the Roman habituation to physical brutality, part of what Keith Hopkins called the 'commitment to cruelty,' which characterized Roman culture and which particularly marked master/slave relations.[42]

In focusing on this minor artistic motif and its variants, I have tried to show that Roman art provides another dimension of human experience from which we can glean a more nuanced view of Roman slavery. From the public and monumental to the private and decorative, Rome's visual culture demonstrates the extent to which slavery was embedded in the Roman mindset in ways that conventional historical sources, such as the occasional comment of Cicero or the declarations of juridical texts, do not. Images such as 'Cupid Punished' lead us into what Tonio Hölscher has called the 'autonomous world of visual experience,' a meaningful and essential aspect of Roman life that we can ill afford to ignore. Far from being mere illustration, imagery must be understood as a product, and therefore a representation, of the Roman cultural imagination; as such, it presents a rich, and as yet largely untapped, source for slavery studies.[43]

NOTES

For help with the illustrations, I would like to thank Katherine Dunbabin, Shari T. Kenfield, Curator, Research Photographs, Department of Art & Archaeology, Princeton University, and Daria Lanzuolo, DAI Rome Fotothek. This chapter was written with the financial support of the Social Sciences and Humanities Research Council of Canada, which I acknowledge with gratitude.

1 Borghese statue: Curtius 1930; Moreno and Viacava 2003: 228–9 and fig. 215; see also *LIMC* 'Amor/Cupido' no. 78 (Blanc and Gury 1986); the statue is 72 cm high.

2 For the Greek motif of 'Eros punished,' see *LIMC* entry (by A. Hermary, H. Cassimatis, R. Vollkommer) vol. 3, 884–5, nos. 417–426, and *LIMC* supplement vol. 1 (by A. Hermary) 210 nos. 420–22 on Delian seals. See also Guzzo 1980 for 163 terracotta counters found at Cosenza in Italy with impressions of Eros bound, dated to the early third century BCE. Fugitive love: *AP* 9.444; see also Gutzwiller 2007: 96; *AP* 3.440 (Eros as runaway); 5.195–199 (statues of Eros with bound hands).

3 On the lack of a clear distinction in Roman art between Cupid, Venus's son in mythological narrative, and the more generic winged putto, see Stuveras 1969: 109–21 and passim; Sichtermann 1969: 268; Blanc and Gury 1986: 1042–9.

4 Pitti Palace example: Curtius 1930, who relates the statue type to an unknown lost Greek original; contra, however, see Sichtermann 1969: 280–1. See also Blanc and Gury 1986: no. 77. For another example of the same type, see Matz and Duhn 1881: no. 1155.

5 For the two Vatican torsos, which are dated to the Roman era, but no more specifically than that, see Lippold 1936: no. 29, pl. 58; no. 63, pl. 69. Terme torso (also identified as Roman, but assigned no other date): extant to 47 cm: D. Candilio (in Giuliano 1981: 340–1) identifies it only as a 'fanciullo' due to the absence of wings, but refers to nine other examples *in toto* (w. bibliography) once extant (including those in the Borghese, Terme, and Pitti Palace), all only partially preserved and dated only as 'Roman.' These include: the two Vatican torsos; one at the Palazzo Corsetti in Rome (DAIR inst. Neg. 67.85), which is distinct from the one described in Matz and Duhn (1881: no. 1155); one in the Palazzo Corsini at Prato; one in the Louvre (as cited by Reinach 1884); one from Baia, now in Naples. Blanc and Gury (1986), however, include the Terme torso in their *LIMC*

entry on Amor/Cupido (no. 79), referring to twelve known versions of this type. Moreno and Viacava (2003: 228–9) also cite an example in the Barracco Museum in Rome, which appears to be unpublished, presumably of the same child's body type as the Borghese statue.

6 Candilio (in Giuliano 1981: 341) hesitates to identify the Terme torso as Cupid due to the absence of wings, but cannot furnish another explanation ('rimane sempre più misterioso il significato di questa iconografia, forse legata ad un culto'). Blanc and Gury (1986), however, include it in their *LIMC* entry on Amor/Cupido (no. 79), and in their summary of the motif argue that Eros/Amor/Cupid is often depicted without wings (Blanc and Gury 1986: 1044). On Cupid without wings, see also Sichtermann 1969: 268 and Stuveras 1969: 168–70. On the tradition of the Eros of Praxiteles and its influence, see Ajootian 1996: 113–16; Pasquier and Martinez 2007: 26.

7 Vatican: Kaschnitz-Weinberg (1937: no. 364, pl. 38) identifies it as Cupid, because of the wings, but not specifically as Cupid Punished. Vettii statues: Sogliano (1898: col. 285) records that traces of yellow paint were found on their hair; Jashemski 1993: 153–5, fig. 172, 173; V. Sampaolo (in Pugliese Carratelli 1990–2003: vol. 5, 524–5, fig. 84, 102, 103) identifies them as 'due bambini'; Mau (*RM* 11 [1896]: 37, considering them the least attractive pieces in the Vettii garden's sculptural ensemble, gives them short shrift and calls them 'fanciulli ..., l'espressione del viso è stupida, un po' sorridente.' Elaborate hairstyle on erotes/putti: Trillmich 1976: 46–7 and n. 160.

8 Casa di Amore Punito (VII 2, 23). Blanc and Gury 1986: 968, no. 81; V. Sampaolo (in Pugliese Carratelli 1990–2003: vol. 6: 665–78, fig. 14) identifies the woman on the left as Peitho, rather than Nemesis; Simon (2000) identifies Anteros as Psyche, despite the absence of the usual butterfly wings. There is a similar motif on a household lamp, where chains on the legs are visible: Blanc and Gury 1986: no. 80. As a comparandum, Herrmann (1904–50: 6, fig. 1) provides a drawing of a woman (Venus?) with one putto at her shoulder and another at her feet, hoe in left hand, right hand to his eyes as if weeping, and fetters on both his ankles (but no chains on his legs). It is described as having been found after the painting in the House of Cupid Punished and in the possession of the German Archaeological Institute. No reference is given, however, and it is otherwise unattested in the subsequent literature, suggesting that it might in fact be an artistic variation inspired by a nineteenth-century visitor to the site, rather than another ancient example of the theme.

9 Blanc and Gury 1986: 967, nos. 68–70, 74, 75; similar composition on statuettes of Roman date: nos. 71–3, 76; Henig 1994: 297.

10 Both fig. 6.5 and 6.6 are dated 50 BCE–50 CE, fig. 6.7 is dated to the second half of the first century BCE. Cupid with a hoe: cast of a gem no longer extent, in the Hanover Museum: Blanc and Gury 1986: no. 84; see also nos. 82, 83 with more bibliography: Zwierlein-Diehl 1969: vol. 2, no. 449 (in Berlin), with

bibliography and more examples; Zwierlein-Diehl 1986: nos. 212, 213, with bibliography and more examples; Sena Chiesa 1960: nos. 287, 288 (Aquileia); Henig 1978: no. 134; Spier 1992: nos. 319, 320. Cupid and Psyche: Blanc and Gury 1986: no. 84.

11 Cupid as captive under trophy: Blanc and Gury 1986: nos. 292 and 293; the latter is dated to the Roman era by Furtwängler and Vollenweider (Furtwängler 1965: p. 49, 27; Vollenweider 1966: 41, n.17, and 104, pl. 33.1, 2, and 4). For *LIMC* no. 292, see Zwierlein-Diehl 1969: vol. 2 no. 593, pl. 6. Psyche bound beneath a trophy: Zwierlein-Diehl 1986: no. 204.

12 Volubilis: Blanc and Gury 1996: no. 66; Lancha 1983: 387–8 fig. 7, 8. See also Dunbabin 1978: 86–7 and n. 99, for a Gallic medallion with the punishment of Cupid for being an *incendiarius*: on the upper register, a tribunal condemns Cupid; on the lower register he is led to be tortured; on the middle register, he is tied to a stake on the *catasta* of the arena, while two doves are set free from a cage (Wuilleumier and Audin 1952: no. 40, pl. III). Thina: Blanc and Gury 1996: no. 65; Dunbabin 1978: 273, no. 7 (a). Utica: Blanc and Gury 1996: no. 64; Dunbabin 1978: 276 no. 4 (ii).

13 Ausonius 8 (see Fauth 1974); Blanc and Gury (1996: no. 87) include this in their *LIMC* entry. To judge from Philostratus, literary descriptions of putti as they were portrayed in art were favourite exercises in rhetorical training and are congruent with the genre of putti in painting and mosaic (*Imagines* 1.6, 1.9, 1.16).

14 Natural slavery: Garnsey 1996: 105–27. Generally on corporal punishment of slaves, see Garnsey 1970: 126–52; Hopkins 1978: 118–23; Robinson 1981: 227–33; Bradley 1987: 113–37, 139–41; Bradley 1994: 28–9, 165–70; Saller 1994: 133–53. Re: hired contractors for punishing slaves, see the famous Puteoli inscription, *AE* 1971, no. 88 (translated in Gardner and Wiedemann 1991: 24–7).

15 Millar 1984: 131–2. Cf. Pliny the Elder's famous lament that farming was now the purview of slave chain gangs (*vincti pedes*) rather than of senators (*Nat. Hist.* 18, 21), or Apuleius's famous description of workers in a mill, probably slaves, and some with shackled feet (*pedes annulati, Met.* 9, 12).

16 Whips and chains: Saller 1994: 138. Ulpian, *Dig.* IV, 6, 10 (as cited in Millar 1984: 132): 'For we have defined those as being *in vinculis* who are bound in such a way that they cannot appear in public without indignity (*sine dedecore*).' Flogging: see Saller 1994: 134–9, citing Aulus Gellius's account (10.3.17) of a speech by Cato on the public whipping of decemvirs: 'Quis hanc contumeliam, quis hoc imperium, quis hanc servitutem ferre potest?' (Who could endure such an insult, such tyranny, such slavery?). Whips versus *fustes: Dig.* XLVIII, 19, 10; see Millar 1984: 128–29; public flogging: Wiseman 1985: 5–10, nn. 17, 18.

17 *Lex Petronia: Dig.* 48.8.11.2; Garnsey 1970: 129–31; Coleman 1990: 54–7; Bradley 1987: 127.

18 Slavery and Latin literature: Fitzgerald 2000. Roman comedy: Segal 1968: 136–69 remains the most focused treatment of physical punishment in Plautus; see also Saller 1994: 148; McCarthy 2000. Plaut. *Asin.* 549–51, which Segal translates to great effect (Segal 1968: 145).

19 For *servitium amoris*, see Copley 1947, Lilja 1965: 76–89; Lyne 1979; Murgatroyd 1981; James 2003: 145–50.

20 Trans. J.P. Postgate, Loeb edition. See also, e.g., Tib. 2.3.80: 'Take me away; I will plough the fields at a mistress' command. / From chains and stripes my body shall not shrink.' For more citations from elegy, see Murgatroyd 1981.

21 Putti generally: Stuveras 1969; as escapist: Muth 1998: 328–36. Putti in the House of the Vettii: Clarke 2003: 98–105; scenes of work romanticized through putti: de Angelis 2011. Connection with children: Sichtermann 1969: passim, but especially 280–92.

22 Hopkins 1978: 121; Bradley 1984: 26–9.

23 Irony: Curtius 1930: 61. For innate character flaws that were shared by children, slaves, women, and barbarians, see Dauge 1981: 494–500, 609. *Domina*: Juv. *Sat.* 6. 219–23, 474–93. Blanc and Gury (1996: no. 66) tie this imagery to school-room beatings, despite the absence of a pedagogue to inflict them.

24 The word was also used of household pets, but the most common usage refers to a particular group of child slaves. On *deliciae* generally, including related terminology (e.g., *delicium, -a, delicatus*) in different contexts, see Slater 1974; Nielsen 1990; Laes 2003, 2011: 222–68.

25 Slave market: Varro, cited in Nonius Marcellus 141.13, refers to a special-ized slave market at Capua for *deliciae*: 'Si venisses Capuam, quod et pueros minute vides libenter et/maiores animadvertere non vis (multos vidisses?)'; see Dahlmann 1950.

26 *Deliciae* as luxury good: *Dig.* 40. 2, 16; Laes 2003: 300–4; 2010: 269; Rawson 2003: 261–3. Anecdotes involving emperors are especially common, e.g., Augustus, who played children's games with *pueri minuti*, preferring the most beautiful and loquacious (*facie et garrulitate amabilis*), especially Syrians and Moors (Suet. *Aug.* 83), or Domitian's *puerulus coccinatus* (little boy dressed in red), with his abnormally small head (Suet. *Dom.* 4.2); see also Cassius Dio 48.44.3 (Augustus); 67.15 (Domitian); Commodus: Herodian 1.17; on these and others, see Slater 1974; Laes 2003. Chatter: Statius *Silv.* 2.2.72–75; 5.5.66–69.

27 Loeb translation, J. W. Basore, 1928. See also Quint. *Inst. Or.* 1. 2,7, in which he decries the freeborn child who is permitted to speak inappropriately (*licentius*) in ways that would not be tolerated even by an Alexandrian *deliciae*. *Deliciae* as court jester, see Nielsen 1990: 79; Laes 2003: 316–17.

28 Cf. the young children, probably slaves, who played the role of putti in Cleopatra's attempt to seduce Antony by reclining like a painted Venus, flanked and fanned by boys 'like Loves in paintings' (Plut. *Vita Ant.* 26); see Apuleius

(*Met.* 10. 32) for a tableau of Venus with a cadre of little children serving as putti in a theatrical setting; Slater 1974: 135, on the possible reflexive relationship between art and ownership of *deliciae*. In poetry, the troupe of small boys (*pueri minuta turba*), using Cupid's weapons of torch, arrow, and chains, who seize the drunken poet/lover Propertius on Cynthia's behalf, thus making her a veritable Venus with a band of erotes at her command (Propertius 2.29; Slater 1974: 136–7); see also the *garrulus verna* (chatty house-born child slave) on the lap of Tibullus's Delia (1 5.26).

29 Sarcophagi, see Amedick (1991: 19–22), who argues that erotes and *deliciae* are indistinguishable in these scenes and serve the same function, i.e., as figurative allusions to wealth and happiness. See Lenski in this volume for anthropomorphic *lychnouchoi* (lamp bearers) and tray bearers which imitate real slaves.

30 Abuse: Kolendo 1981; Bradley 1994: 28, 49; Finley 1998: 163–4 and Shaw introduction in Finley 1998: 46–7; Williams 1999: 30–8; Laes 2003: 317–320. Emperors, e.g., Tiberius's *pisciculi* (Suet. *Tib.* 44); political invective: Laes 2003: 301–2. Cf. Sen. *Contr.* 4, pr. 10: 'impudicitia in ingenuo crimen est, in servo necessitas, in liberto officium' ('Losing one's virtue is a crime in the freeborn, a necessity in the slave, a duty for the freedman' Loeb translation, M. Winterbottom, 1974).

31 *Deliciae* in Statius and Martial, see Asso 2010; Laes 2010. In Statius *Silv.* 2.1, Glaucias is referred to both as *delicatus* and *deliciae*; as well as a *verna*, a houseborn slave whom Melior freed as an infant and raised as an *alumnus* (foster child); on the ambiguities of his status, see Asso 2010, who argues for a homoerotic relationship between Glaucias and Melior, which is presented as parental/filial in a nod to social convention. Erotion: *Ep.* 5.34, 5. 37, 10 61; see Watson 1992, esp. 258–63. See also Rawson, 'The line between indulgent affection and sexual exploitation must have been blurred' (2003: 261–2).

32 E.g., the eventual liberation of the fictional Trimalchio, a *deliciae* to his former master and mistress: Petr. *Sat.* 76; for Trimalchio's own *deliciae* Croesus, described mockingly as bleary-eyed and with discoloured teeth, see *Sat.* 28 and 64. Homoerotic: Williams 1999: 17–19, 30–7; Laes 2003: 301–2, 317–20. In art, e.g., the Warren cup: Clarke 1998: 59–90; Pollini 2003; see also Marabini Moevs 2008, who argues that the Warren cup is a forgery.

33 Philo, *De Vita Contemplativa* 50: καὶ τὰς τῆς κεφαλῆς τρίχας εὖ πως διαπλέκονται σφηκούμενοι; for the 'Scheitelzopffrisur' on putti and children, see Trillmich 1976, with further bibliography. Hairstyles of *pueri delicati*: Pollini 1999; 2003.

34 Such abuse might not necessarily have included intercourse, although it cannot be ruled out. See Néraudau (1984: 351–68); Watson: 'All slaves in this position were sexual playthings, whether potential or actual' (1992: 261). Pederasty

generally: Williams 1999: 63–77; fear of sexual abuse by male slave childminders (*paedagogi*): Bradley 1991: 53–4; Rawson 2003: 160.

35 Eros / erotes as birds: Anacreon's poetic image of a nest of Loves (fr. 25) has an incarnation in Roman art in Pompeian wall painting, in sculpture fragments, and one gem (Blanc and Gury 1986: nos. 48–53; Micheli 1992), and enjoyed a revival in the eighteenth and nineteenth centuries (Ascione 2001). Moschus (second century BCE) describes Eros as a fugitive who, like a bird, alights on his unknowing victims (Moschus *AP* 9.440 16–17).

36 Villa Arianna: Allroggen-Bedel 1977: 37; Adamo Muscettola 1980; Blanc and Gury 1986: 964–5; Micheli 1992; Mastroroberto (2001: 124) notes that in the adjoining room of similar size (W26), also called a *cubiculum*, were found the four famous panels of female figures that included Flora, Medea, Diana, and Leda, leading her to suggest that the decoration of this part of the villa reflects use by women above all. The scene of the Cupid-seller also appears on a Roman gem, now in Vienna: Zwierlein-Diehl 1973: vol. 1, no. 200.

37 Eighteenth- and nineteenth-century reception of scene: Kimball 1953; Micheli 1992; Ascione 2001; Mühlenbrock and Richter. 2004: 334–5. The motif was also celebrated by Goethe in his poem 'Wer kauft Liebesgötter?'

38 1763, Musée National du Château, Fontainebleau; see Rosenblum 1969: 3–10.

39 Rosenblum 1969: 19–20. There are two versions of this painting by Vien, one in the Musée des Augustins in Toulouse and the other in the Princeton Museum of Art; in the former, the cage is empty, in the latter, another putto watches his comrade flee through the cage's bars.

40 Coloured Capitals: Birt 1919: 157–60 (who first made the connection between the Cupid-seller motif and a real slave market); J.-P. Descoeudres in Pugliese Carratelli 1990–2003: vol. 6, pt. 1: 1031–44, figs. 52–3; Venus and Adonis, fig. 60; Bragantini in Pugliese Carratelli 1995: 200–2, figs 84–6.

41 Antioch mosaic: Levi 1947: 191–5, pl. XLIII a; Cimok 2000: 172–3. See also two Roman cameos in Naples, on which Venus holds a receptacle (a basket?) containing a captured putto, while two attendants try to catch two other runaways, one in mid-flight and another in a tree (Richter 1971: nos. 144 and 145).

42 Hopkins 1983: 29.

43 Hölscher 2003: 2. For a valuable survey of recent developments in the role of visual culture within ancient culture, see Smith 2002, and Elsner's introduction to the English translation of Hölscher 1987; for slavery in visual culture, see Kolendo 1979; Schumacher 2001; George 2009. For visual evidence as 'illustration,' see Scheidel 2003: 581.

7

Slaves and *Liberti* in the Roman Army

†NATALIE BOYMEL KAMPEN

Introduction

The stela of Marcus Caelius, a soldier in the Eighteenth Legion of the Roman army (fig. 7.1), is especially famous because the inscription tells us that he died in the Varian wars in Germany in 9–10 CE. A substantial literature debates the precise meaning of the inscription that reads: 'Marcus Caelius, the son of Titus, a member of the Lemonia tribe from the city of Bologna. He served as [first centurion] or [in the first cohort] of the Eighteenth Legion. He was fifty-three years old and was killed in the Varian wars. It is permitted that the bones [of his freedmen or his bones] be buried. Publius Caelius, son of Titus and member of the Lemonia tribe, Marcus's brother, made (this monument).'[1] Discussion of the vagaries of the inscription follows shortly, but for now, it is important to note how little interest scholars have shown in the extraordinary and perhaps unprecedented image above the inscription. Perhaps one should have expected this general neglect of the two portrait busts on bases flanking the image of the soldier, the first and only time, to my knowledge, that such a combination had occurred in Roman art. Given that much of the scholarship on provincial Roman tombstones has been devoted to their physical and thematic typology, their workshops and their relation to specific historical questions such as whether this monument was a tombstone or a cenotaph marker for Caelius, the actual composition seems to have fallen between the two stools of traditional historical and art historical scholarship. The busts of the *liberti* Thiaminus and Privatus have inscriptions that provide their names and their legal status, and yet the discussion has focused mainly on whether these men died with Caelius in the field or were alive when the monument was made.[2] The possibilities for understanding more about the patronage and social relations behind the stela are still unclear because of the rarity of work in this area. My paper attempts to open up the discussion a bit further, and in the process, to explore the visual connections between owners or patrons and their slaves and *liberti* in the context of the Roman army.[3]

This essay focuses on the Roman army specifically along the northern frontier to ask how we can use military stelae and the physical remains of the military fortresses and camps to think about social and artistic relationships. Of particular interest are the relationships between slaves, freedmen, and soldiers who were actively serving in the military when they died. Veterans will not be discussed specifically because one cannot tell from their monuments whether the slaves and *liberti* mentioned on them were acquired before or after their retirement. Thus an example from Pisidian Antioch names a veteran of the Fifth Legion Gallica whose stela was erected by a freedman named Urbanus and a woman named Vivia, while a Flavian stela from Pannonia tells us that a veteran of the Fifteenth Legion Apollinaris, who came originally from Milan, and his wife were commemorated by their freedman L. Naevius Silvanus. We get no information about the *liberti* and their history with the deceased.[4] The choice of geographical region has more to do with the current availability of the evidence than with its actual occurrence. Excavation of military sites has been particularly good, as has publication of military sculpture, in Britain, Germany, Austria, and Hungary, with material readily available in the ever-growing set of volumes of the *Corpus Signorum Imperii Romani* (The corpus of Roman imperial sculpture) and online on the Austrian website Ubi Erat Lupa.[5] Although the Danube stelae are more plentiful in the second and third centuries than in the first and the camps of Britain more visible in the second century than earlier, the essay concentrates on material from the first century CE, in order to understand the context of the Caelius stela as the earliest known example of a soldier represented with his *liberti*.[6]

The hypothesis here is that slaves and *liberti* were present in the military camps in a variety of roles, some of which created a degree of intimacy between them and their masters or patrons. They might be grooms and baggage handlers, fire stokers and craftsmen, personal servants and even children's attendants.[7] Nevertheless, it was extremely unusual for them to be represented or named on the tombstones of their masters or patrons even though they are sometimes revealed as the heirs of those men and the people who set up the tombstones for them.[8] The divide between personal servants and other enslaved workers may have played a major role in who was manumitted, who made an heir, who depicted on a tombstone. Certainly, the humans who wore the chains found in camps such as that of Novaesium (Neuss, Germany) were hardly the ones to be named or shown on stelae.[9] As we will see, the evidence is neither plentiful nor clear and often speaks more from silence than from sound, but sometimes the silence forms a useful pattern.

The Portraits

To return to the Caelius stela for a closer look at it and its inscriptions, it seems useful to describe it before dealing with its context, particularly because the description can set up the conditions for a discussion of iconographies of military slavery, and this in turn can help us to understand more of the artistic and social setting. The most striking element of the limestone stela is of course Caelius in his elaborately ornamented breastplate, his baton or *vitis* crossing from his space in the recessed *aedicula* down in front of the inscription. His head rises before the entablature, the triangular pediment with its floral motif above him. Two pilasters frame the space, and foliate motifs fill in above the gable and below the pilasters. On either side of the soldier, seen above the hips, are simple inscribed bases with heavy upper and lower mouldings. On each is a portrait head with the neck and clavicle area, each face looking inward slightly, oriented towards the frontal Caelius. The semiotics of power are obvious in these poses and positions.

The stela is more than three feet high and was not set into a grave structure.[10] This is of interest because the window or aedicular form was common for funerary reliefs in Rome and northern Italy in the later first century BCE and the early first century CE, when many were attached to the front of an enclosure or an architectural tomb monument; the individuals or families seem to stare out at passersby through a window, and the portrait of the frontal Caelius resembles that contemporary composition. The most familiar examples of the type can be found along Via Appia, as with the Tomb of the Rabirii.[11] This physical presentation, along with the use of half-length frontal portraiture and aedicular niches in northern Italy, led Hans Gabelmann to trace the ancestry of this kind of stela, and the workshop itself, to cities such as Milan, Aquileia, and even Bononia, from which Caelius and his brother came.[12] The discovery of the stela in the seventeenth century at the site of the military camp of Vetera suggests that it was part of a military necropolis, but no foot or base remains to indicate whether it once was set into the ground.[13] The lower left corner, including the beginning of the first four lines of the inscription, is broken off irregularly, but the rest of the stela is in fairly good condition except for some abrasion and loss of noses and chins consistent with falling or being placed face down.

The portrait of Caelius, like that of the *liberti*, renders him beardless and youthful, with short thick wavy hair on a broad cranium above protruding ears. The eyes are close-set on all three men, but Caelius is represented as having a broader face with less pronounced naso-labial lines. Each portrait is individualized, testimony to the fact that even the *liberti* are meant to be portraits. They, however, are without the glorious military costume that identifies Caelius and his rank.

Caelius wears a cuirass with flaps, *pteryges*, at the sleeves and skirt, with a tunic beneath and a *paludamentum* or cloak over the ensemble. In addition to his *vitis* or staff, he wears a *corona civica* on his head and *armillae* on his wrists. These attributes all attest to his having been honoured by the military, as do the decorations on the cuirass.[14] At the shoulders are two large torques or thick metal loops to which are attached lion-headed clips to hold the fabric of his cloak, and on his chest are five metal disks with relief ornament. These are the *phalerae*, normally nine in number but here fewer presumably because of the artist's sense of the relation between the space of the cuirass and the need for legibility. Two have visible heads with ivy crowns, perhaps Bacchic, and one is a *gorgoneion*; the fourth is a lion head, and the fifth is hidden by the soldier's arm. All these elements, the *dona militaria*, clearly were meant to stand as documents of the deceased's rank and status within the army, and they supplement the inscription in crucial ways.

The portraits of the *liberti* may have a similar function: they supplement the inscription to speak about the status of Caelius. But this is not the entire story. Certainly, the patron of the stela, Caelius's brother, felt that the *dona militaria* and the *liberti* portraits were both important for the stela and its representation of the deceased, since having *liberti* meant that Caelius had been a man of property. But several other issues are worth investigating, beyond this bit of status enhancement. First, the *liberti* are prominently shown and their portraits inscribed with their names; they appear specifically as portraits on bases and not as living men with bodies. The idea of their being alive at the time of the stela's production is founded exclusively on the reconstruction of the inscription's missing fourth line: OSSA / [] []NFERRE LICEBIT.[15] If we assume that the *ossa* are not those of Marcus Caelius, left on the battlefield, but rather those of the *liberti*, the bust portraits have to be taken as depicting living men. But if the inscription is not restored with *libertorum* inserted, then the *ossa* can be those of the deceased, the brother, or some other family members. In that case, the *liberti* appear in the pictorial field but go unmentioned in the inscription. They are thus important enough to depict but for unknown reasons find no place in the main body of the inscription. As it happens, we will see that this is by no means unusual in military stones, where *liberti* may be shown and not mentioned or mentioned and not shown. For the moment, it seems preferable to see the portraits of the *liberti* as representations of the dead, as is at least occasionally the case with portraits busts, and the inscription as referring to the bones of others.

A second point of interest in relation to the portraits of Thiaminus and Privatus is whether they were part of that extraordinary moment in 9–10 CE when Augustus permitted the military recruitment of slaves, who were immediately manumitted in order to serve.[16] And finally, since neither *liberti* nor slaves will ever again be represented in quite this way on a military tombstone, at least as far as the evidence tells us today, we need to ask what their exceptionality might mean.

The way the *liberti* are shown is unique for tombstones of soldiers although it is predictable for the commemorations of *liberti* themselves. Whether on contemporary stelae, grave reliefs, or funerary altars, *liberti* and their families in Rome occasionally had themselves depicted not only as half-length and full-length figures but as busts.[17] Older men routinely took up the old-fashioned style of the Republican *paterfamilias*, their faces lined and haggard as if with the burdens of a life of care and service, whereas younger men repeated the bony structure of their elders with fewer lines and a tendency to a more mask-like idealization. By the early first century CE this set of portrait conventions was common, although younger men and boys were increasingly shown with the short thick hair and broad cranium typical for portraits of the emperor Augustus and the youths of the imperial family. So the portraits of Caelius and his *liberti* are stylistically and iconographically related to contemporary modes in Rome as well as in northern Italy.

The use of bust portraits tended to suggest not only an honorific presentation but a funerary one. The bust comes into fashion on funerary monuments in Rome from the time of Augustus and grows more frequent in the later first and early second centuries, but it is seldom combined with a tall base as it is here.[18] Instead, it takes on a funerary connotation both from its regular use on monuments such as the tomb reliefs from Rome and the later statues of figures reclining on a couch (*kline*) and holding a sculpted bust, and because it appeared on statues of people such as the 'Barberini Patrician,' a *togatus* holding two busts, with portraits of their ancestors or family members.[19] And with the inscribed bases, clearly meant to show that these are statues, the portraits evoke honours rather than simple presence. As we can see, then, contrary to the conclusions of many scholars focused on the question of the relationship of Caelius and his *liberti* to the Varian wars, the *liberti* shown here may already be dead, although whether they died with Caelius cannot be known from the imagery.

Slaves in the Army

Nor can we know for sure the circumstances of Thiaminus and Privatus's enslavement or their manumission, but it is certainly useful to propose a few suggestions, especially since the historical moment when the stela was made was unusual in apparently allowing slaves and *liberti* entry into the military. Although there is evidence for the use of slaves in the military during the Republic and the Triumvirate, prohibitions against such use seem to have been enforced more rigorously during the imperial period. However, two episodes during the reign of Augustus precipitated a relaxation of the prohibition. The first case was connected with the crisis of 6–7 CE in Illyricum and the second with the crisis on the Rhine, as Suetonius explains: 'Except as a fire-brigade in Rome, and when there was fear of riots in times of scarcity, he (Augustus) employed freedmen as soldiers only twice: once as a guard for the colonies in the vicinity of Illyricum, and again to defend the bank of the river Rhine; even these he levied, when they were slaves, from men and women of means, and at once gave them freedom; and he kept them under their original standard, not mingling them with the soldiers of free birth or arming them in the same fashion' (*Aug.* XXV.2).[20] The texts confirm that Augustus levied slaves for service in two specific emergencies and immediately manumitted them but kept them in their own units. The *liberti* served as guards at the frontiers but probably not with the same equipment as the regular army. It is unclear whether we should read the texts as indicating that the use of *liberti* on the Rhine was in response to the defeat at the Teutoburg Forest in 9 CE or to the Varian wars in general and whether they tell us that the levy occurred during or after these wars. That being so, we are not likely to learn the relationship of the levy to Caelius's *liberti*, who may be shown here simply because they were his and served him while he served in the army. They may have come with him from home or have been acquired by him along the way, just as they may have been levied from him to serve in another unit near enough to be commemorated with him when they died (if indeed they were dead when the stone was made). No tombstone inscription except for those that use the word *verna* can tell us precisely how and when a soldier acquired a slave.[21] The time and circumstances of manumission, likewise, are not often visible from the inscriptions, although the military inscriptions seem to mention *liberti* rather than slaves when they mention such dependents at all.[22] The levy connected with the army on the Rhine in 9–10 CE seems to suggest both what we don't know and what we might not want to take for granted. The *liberti* of Marcus Caelius may be here because they themselves saw action and died in military service, although no inscribed words document it. The hypothesis does go some way to explaining the occurrence of the *liberti* in so prominent and honorific a form, unprecedented in a military setting and never to recur in this way again.

Slaves and Liberti on Military Tombstones

The assertion that the representation of the *liberti* Privatus and Thiaminus on Caelius's stela is unique now requires documentation using a number of examples of forms in which slaves and *liberti* were shown on military tombstones. This occurs in two distinct ways. First, very rarely, and without as much clarity as the Caelius stela, *liberti* are shown in portrait form, but there are far more tomb monuments that show dependents serving the deceased. Whether in the form of male attendants with horsemen or as male and female servants at the funerary banquet, these dependents are not portraits, are usually distinguished by size from the deceased and his family, and are utterly stereotypic in their presentation.[23]

The only case of a dependent's portrait with an identifying inscription besides that of Caelius comes again from the Rhine. The stela of Firmus was found in Andernach and is in the Rheinisches Landesmuseum in Bonn although not included in that volume of CSIR; published by Rinaldi Tufi twenty years ago in his catalogue of first-century military stelae from the Rhine, it is normally dated to the Julio-Claudian period (fig. 7.2).[24] The stela is thick enough to have two mournful Attis figures in relief below *peltae* on the sides, and the front contains a shell-niche with figures. In the centre the soldier Firmus stands on a high rectangular pedestal on which we read: 'Firmus the son of Ecco, a soldier with the Raetian cohort who belonged to the Montanus nation. He was 36 years old and served (more than 12) years. His heir set up this monument by order of the will.'[25] To either side of the large soldier and at a lower level of the socle stand two small figures. On the right is the larger of the two, a youthful *togatus*, not a boy because he lacks a *bulla*; the inscription is no longer legible but *CIL* 13.7684 reads it as SSAVIES. At left stands the smallest of the figures. He is now headless but wears a *cucullus* or *paenula* over a tunic; his arms and legs are visible, and in his hand he carries a purse or sack. The base beneath him identifies him as *Fuscus servus*, Fuscus the slave.

The stela is a tease. Firmus is represented in a way typical of early first-century soldiers from northern Italy to the Rhine and into Britain, and the presentation of his name, without tribal designation or *tria nomina*, is not unusual. Age and length of service are there, but no kin are named nor is the heir. We are looking at Firmus, then, and at his slave Fuscus, but the *togatus* may be the free heir, perhaps kin or an *alumnus* given Firmus's protective or possessive gesture. Unlike the Caelius stone, which now starts to seem positively explicit, the Firmus stone leaves many questions open, including how Fuscus came to be here and what his connection was to Firmus and his life.

Even more problematic is the stela of Faltonius because it seems to echo elements of the Firmus stela while providing even less secure information (fig. 7.3).[26] Found in Mainz and on display there, the stone uses a broad niche to accommodate three figures, although size rather than a raised socle differentiates the relative status of the men. In the centre stands the soldier C. Faltonius Secundus; he wears a short military tunic and a cloak over it; both the skirt of the tunic and the back of the cloak are curved in an inverted U typical of the garments on military stelae from the Rhine.[27] None of the faces is visible, but the two flanking figures, each about the same size but considerably smaller than Faltonius, wear a long tunic beneath a hooded cloak, and no one touches anyone else. The figure on the left holds a tablet and stylus, the one on the right a *mappa* and two *soleae*, according to Rinaldi Tufi, who suggests he may be a *vestiarius*.[28] To Walburg Boppert, the object is the pack of a *capsarius*, but it may be an ordinary sack.[29]

The inscription is set below the niche without a frame or tabula, and below it is the rough stone that will have been set into the ground. The inscription tells us that Caius Faltonius Secundus, son of Caius and member of the Pomptina tribe, having come from Dertona (modern Tortona in northern Italy), was forty-six years old and had served with the Twenty-second Legion Primigenia for twenty-one of those years. The inscription then says, 'Here he lies,' and we learn nothing about the commissioner of the stela, the heir, or the identity of the two men, whom many scholars simply refer to as slaves or servants.[30] By analogy to the grouping around Firmus, where the inscription of one similarly dressed figure makes his status explicit, the Faltonius stela, dated to the time of Nero by Boppert, probably does show us slaves or *liberti*, but nothing will prove that. No more explicit cases remain.

I mentioned a distinction earlier between those stelae with portraits of slaves and *liberti* and those with conventionalized images of servants, but there are several transitional examples where the divide is far from clear. One, naming Maris, comes again from Mainz and is dated by Boppert to the period prior to Claudius (fig. 7.4).[31] The space depicted makes this date seem right. The stone was set into the ground as was the Faltonius stela, but above the foot is a handsome arch on pilasters. Several layers of depth appear in the relief within the arch; the inscription panel was meant to be seen as within and slightly behind the pilasters but creating a layer of space on which the figures can stand in front of the background. Within the arch, then, a bowman sits astride a rearing horse and prepares to shoot, and a soldier in a military tunic stands on a slightly lower level just to the rear of the horse.

The relation of the figures to reality is tentative, but the standing man, who holds a bundle of arrows in one hand and a single arrow in the other, is dressed as a soldier and not in a *cucullus* or *paenula*. The curved drape of the skirt and the short sleeves seem to confirm his status as a free man if not his role, although Michael Speidel argues that the only consistent and necessary difference between soldiers' garb and servants' is that the latter never have swords or swordbelts.[32]

The inscription reads: 'Maris, the son of Casitis, aged fifty, served thirty years. He was part of the *Variagnis turma* of the *Ala Parthorum et Araborum*. His brother Masicates and Tigranus set up the commemoration.'[33] He and the others all have names considered Eastern, and he served in an Eastern auxiliary troop.[34] No name attaches to the standing man, but his garment and his size make me uneasy about agreeing with Boppert and Speidel that the man is a *calo*, a slave whose work involves looking after the troops and their property.[35] One simply cannot tell from the inscription and image whether the man is a slave, is Tigranus (who may or may not be a slave), or is Masicates (the brother of the deceased). Nevertheless, size and attributes distinguish this figure from the small attendants who accompany riders on many stelae by the second half of the first century.[36] One of many possible examples is the stela of Oclatius, a *signifer* with the *ala Afrorum*, whose brother and heir set up the stone sometime around 69 CE.[37] The stone, found and displayed in Neuss, shows the standing *signifer* in the arch above, the inscription without a frame below him, and then, on the lowest section, a small rectangular niche accommodates a small horse and a taller man leading it. This bottom element will become a standard part of many rider stelae, as will the placement of a small attendant at the front or the rear of the horse and rider. The type can be seen in the stela from Mainz of Romanius Capito, an *eques* with the *ala Noricorum* whose unnamed heir set up the stone by order of the will.[38] Dated to the time of Nero or Vespasian, the stone combines the rider trampling a fallen barbarian with the standing attendant behind the horse's flank, and it will represent a popular form for the next two centuries over many parts of the Empire. One can easily see the difference between this kind of image and that of Maris.

The parallel to the rider's small attendant is the stereotypic servant type in the banquet or funerary feast.[39] The standard composition for civilians and veterans shows the deceased reclining on a *kline* with a tripod table before him and sometimes a wife seated on a chair at the foot of the couch. Nearby or in a panel beneath this one are one or two small servants usually with wine-drinking equipment or a platter. Clearly, the servants are generic attributes just like the table and the pitcher. A nice example of the blending of the two types appears in the tombstone of Muranus from Wiesbaden (fig. 7.5).[40] The inscription, placed between the upper niche with the banquet and the lower rectangular niche with the horse, names the deceased and his cavalry unit.[41] The upper section shows the large reclining figure of the deceased, his table and wine jar near to hand and his small servant standing at the ready by the foot of the *kline*. Equally conventional is the riderless horse followed by an attendant who, in this case, seems to be nude and whose head is missing.

The banquet and the horse or horse and rider with their servants tell us a good deal about the preferences of patrons both military and civilian in the provinces, the dependency of workshops on earlier Hellenistic prototypes, and the spread of artistic types and conventions throughout the empire. What they cannot tell us, however, is who the servants were, what their lives and status were, and what their relationships were to the soldiers and to the army. In short, we can conclude that only a small number of extremely early stelae provide portraits and naming inscriptions of the servants of soldiers. By the middle of the first century, names of freedmen and slaves are rarely included on military tombstones. More and more, soldiers' tombstones name the deceased and their years and service, and conclude by reminding the viewer that they are buried here. Even the heirs and brothers who continue to be mentioned as donors of the stelae are rarely named. And overall fewer and fewer military gravestones will contain portraits of the deceased as they are numerically overwhelmed by inscription stones without human or animal images. The pattern is true not only for the Rhineland but for the Danube frontier and Britain as well.[42]

If we are dealing with a phenomenon particular to the earliest years of the Roman military's involvement along the northern frontier, then it might be of interest to look at the military camp remains from the first century in these same areas to see whether there is any information to be gained from them about slaves and freedmen. Most textual evidence suggests that the main roles for slaves in the army involved heavy work such as baggage handling and care of the animals, but it seems likely that officers with houses of their own rather than barracks housing would have had someone to serve them and their families, if they were in camp.[43] The question is whether the archaeological material can tell us anything about where men such as Fuscus and Privatus did their work.

The camps and even the great fortresses were cramped places, with no obvious mess halls or dining spaces, hardly enough space for a soldier to turn over in his sleep.[44] The grain storage and barracks took up most of the space, with the *principia* for headquarters and sometimes for housing of the commander, smaller officers' houses, baths, and latrines as consistent elements occupying the rest of the space.[45] Even though there are parade grounds or at least some sort of open or basilical covered space, in most camps they too seem rather small for the number of people and animals who might have needed to use them.⁴⁶ Further, since there are no evident communal eating spaces that might imply a kitchen and service staff except in officers' quarters, one might imagine a soldier cooking for himself as some of the literary sources say the emperors did when in the field.⁴⁷ There is one place, however, where it is hard not to imagine slave workers, and that is the communal ovens.⁴⁸ Many fortresses had large ovens placed along the ramparts and often oriented to the ends of barrack blocks as if to allow each group to claim an oven for itself. In order to make efficient use of the ovens, the camp will have needed someone to pay regular attention to them. Since the hard and menial labour went to slaves in civilian life, perhaps it did in a camp too. The heating for officers' housing and for the camp's baths will also have demanded such labour, and it is unlikely that legionaries and fighting forces would have been used this way.⁴⁹ Similarly, the men who prepared and served food in the officers' quarters may have been slaves supervised by military staff rather than soldier servants, and slaves may have taken care of other domestic tasks in those houses. Even centurions often had houses of more than one room, and thus they may have had space, now undetected by us, for a slave or *libertus* to live in.⁵⁰ In other words, slave labour for menial and domestic labour in the fortresses will have permitted regular troops the freedom to do other kinds of work and the dignity not to do work that may have been associated with slaves.

The question of where slave *calones* would have been, whether as baggage handlers or grooms, as personal attendants or over-stokers, is even more difficult to assess, and it is not possible, given the state of our knowledge of the areas outside the ramparts of the fortresses, to say whether stables or paddocks and slave housing for the baggage handlers and dray horses were located there or within the walls. The results of recent re-excavation at South Shields have shown that cavalry troops and their horses occupied a single barracks building, the horses in the *arma* area, a front room, the humans in the back room.⁵¹ Whether grooms were accommodated there, in what must have been stifling quarters in summer but toasty in winter, remains unknown. It does seem possible that cavalry horses got better accommodation than freight animals and that slave grooms managed more easily than baggage handlers. Such slaves may have bedded down wherever they might, and animals will have stood tethered or hobbled in the open or loose in fenced paddocks rather than indoors.

To return to Caelius and his freedmen, several lines of interpretation have emerged from this rather speculative investigation. We have seen that the depiction of slaves and freedmen in portraits with soldiers is a rarity and a phenomenon of the Rhineland in the very earliest years of the Roman military presence there. Most slaves and freedmen, when they are present on military tombstones, are anonymous, although a few have names given, especially if they were responsible for setting up the monument. Further, most military stelae are aniconic, but when they represent soldiers with servants, they depict the deceased banqueting in the presence of a tiny servant or two or mounted on a charging horse and accompanied by a small attendant. This is the case in Britain, Germany, and the Danube provinces alike.

Two more early first-century examples make it clear that there were also significant regional variations on these themes. One comes from the Klagenfurt area of modern Austria, ancient Noricum, and dates to the time of Claudius (fig. 7.6).[52] The upper part of the stone contains disk niches for four portrait busts, while below the inscription panel is a square space flanked by columns in which a profile rider appears. The inscription names T. Claudius Attucius of the first Cohort Noricorum and says that his will ordered that the tomb be made for himself and Primus Fuscus Priscus and their *liberti* by those same *liberti* and heirs.[53] The individuals in the disks are unnamed and one cannot tell whether the *liberti* are depicted here, although Attucius is surely the horseman. Disk niches with busts can be found in Rome in the Augustan period, and the stela type is related to first-century examples such as those from the area around Ravenna and Aquileia in northern Italy.[54] And a final example of local representation comes from the legionary camp at Carnuntum in Pannonia; dated to the Julio-Claudian period, its large inscription panel names Attius Exoratus as a soldier of the Fifteenth Legion Apollinaris and says that Marcus Minucius and the *libertus* Sucessus set up the stone (fig. 7.7).[55] The arched upper space shows a high-wheeled flatbed cart drawn by a yoke of oxen. A man stands on the cart to drive it, and a man wearing a tunic stands at the head of the oxen but on a downward slope that allows greater prominence to the figure on the cart. Again we cannot tell whether we are seeing any of the men whom the inscription names, let alone identify them, but we do gain a sense of the kind of early tombstone a soldier in Pannonia might have. Like Caelius and others of the legionaries in this period, Exoratus was from Italy, far from home, closest in life to his *commilitones* and perhaps to the slaves whom his will would free.[56]

Conclusion

The men whom military tombstones identify in inscription or portrait as slaves and freedmen of soldiers were not *calones* or the stokers of ovens. They had a special connection to their owners and patrons that got them manumitted, that made them heirs, that gave them the place and confidence to become visible. The fundamental quality of slavery is its invisibility to the free people whose interests it serves, to those who benefit by it as individuals as well as institutionally. The few dependents who came into visibility were, thus, *liberti*, and their closeness to their owners led to their manumission and thus to their presence on the tombstones. Even so, the majority of such *liberti* remained anonymous on the tombstones whether they were heirs or not, and thus they seem to have observed an unspoken convention in which the deceased takes the spotlight, his kinfolk come next, and his *liberti* remain discreetly in the shadows.

NOTES

1 *M(arco) Caelio T(iti) f(ilio) Lem(onia tribu) Bon(onia) / [I] o(rdini) leg(ionis) XIIX ann(orum) LIII s(emissis). / [ce]cidit bello Variano. Ossa / [lib(ertorum) i]nferre licebit. P(ublius) Caelius T(iti) f(ilius) Lem(onia tribu) frater fecit.* Bauchhenss 1978: 18–22, no. 1, pl. 1–4 with earlier literature. My translation is based on text in Bauchhenss 1978 and on update from 2006 of the Epigraphische Datenbank Heidelberg HD019187. On the history of the object in modern times, see Wiegels 2002: 35–70.

2 On the discussion about the inscription and its meaning, see, for example, Wells 2004: 101–2; Bauchhenss 1978: 19–20; Welwei 1988: 90–1 and note 135; and many others.

3 Of the very few papers on this question, the most interesting is still Speidel 1992: 239–48. The essay focuses on the number of servants and their roles, particularly those attached to cavalry, and it concentrates on the evidence from late literary sources. However, its approach to the visual material, especially the tombstones, is typical of many historians in its use of this material as support for textual evidence and its tendency to see motifs such as small figures following riders as either 'a meaningless, handed-down icon' or something that 'sets forth what mattered' to the patrons (241). That the motifs were no more likely to be literal depictions of 'reality' than the tiny male and female servants at the 'Totenmahl' but still reflective of important social and psychic needs and preferences of patrons seems a far more likely alternative, and one that art historians have long understood in their efforts at interpretation.

4 L. Pomponius Nigro, Urbanus and Vivia: *AE* 1920: no. 75, *AE* 1924: 40, n. 138, and *EDH* 27466. L. Naevius Rufus and his *libertus* Silvanus: Buócz et al. 1994: no. 58 and *EDH* 9598; other examples are plentiful throughout the Empire, although I do not know of studies of the subject.

5 *Corpus Signorum Imperii Romani* has published much of the material from Austria, Germany, and Britain already. The website www.ubi-erat-lupa.org provides images as well as searchable databases for large numbers of stelae and altars from the Danube provinces.

6 Although I find the late textual evidence important, I use primarily first-century sources in this paper in an attempt to avoid taking for granted the relatively unchanging nature of military structures and practices.

7 On grooms and baggage handlers, see Welwei 1988 and Speidel 1992; on crafts-people, see for example Bishop 1985: 1–42, but see also inscriptions concerning craft *collegia* in military areas, esp. *RIB* 156 from Bath for Julius Vitalis, a Belgian *fabriciensis* of Legio XXVV who died at age twenty-nine and was buried at the expense of his *collegium*.

8 The most important text-based study of military slavery is Welwei 1988. He does not deal with the visual and archaeological evidence but does pay attention to inscriptions as well as other kinds of texts.

9 Chains that seem to be for groups of humans rather than for animals, at least to judge by the size of the neck irons, are recorded in Simpson 2000: 99–100, and pl. 34–5.

10 Height 1.27 m, width 1.08 m, depth 0.18 m; Bauchhenss 1978: 19. An attempt to think through the style questions raised by the stela: von Petrikovits 1965: I.145–52, II, Pl. 7, no. 2.

11 Rabirii: Kockel 1993: 138–9, no.H2, pl. 2a.

12 Gabelmann 1972: 65–140, esp. 73–8; Gabelmann 1977: 101–17; Gabelmann 1979; Gabelmann 1987: 291–308; Gabelmann 1994: 103–7. From this list, Gabelmann's central role in exploring this material and the cultural relations between the Rhine and northern Italy should be obvious.

13 Bauchhenss 1978: 19 and Wiegels 2002.

14 Robinson 1975: 147–86 on cuirasses.

15 Epigraphische Datenbank Heidelberg 2006: HD019187.

16 Welwei 1988: 18–22. Vegetius III.6, saying that *calones* had their own unit and standards, may be basing his comments on the Augustan period as recounted by Suetonius (see below, note 20).

17 Kockel 1993: 161 J7 pl. 74a, 179 L5, pl. 90c, 18182, L8, pl. 952, and 187 L 17 pl. 101a and 102 a and b. Gabelmann (1972: 127) suggests a very early use for them in the Rhineland during the Julio-Claudian period as devices to associate the deceased with ancestor portraits, but he makes no reference to the *liberti* in the Caelius relief in relation to this useful comment. Kockel (1993: 161) makes a similar comment about a bust portrait in a niche the lower edge of which contains the inscription of the deceased: he notes the way this arrangement recalls the ancestor portraits in the atria of elite families. On the reliefs at Rome, see also Zanker 1975; Kleiner 1977; George 2005.

18 Kockel 1993: 60, on the fashion for busts, with the early example (late Augustan) of the Vettii relief, Museo Nationale Romano, inv. 125 830: Kockel (1993: 102–3, C3, pl. 17 c–e), who mentions the likelihood that people represented in bust form were already dead. Busts set above inscriptions of those who

have died on funerary reliefs of architectonic form may be seen in the Augustan period in examples such as the L. Petronius monument in the Museo Nazionale Romano, inv. 78 145, dated late Augustan by Kockel (1993: 179, L. 5, pl. 90c, 91 a and b,) or the Licinii relief in the British Museum, inv. 1954.12–14.1 (Kockel 1993: pl. 101a, 102 a and b). For images of the deceased as figures standing on an inscribed base, see the Altar of Tonneia Delicata, dated to the second half of the first century CE: Maria Elisa Micheli and Marina Bertinetti, in Antonio Giuliano 1984: 58–60, no. III.1.

19 *Kline* statue: Dayan and Musso in Giuliano 1981: 167–8, no. 58, fig. II, 58. The Barberini Patrician: Helbig 1966: 418–19, no. 1615. And see as well the heads on bases on the later Tomb of the Haterii in the Vatican Museo Gregoriano Profano.

20 Translation from the Loeb edition. Later sources confirm but also confuse the story given by Suetonius, e.g., Velleius speaks further of the recruitment as a levy: Velleius Paterculus II.111.1: *Habiti itaque dilectus, revocati undique et omnes veterani, viri feminaeque ex censu libertinum coactae dare militem* (Accordingly levies were held, from every quarter all the veterans were recalled to the standards, men and women were compelled, in proportion to their income, to furnish freedmen as soldiers). Dio, in his usual way, amplifies the story: Cassius Dio LV.31.1: 'When Augustus learned of these things, he began to be suspicious of Tiberius, who, as he thought, might speedily have overcome the Dalmatians, but was delaying purposely, in order that he might be under arms as long as possible, with the war as his excuse. He therefore sent out Germanicus, although he was only a *quaestor*, and gave him an army composed not only of free-born citizens but also of freedmen, including those whom he had freed from slavery by taking them from their masters and mistresses on payment of their value and the cost of their maintenance for six months.'

21 E.g., AE 1929: no. 106; AE 1932: no. 50: Stela of Diadumenus, sixteen-year-old *verna* and *alumnus* of Marcus Ulpius Vannius, a centurion of the Eighth Legion Augusta, from Germania Superior, and see also AE 1914: no. 253 from Rome.

22 Saller and Shaw 1984: 124–56, esp. tables pp. 152–5. The numbers are quite small everywhere compared with those of kin, but the data are not separated according to date, so one cannot tell from their statistics whether the *liberti* are commemorating patrons in a particular time. My data make it clear that the Rhineland military monuments with such commemorations are early.

23 Interesting exceptions occur among the rider stelae in the first century but rarely later. A good example is the stela of Titus Calidius Severus from Carnuntum, dated to the Flavian period and showing the armour in one panel and a large man holding the reins of a horse in the panel below: Krüger 1970: 54, no. 319, pl. 62. A late exceptional case is the stela of Aurelius Flavinus from Aquileia, dated by Claudio Franzoni to the fourth century by style (Franzoni

1987: 31–2, no. 15, pl. VI.1). The soldier stands before the horse, his unusually large and mature *calo* holding the bridle.

24 Rinaldi Tufi 1988: 26–7, no. 13 pl. XIV–XV.

25 *Firmus / Ecconis f(ilius) / mil(es) ex coh(orte) / Raetorum / natione M / ontanus / ann(orum) XXXVI / stip(endiorum) X … II / heres [e]x tes(tamento) / po[suit].* Base on left with inscription: *Fuscus servus;* base on right: *SSAVIES (?)*: Rinaldi Tufi 1988: 27.

26 Rinaldi Tufi 1988: 30–1, no. 19 pl. XVIII.1; Boppert 1992: 96–8, no. 5, pl. 6.

27 E.g., stela of Q. Petelius Secundus in Bonn inv. U86: Bauchhenss 1978: 27–8, no. 6 pl. 11; fragment of a stela of a standing soldier, Mannheim inv. Haug 68: Boppert 1992: 94–6, no. 4 pl.4–5; or stela of Annaius, Bad Kreuznach, Karl-Geib Museum: Rinaldi Tufi 1988: 19–20, no. 4 pl. IV.1.

28 Rinaldi Tufi 1988: 31.

29 Boppert 1992: 97.

30 *C(aius) Faltonius C(ai) f(ilius) Pom(ptina tribu) / Secundus Dertona mil(es) / leg(ionis) XXII Pr(imigeniae) an(norum) XLVI / stip(endiorum) XXI / H(ic) S(itus) E(st): CIL* XIII. 6960, Boppert 1992: 97.

31 Boppert 1992: 130–1, no. 29 pl. 27.

32 Speidel 1992: 244, 245.

33 *Maris Casiti f(ilius) annor(um) L / stip(endiorum) XXX ala Part(h)o(rum) et / Araborum turma / Variagnis Masicates / frater et Trigranus / posierunt (sic).*

34 Boppert 1992: 131.

35 Boppert 1992: 130–1.

36 Gabelmann 1973: 132–200; and for monuments of the second and third centuries, see especially Speidel 1994; for example, the stela of Andes, Mainz inv. S 608 (Boppert 1992: 141–4, no. 35 pl. 33).

37 Rinaldi Tufi 1988: 42–3, no. 35 pl. XXVI.2. From Neuss and now in the Clemens-Sels Museum there. The inscription reads: *Oclatio Carvi f(ilio) / signif(er) alae Afror(um) / Tungro. Frater h(eres) f(aciendum) c(uravit).*

38 Boppert 1992: 133–6, no. 31 pl. 29.

39 Noelke 1998: 399–418.

40 Bauchhenss 1978: 44–6, no. 29 Pl. 30. Cf. Piccottini 1977 for the diverse forms the servant image could take.

41 *Muranus eq. ala I. Flavia Andiouri f. vicus Secuanus.* Henzen et al. 1884: 236.

42 E.g., Roxan 1991: 462–7.

43 Welwei 1988: 56, 84–5, 87–90, 92–100, 104–11; and Speidel 1992 passim.

44 von Petrikovits 1975; Webster 1998: 167–230 on forts. Wells 1977: 659–65; Sommer 1995: 149–68; and most recently, Hodgson 2002.

45 von Petrikovits 1977: 633–4; Chantraine et al. 1984.

46 Blagg 2000: 139–47; Davies 1989: 93–124. See also the possibility of paddock or riding school space in Kandler 1997: 89–96.

47 Vegetius III.8 on camps; I.18 and II.23 on covered exercise halls. On the emperors eating simple rations while in camp or on the march: *SHA* Hadrian X.2, behaving like Scipio Aemilianus, Metellus, and Trajan and eating simple camp fare out of doors; Herodian IV.7.5 on Caracalla doing his own cooking in the field. On the question of whether there were mess halls in camps, two different issues are at play here: the translation of the word *contubernales* as tentmates or as messmates, the latter seeming to be a particularly British usage, and the archaeological remains in relation to ovens. For *contubernales* as 'messmates,' see Bowman 1983: 45–6. The sources, including Vegetius II.8.13, Suetonius *Caes.* 42, Tacitus *Agr.* 5, among others, specify tentmates who may also eat together, although there seems to be no discussion of this issue in any of them. On the archaeology, I have found no clear evidence for mess halls or large dining spaces within the walls of the fortresses or camps. However, a number of scholars have concluded that mess halls can be seen in relation to communal ovens. For example, Webster 2002, describes a large oven along the interior of the rampart. He suggests that each century of men had an oven and that in the second legionary phase, a tile oven near the back of area 91 on the rampart was once covered by a timber building, which he called mess hall 3. He sees several other such structures, each 4.3 metres wide, which seems unlikely as an eating area for large numbers of people and the space for an oven at work (29–30). Richmond once said that soldiers' barracks had *triclinia*, but this seems to be based both on minimal textual material and on the highly speculative interpretation of remains at Masada, where he sees a very large *triclinium* for an 'officers' mess' (Richmond 1962: 143–55, esp. 146, 148, and 150–1). By contrast, the very careful excavations at the Flavian legionary fortress at Inchtuthil (Pitts and St Joseph 1985: 128–32) indicate kitchen and dining areas in courtyard houses, presumably for officers and ovens, 'cook-houses,' tanks and latrines in the *intervallum* area opposite barracks (195–200). They find no communal dining areas here, nor in the continental camps. Contrasting evidence comes from the *Digest* 44.16.12, which says that an officer should be present at mealtimes in camp to supervise food quality. Perhaps the very large and often basilical spaces of the *principia* were used for communal dining, but the archaeological evidence does not clarify the matter. Barracks at some forts show evidence of braziers, whether for cooking or for heating or both is not obvious, e.g., Crow 1995: 54. I have not so far found comparable evidence outside of Britain.

48 Ovens found at camps including those mentioned in n. 34 and also Housesteads: Crow 1995: 37–8); Balmuidy: Miller 1922: 39–40; and Isca: Boon 1972: 24. I have as yet found no examples of such ovens in continental camps but have just begun to search for them.

49 The uncertainty about what legionary soldiers actually did as work in camp remains a problem not only because of lack of evidence but because our modern

Western assumptions about what slaves and *liberti* were for may be alien to the Romans themselves. On hypocausts in officers' houses, see, for example, Hoffmann 1997: 195–8, esp. 196.

50 Centurion houses: e.g., those of Inchtuthil: Pitts and St Joseph 1985: 146–50; Hoffmann 1997.

51 Hodgson 2002.

52 AE 1974: 475; Piccottini 1972: no. 635.

53 *Ti(berius) Claudius Trausi fil(ius) / Attucius missicius coh(ortis) I / Nor(icorum) ann(orum) L stip(endiorum) XXVII t(estamento) f(ieri) i(ussit) sibi et / Primo Fusco Prisco lib(ertis) isdem / liberti et heredes fecer(unt).*

54 Pflug 1989; Kockel 1993: 191–2, L21, pl. 106a-c, 107 a and b: Relief of the Bennii. Cf. Longidienus relief in Ravenna, most recently in Clarke 2003: 188–21.

55 Krüger 1970: 57, no. 330 pl. 67; Mosser 2003: no.121: *C(aius) Attius C(ai) f(ilius) / Voturia Exor / atus miles leg(ionis) XV / Apo(llinaris) annor(rum) XXXXIV / stipen(diorum) XXIIII / h(ic) s(itus) e(st) / M(arcus) Minicius et / Suces(s)us l(ibertus posierunt (sic).*

56 On commemoration for soldiers far from home, see Hope 2003: 113–40, esp. 132–3. She also notes the fact that in Britain, along with the rarity of soldiers' tombstones, those that do exist tend not to use visual imagery.

REFERENCES

AA.VV. 1982. *I Volusii Saturnini. Una famiglia romana della prima età imperiale.* Archeologia. Materiali e problemi 6. Bari.

Abel, L. and B.E. Buckley. 1977. *The Handwriting on the Wall: Towards a Sociology and Psychology of Graffiti.* Westport.

Abramenko, A. 1993. *Die munizipale Mittelschicht im kaiserzeitlichen Italien. Zu einem neuen Verständnis von Sevirat und Augustalität.* Frankfurt.

Adamo Muscettola, S. 1980. *Civiltà del '700 a Napoli 1734–1799. Catalogo della mostra: Napoli, dicembre 1979-ottobre 1980* 2, 71–2. Florence.

Adams, J.N. 1982. *The Latin Sexual Vocabulary.* London.

– 2003. *Bilingualism and the Latin Language.* Cambridge.

Adams, J.N., M. Janse, and S. Swain, eds. 2002. *Bilingualism in Ancient Society. Language Contact and the Written Text.* Oxford.

Ajootian, A. 1996. 'Praxiteles,' in Olga Palagia and J.J. Pollitt, eds., *Personal Styles in Greek Sculpture. Yale Classical Studies* 30, 91–129. Cambridge.

Ako-Adounvo, G. 1999. *Studies in the Iconography of Blacks in Roman Art.* PhD diss., McMaster University, Hamilton, ON.

Alföldy, G. 1986. *Die römische Gesellschaft.* Stuttgart.

Allison, P. 1999. 'Artefact Distribution and Spatial Function in Pompeian Houses,' in B. Rawson and P. Weaver, eds., *The Roman Family in Italy: Status, Sentiment, Space*, 321–54. Oxford.

– 2004. *Pompeian Households: An Analysis of the Material Culture.* Los Angeles.

– 2006. *The Insula of the Menander at Pompeii. Volume III: The Finds, a Contextual Study.* Oxford.

Allroggen-Bedel, A. 1977. 'Die Wandmalereien aus der Villa in Campo Verano,' *RM* 84: 27–89.

Amedick, R. 1991. *Die Sarkophage mit Darstellungen aus dem Menschenleben* 1.4: *Vita Privata.* Berlin.

Amelung, W. 1927. 'Bronzener Ephebe aus Pompei,' *JDAI* 42: 137–51, Beilage 11–23.

Andreau, J. 1999. *Banking and Business in the Roman World*. Cambridge.

Anti, C. 1926. 'Il nuovo bronzo di Pompei,' *Dedalo* 7: 3–85.

Armstrong, D. 1990. *The Old Village and the Great House: An Archaeological and Historical Examination of Drax Hall Plantation, St Ann's Bay, Jamaica*. Urbana and Chicago.

– 1999. 'Archaeology and Ethnohistory of the Caribbean Plantation,' in T. Singleton, ed., *'I, Too, am America' – Archaeological Studies of African-American Life*, 173–92. Charlottesville.

Asche, S. 1978. *Balthasar Permoser: Leben und Werk*. Dresden.

Ascione, G.C. 2001. 'Wer kauft Liebesgötter? Anyone for gods of love?' in *In Stabiano; cultura e archeologia da Stabiae; la città e il territorio tra l'età arcaica e l'età romana–catalogo della mostra Castellamare di Stabia palazzetto del mare 4 novembre 2000–31 gennaio 2001*, 87–9. Naples.

Asso, P. 2010. 'Queer Consolation: Melior's Dead Boy in Statius' *Silvae* 2.1,' *American Journal of Philology* 131, no. 4: 663–97.

Avetta, L., ed. 1985. *Roma–Via Imperiale. Scavi e scoperte (1937–1950) nella costruzione di Via delle Terme di Caracalla e di Via Cristoforo Colombo*. Tituli 3. Rome.

Babelon, E., and J.A. Blanchet. 1895. *Catalogue des bronzes antiques de la Bibliothèque Nationale*. Paris.

– 1928. *Choix de bronzes de la Collection Caylus donée au roi en 1762*. Paris and Brussels.

Bailey, C. 1947. *Lucretius De rerum natura*. Oxford.

Bain, D. 1991. 'Six Greek Verbs of Sexual Congress.' *CQ* 41: 51–77.

Baldwin, B. 1978. 'Trimalchio's Domestic Staff,' *AC* 21: 87–97.

Balty, J. 1982. 'Paedagogiani-pages, de Rome à Byzance,' in L. Hadermann-Misguich and G. Raepsaet, eds., *Rayonnement Grec. Hommages à Charles Delvoye*, 299–305. Brussels.

Barbet, A., and P. Miniero, eds. 1999. *La Villa San Marco a Stabia*. Rome.

Barr-Sharrar, B. 1996. 'The Private Use of Small Sculpture,' in C.C. Mattusch, ed., *The Fire of Hephaistos: Large Classical Bronzes from North American Collections*, 104–21. Cambridge, MA.

Barrow, R.H. 1928. *Slavery in the Roman Empire*. New York (repr. London, 1948).

Bauchhenss, G. 1978. *CSIR Deutschland III.1: Germania Inferior: Bonn und Umgebung: Militärische Grabdenkmäler*. Bonn.

Baulez, C. 2007. 'The "Grande Galerie" and Its Furnishings: From Louis XIV to the Present Day,' in A. Amarger et al., eds., *The Hall of Mirrors: History & Restoration*, A. Sautier-Greening, trans., 84–95. Dijon.

Beard, M. 2007. *The Roman Triumph*. Cambridge, MA.

Bek, L. 1980. *Toward Paradise on Earth. Analecta romana Istituti danici*, supp. 19. Rome.

Bellen, H. 1971. *Studien zur Sklavenflucht in römischen Kaiserreich*. Wiesbaden.

– 2003. ed. *Bibliographie zur antiken Sklaverei*. Stuttgart.

Bergmann, B. 1994. 'Roman House as Memory Theatre: House of the Tragic Poet,' *Art Bulletin* 76: 223–56.

– 1995. 'Greek Masterpieces and Roman Recreative Fictions,' *HSCPh* 97: 79–120.

– 2002. 'Art and Nature in the Villa at Oplontis,' *JRA* Suppl. 47: 87–120.

Berlin, I. 1998. *Many Thousands Gone: The First Two Centuries of Slavery in North America*. Cambridge, MA.

Berry, J. 1997a. 'The Conditions of Domestic Life in Pompeii in AD 79: A Case-study of Houses 11 and 12, Insula 9, Region 1,' *PBSR* 65: 103–25.

– 1997b. 'Household Artefacts: Towards a Reinterpretation of Domestic Space,' R. Laurence and A. Wallace-Hadrill, eds., *Domestic Space in the Roman World. JRA* Suppl. 22, 183–95. Portsmouth.

Beschi, L. 2000. 'L'Idolino di Pesaro e gli altri bronzi del suo contesto archeologico,' *SOliv* n.s. 20: 9–54.

Bieber, M. 1961a. *The History of the Greek and Roman Theater*, 2nd ed. Princeton.

– 1961b. *The Sculpture of the Hellenistic Age*, rev. ed. New York.

Binsfeld, A. 2010. 'Antike Sklaverei: Rückblick und Ausblick. Neue Beiträge zur Forschungsgeschichte und zur Erschließung der archäologischen Zeugnisse,' in H. Heinen, ed., *Antike Sklaverei: Rückblick und Ausblick. Neue Beiträge zur Forschungsgeschichte und zur Erschließung der archäologischen Zeugnisse*, 161–77. Stuttgart.

Birt, T. 1919. *Aus Leben in der Antike*. Leipzig.

Bishop, M.C. 1985. 'The Military Fabrica and the Production of Arms in the Early Principate,' in M.C. Bishop, ed., *The Production and Distribution of Roman Military Equipment* (*BAR* International 275), 1–42. Oxford.

Blagg, T.F.C. 2000. 'The Architecture of the Legionary *Principia*,' in R.J. Brewster, ed., *Roman Fortresses and Their Legions*, 139–47. London.

Blanc, N., and F. Gury. 1986. 'Eros / Amor, Cupido,' in *Lexicon Iconographicum Mythologiae Classicae* 3, 966–1049. Zurich and Munich.

Bloch, H. 1947. *I bolli laterizi e la storia edilizia romana*. Rome.

Bodel, J., ed. 2001. *Epigraphic Evidence: Ancient History from Inscriptions*. London and New York.

– 2005. '*Caveat emptor*: Towards a Study of Roman Slave-dealers,' *JRA* 18: 181–95.

Bol, P.C. 2007. *Die Geschichte der antiken Bildhauerkunst. Tom. III. Hellenistische Plastik*, 2 Bände. Mainz.

Bolender, U.M. 2000. 'Repräsentation von Negroiden Typen (Aethiopien) in Hellenistischen Bronzen,' *KJ* 33: 91–101.

Bonifacio, G., and A.M. Sodo. 2001. *Stabiae. Guida Archeologica alle Ville*. Castellammare di Stabia.

Boon, G.C. 1972. *Isca*. Cardiff.

Boppert, W. 1992. *Militärische Grabdenkmäler aus Mainz und Umgebung*. Mainz.

Bourdieu, P. 1977. *Outline of a Theory of Practice*. Cambridge.

Bove, L. 1984. *Documenti di operazioni finanziarie dall'archivio dei Sulpici*. Naples.

Bowman, A.K. 1983. *The Roman Writing Tablets from Vindolanda*. London.

Bowman, A.K., and J.D. Thomas. 1983. *Vindolanda: The Latin Writing-Tablets*. London.

Bowman, A.K., and G. Woolf, eds. 1994. *Literacy and Power in the Ancient World*. Cambridge.

Braconi, P. 2005. 'Il 'Chalcidio' di Lepcis Magna era un mercato di schiavi?' *JRA* 18: 213–19.

Bradley, K.R. 1978. 'Holidays for Slaves,' *Symbolae Osloenses* 54: 111–18.

– 1984. *Slaves and Masters in the Roman Empire. A Study in Social Control*. Brussels.

– 1986. 'Wet-nursing at Rome: A Study in Social Relations,' in B. Rawson, ed., *The Family in Ancient Rome: New Perspectives*, 201–29.

– 1987. *Slaves and Masters in the Roman Empire. A Study in Social Control*. New York.

– 1989. *Slavery and Rebellion in the Roman World 140–70 BC*. Bloomington.

– 1990. '*Servus Onerosus*: Roman Law and the Troublesome Slave,' *Slavery and Abolition* 11: 135–57.

– 1991. *Discovering the Roman Family: Studies in Roman Social History*. Oxford.

– 1994. *Slavery and Society at Rome*. Cambridge.

– 2000. 'Animalizing the Slave: The Truth of Fiction,' *JRS* 90: 110–25.

– 2004. 'On Captives under the Principate,' *Phoenix* 58: 298–318.

– 2008. 'Roman Slavery: Retrospect and Prospect,' *Journal of Canadian History* 43, no. 3: 477–500.

Brana-Shute, R., and R.J. Sparks, eds. 2009. *Paths to Freedom: Manumission in the Atlantic World*. Columbia, SC.

Breuer, S. 1996. *Stand und Status. Munizipale Oberschichten in Brixia und Verona*. Bonn.

Bruneau, P. 1975. 'L'Agora des Italiens servait-elle de marché aux esclaves?' *BCH* 99: 267–311.

– 1985. 'L'Agora des Italiens était-elle un marché aux esclaves?' *BCH* 109: 557–64.

Bruun, P. 1963. 'Symboles, signes et monogrammes,' in H. Zilliacus, ed., *Sylloge Inscriptionum Christianarum Veterum Musei Vaticani 2. Commentarii*, 73–166. Helsinki.

Buckland, W.W. 1908. *The Roman Law of Slavery: The Condition of the Slave in Private Law from Augustus to Justinian*. Cambridge.

Buecheler, F. 1894–1930. *Carmina Latina Epigraphica*, 2 vols., with suppl. by E. Lommatzsch. Leipzig.

Buócz, T., et al. 1994. *Das Lapidarium des Savaria Museums*. Szombathely.

Buonocore, M. 1984. *Schiavi e liberti dei Volusii Saturnini. Le iscrizioni del colombario sulla via Appia antica*. Rome.

Caldelli, M.L., and C. Ricci. 1999. *Monumentum familiae Statiliorum: un riesame*. Rome.

Camodeca, G. 1992. *L'archivio puteolano dei Sulpicii*. Naples.

Camp, S.M.H. 2004. *Closer to Freedom: Enslaved Women and Everyday Resistance in the Plantation South*. Chapel Hill and London.

Carandini, A., ed. 1985. *Settefinestre. Una villa schiavistica nell'Etruria romana*, 3 vols. Modena.

Carandini, A., and S. Settis. 1979. *Schiavi e padroni nell'Etruria romana: la villa di Settefinestre dallo scavo alla mostra*. Bari.

Carrington, R.C. 1931. 'Studies in the Campanian "Villae Rusticae,"' *JRS* 21: 110–30.

Castellan, R. 1978. *Aesthetics of Graffiti*. San Francisco.

Castleman, C. 1982. *Getting Up: Subway Graffiti in New York*. New York.

Chamoux, F. 1950. 'Le Dionysos de Sakha,' *BCH* 74: 70–81.

Chantraine, H. 1967. *Freigelassene und Sklaven im Dienst der römischen Kaiser*. Wiesbaden.

Chantraine, H., et al., eds. 1984. *Das römische Neuss*. Stuttgart.

Cimok, F., ed. 2000. *Antioch Mosaics*. Istanbul.

Clarke, J.R. 1991. *The Houses of Roman Italy, 100 B.C.–A.D. 250: Ritual, Space, and Decoration*. Berkeley.

– 1998. *Looking at Lovemaking: Constructions of Sexuality in Roman Art, 100 B.C–A.D. 250*. Berkeley.

– 2003. *Art in the Lives of Ordinary Romans: Visual Representations and Non-Elite Viewers in Italy, 100 B.C.–A.D. 315*. Berkeley.

– 2006. Review of D. Williams, *The Warren Cup*. *JRA* 19: 509–10.

Cline, L. 2012. 'Imitation vs. Reality: Zebra Stripe Paintings and Imitation Marble in the Late Fourth Style at Oplontis,' in N. Zimmerman, ed., *Actes du XI Colloque de l'Association international pour la peinture murale antique* (Ephesos, 13–27 September 2010).

Coarelli, F. 1982. '"L'agora des Italiens" a Delo: il mercato degli schiavi,' *OIRF* 2: 119–45.

– 2005. 'L'Agora des Italiens': lo *statarion* de Delo?' *JRA* 18: 196–212.

– 2008. *Roma*. Bari.

Coleman, K. 1990. 'Fatal Charades: Roman Executions Staged as Mythological Enactments,' *JRS* 80: 44–73.

Cooley, A., and M.G.L. Cooley. 2004. *Pompeii: A Sourcebook*. London.

Cooper, M., and H. Chalfant. 1995. *Subway Art*. New York.

Copley, F. 1947. '*Servitium amoris* in the Roman Elegists,' *TAPA* 68: 285–300.

Correra, L. 1893. 'Graffiti di Roma,' *Bulletino della Commissione Archeologica* 21: 245–60.

– 1894. 'Graffiti di Roma,' *Bulletino della Commissione Archeologica* 22: 89–94.

Crea, S. 2006. 'Aree sepolcrali all'interno di fondi imperiali: il caso del sepolcreto nella villa dell'*Albanum*,' *RAL* 9, no. 17: 145–70.

Crow, J. 1995. *The English Heritage Book of Housesteads*. London.

Croza, B. 1942. *Edilizia e Technica Rurale di Roma Antica*. Milan.

Curtius, L. 1930. 'Poenitentia,' in *Festschrift für James Loeb zum sechzigsten Geburtstag, gewidmet von seinen archäologischen Freunden in Deutschland und Amerika*, 53–62. Munich.

Dahlmann, H. 1950. 'Bemerkungen zu den Resten der Briefe Varros,' *Museum Helveticum* 7: 200–20.

Dal Lago, E., and C. Katsari, eds. 2008. *Slave Systems: Ancient and modern*. Cambridge.

Darder Lissón, M. 1996. *De Nominibus Equorum Circensium: Pars Occidentis*. Barcelona. Reial Acadèmia de Bones Lletres.

D'Arms, J.H. 1981. *Commerce and Social Standing in Ancient Rome*. Cambridge, MA.

– 1991. 'Slaves at the Roman *Convivia*,' in W.J.S. Slater, ed., *Dining in a Classical Context*, 171–83. Ann Arbor.

Dasen, V., and T. Späth. 2010. *Children, Memory, and Family Identity in Roman Culture*. Oxford.

Daube, D. 1952. 'Slave-Catching,' *Juridical Review* 64: 12–28.

Dauge, Y.A. 1981. *Le Barbare. Recherches sur la conception romaine de la barbarie et de la civilisation. Collection Latomus* 176. Brussels.

Daumas, M. 1993. 'Le nègre Caylus est-il vraiment un faux?' *REA* 95: 191–206.

Davies, R.W. 1989. 'Training Grounds of the Roman Cavalry,' in D. Breeze and V.A. Maxfield, eds., *Service in the Roman Army*, 93–124. New York.

de Angelis, F. 2011. 'Playful Workers. The Cupid Frieze in the Casa dei Vettii,' in E. Poehler, M. Flohr, and K. Cole, eds., *Pompeii. Art, Industry and Infrastructure*, 62–73. Oxford.

de Caro, S. 1994. *La villa rustica in località Villa Regina a Boscoreale*. Naples.

de Caro, S., and L. Pedicini. 1996. *The National Archaeological Museum*. Naples.

de Certeau, M. 1984. *The Practice of Everyday Life*. S. Rendell, trans. Berkeley.

de Franciscis, A. 1975. 'La Villa romana di Oplontis,' in B. Andreae and H. Kyrieleis, eds., *Neue Forschungen in Pompeji*, 9–17. Recklinghausen.

Della Corte, M. 1923. *NS*: 275–80.

Delle, J.A. 1998. *An Archaeology of Social Space – Analyzing Coffee Plantations in Jamaica's Blue Mountains*. New York and London.

Desanges, J. 1976. 'The Iconography of the Black in Ancient North Africa,' in J. Vercoutter, J. Leclant, F.M. Snowden, and J. Desanges, eds., *The Image of the Black in Western Art, Vol. 1: From the Pharaohs to the Fall of the Roman Empire*, 246–68. New York.

de Vos, A., and M. de Vos. 1982. *Pompei Ercolanao Stabia*. Guida archeologica Laterza, 11. Rome.

Dixon, S. 1992. *The Roman Family*. Baltimore and London.

Donderer, M., and I. Spiliopoulou-Donderer. 1993. 'Spätrepublikanische und kaiserzeitliche Grabmonumente von Sklavenhändlern,' *Gymnasium* 100: 254–66.

Drerup, H. 1959. 'Bildraum und Realraum in der römischen Architektur,' *Römische Mitteilungen* 66: 145–74.

Dubin, S.C. 1987. 'Symbolic Slavery: Black Representations in Popular Culture,' *Social Problems* 34, no. 2: 122–40.

DuBois, P. 2003. *Slaves and Other Objects*. Chicago.

Duckworth, G.E. 1952. *The Nature of Roman Comedy: A Study in Popular Entertainment*. Princeton.

Dunbabin, K.M.D. 1978. *The Mosaics of Roman North Africa – Studies in Iconography and Patronage*. Oxford.

– 2003a. *The Roman Banquet: Images of Conviviality*. Cambridge.

– 2003b. 'The Waiting Servant in Later Roman Art,' *AJP* 124: 443–68.

Dupont, F., and E. Valette-Cagnac, eds. 2005. *Façons de parler grec à Rome*. Paris.

Dyson, S.L. 2003. *The Roman Countryside*. London.

Eck, W. 1972. 'Die Familie der Volusii Saturnini in neuen Inschriften aus Lucus Feroniae,' *Hermes* 100: 461–84.

– 1978. 'Zum neuen Fragment des sogenannten testamentum Dasumii,' *ZPE* 30: 277–95.

– 2007. 'Befund und Realität. Zur Repräsentativität unserer epigraphischen Quellen in der römischen Kaiserzeit,' *Chiron* 37: 49–64.

Eck, W., and J. Heinrichs. 1993. *Sklaven und Freigelassene in der Gesellschaft der römischen Kaiserzeit*. Darmstadt.

Edmondson, J.C. 1996. 'Dynamic Arenas: Gladiatorial Presentations in the City of Rome and the Construction of Roman Society During the Early Empire,' in W.J.S. Slater, ed., *Roman Theater and Society*, 69–112. Ann Arbor.

Edwards, C. 1993. 'Unspeakable Professions: Public Performance and Prostitution in Ancient Rome,' in J. Hallett, and M. Skinner, eds., *Roman Sexualities*, 66–95. Princeton.

Ellis, S. 2002. *Roman Housing*. London.

Fauth, W. 1974. 'Cupido cruciatur,' *Grazer Beiträger* 2: 39–60.

Fenoaltea, S. 1984. 'Slavery and Supervision in Comparative Perspective: A Model,' *Journal of Economic History* 44: 635–68.

Fentress, E. 2005. 'On the Block: *Catastae, chalcidica* and *cryptae* in Early Imperial Italy,' *JRA* 18: 220–34.

Fergola, L., and M. Pagano. 1998. *Oplontis: Le splendide ville romane di Torre Annuniziata*. Itinerario Archeologico Regionato. Naples.

Finley, M.I. 1971. 'Archaeology and History,' *Daedalus* 100: 168–86, repr. in M.I. Finley, 1975, *The Use and Abuse of History*, 87–101. New York.

– 1973. *The Ancient Economy*. London.

– 1998. *Ancient Slavery and Modern Ideology* (expanded ed. of 1980 original with intro. and notes by B. Shaw). Princeton.

Fitzgerald, W. 2000. *Slavery and the Roman Literary Imagination*. Cambridge.

Flory, M.B. 1978. 'Family in *Familia*: Kinship and Community in Slavery,' *AJAH* 3.1: 78–95.

Foerster, W. 1964. 'σωτήρ C-D,' *ThWNT* VII: 1014–18.

Forbes, C.A. 1955. 'Supplementary Paper: The Education and Training of Slaves in Antiquity,' *TAPA* 86: 321–60.

Foss, P. 1997. 'Watchful Lares: Roman Household Organization and the Rituals of Cooking and Eating,' in R. Laurence and A. Wallace-Hadrill, eds., *Domestic Space in the Roman World. JRA* Suppl. 22, 196–218. Portsmouth.

Frank, T. 1916. 'Race Mixture in the Roman Empire,' *AHR* 21: 689–708 (repr. in D. Kagan, ed., 1965, *Decline and Fall of the Roman Empire*, 44–56. Boston).

Franzoni, C. 1987. *Habitus atque habitudo militis: Monumenti funerari di militari nella Cisalpina Romana*. Rome.

Fröhlich, T. 1991. *Lararien- und Fassadenbilder in den Vesuvstädten: Untersuchungen zur 'volkstümlichen' Pompejanischen Maleri*. Mainz.

Fuchs, W. 1963. *Der Schiffsfund von Mahdia*. Bilderhefte des Deutschen Archäologischen Instituts Rom 2. Tübingen.

Furtwängler, A. 1883–7. *Die Sammlung Sabouroff*, 2 vols. Berlin.

– 1965. *Die antiken Gemmen*. Amsterdam.

Futrell, A. 2001. *Blood in the Arena: The Spectacle of Roman Power*. Austin.

Gabelmann, H. 1972. 'Die Typen der römischen Grabstelen am Rhein,' *BJb* 172: 65–140.

– 1973. 'Römische Grabmonumente mit Reiterkampfszenen im Rheingebiet,' *BJb* 173: 132–200.

– 1977. 'Römische Grabbauten in Italien und den Nordprovinzen,' in U. Höckmann and A. Krug, eds., *Festschrift für Frank Brommer*, 101–17. Mainz.

– 1979. *Römische Grabbauten der frühen Kaiserzeit*. Stuttgart.

– 1987. 'Römische Grabbauten der Nordprovinzen im 2. und 3. Jh. n.Chr.,' in H. von Hesberg and P. Zanker, eds., *Römische Gräberstrassen. Selbstdarstellung, Status, Standard. Kolloquium in München vom 28. bis 30. Oktober 1985*, 291–308. Munich.

– 1994. 'Denkmäler römischer ritterlicher Offiziere,' in K. Rosen, ed., *Macht und Kultur im Rom der Kaiserzeit: Symposium in Bonn am 24. und 25. November 1989*, 103–7. Bonn.

Gaca, Kathy L. 2010. 'The Andrapodizing of War Captives in Greek Historical Memory,' *TAPhA* 140: 117–61.

Garcia y Bellido, A. 1949. *Esculturas Romanas de España y Portugal*, 2 vols. Madrid.

– 1969. 'Der Bronzene Mellephebe von Antequera,' *Antike Plastik* 9: 73–8.

Gardner, J., and T. Wiedemann. 1991. *The Roman Household: A Sourcebook.* London and New York.

Garfinkel, H. 1967. *Studies in Ethnomethodology.* Englewood Cliffs.

Garnsey, P. 1970. *Social Status and Legal Privilege in the Roman Empire.* Oxford.

– 1975. 'Descendants of Freedmen in Local Politics, Some Criteria,' in B. Levick, ed., *The Ancient Historian and His Materials. Essays in Honour of C.E. Stevens,* 167–80. Farnborough.

– ed. 1980. *Non-Slave Labour in the Greco-Roman World.* Cambridge.

– 1996. *Ideas of Slavery from Aristotle to Augustine.* Cambridge.

Garnsey, P., and R.P. Saller. 1987. *The Roman Empire. Economy, Society and Culture.* London.

Garrucci, J.R. 1879. *Storia della arte cristiana nei primi otto secoli della chiesa.* Prato.

Gazda, E.K. 1991. *Roman Art in the Private Sphere: New Perspectives on the Architecture and Décor of the Domus, Villa, and Insula.* Ann Arbor.

George, M. 1997a. 'Repopulating the Roman House,' in B. Rawson and P.R.C. Weaver, eds., *The Roman Family in Italy,* 299–319. Oxford.

– 1997b. '*Servus* and *domus*: The Slave in the Roman House,' in R. Laurence and A. Wallace-Hadrill, eds., *Domestic Space in the Roman World. JRA* Suppl. 22, 15–24. Portsmouth.

– 2003. 'Images of Black Slaves in the Roman Empire,' *Syllecta Classica* 14: 161–85.

– 2005. 'Family Imagery and Family Values in Roman Italy,' in M. George, ed., *The Roman Family in the Empire. Rome, Italy, and Beyond,* 37–66. Oxford.

– 2006. 'Social Identity and the Dignity of Work on Freedmen's Reliefs,' in E. D'Ambra and G.P.R. Métraux, eds., *The Art of Citizens, Soldiers, and Freedmen in the Roman World,* 19–29. Oxford.

– 2009. 'Archaeology and Roman Slavery: Problems and Potential,' in H. Heinen, ed., *Antike Sklaverei: Rückblick und Ausblick. Neue Beiträge zur Forschungsgeschichte und zur Erschließung der archäologischen Zeugnisse,* 141–60. Mainz.

Gigante, M. 1979. *Civiltà delle forme letterarie nell'antica Pompei.* Naples.

Giuliano, A., ed. 1981. *Museo nazionale romano: Le Sculture* I.7. Rome.

Glymph, T. 2008. *Out of the House of Bondage: The Transformation of the Plantation Household.* Cambridge.

Goffman, E. 1959. *The Presentation of Self in Everyday Life.* New York.

Goings, K.W. 1994. *Mammy and Uncle Mose: Black Collectibles and American Stereotyping.* Bloomington.

Gordon, M.L. 1924. 'The Nationality of Slaves under the Early Roman Empire,' *JRS* 14: 93–111.

Goulet, C.C. 2000. 'The "Zebra-Stripe" Design: An Investigation of Roman Wall Painting in the Periphery,' *AJA* 104: 366–7.

– 2001–2. 'The "Zebra-Stripe" Design: An Investigation of Roman Wall Painting in the Periphery,' *RSt Pomp* 12–13: 53–94.

Grahame, M. 1997. 'Public and Private in the Roman House: Investigating the Social Order of the *Casa del Fauno*,' in R. Laurence and A. Wallace-Hadrill, eds., *Domestic Space in the Roman World. JRA* Suppl. 22, 137–64. Portsmouth.

– 2001. *Reading Space: Social Interaction and Identity in the Houses of Pompeii: A Syntactical Approach to the Analysis and Interpretation of Built Space.* Oxford.

Grandjouan, C. 1961. *The Athenian Agora, vol. VI, Terracottas and Plastic Lamps of the Roman Period.* Princeton.

Granino Cecere, M.G., and C. Ricci. 2008. 'Monumentum sive columbarium libertorum et servorum. Qualche riflessione su motivazioni e successo di una fisionomia edilizia,' in M.L. Caldelli, G.L. Gregori, and S. Orlandi, eds., *Epigrafia 2006. Atti della XIVe Rencontre sur l'épigrafie in onore di Silvio Panciera con altri contributi di colleghi, allievi e collaboratori,* 323–37. Rome.

Greene, K. 1990. *The Archaeology of the Roman Economy.* Berkeley and Los Angeles.

Gregori, G.L., ed. 2001. *La collezione epigrafica dell'Antiquarium Comunale del Celio.* Tituli 8. Rome.

Grewing, F. 1997. *Martial Buch VI. Ein Kommentar.* Göttingen.

Gundaker, G. 1998. *Signs of Diaspora / Diaspora of Signs.* Oxford.

Gutzwiller, K. 2007. *A Guide to Hellenistic Literature.* Malden, MA.

Guzzo, P.G. 1980. 'Pene d'Amore,' *Boll d'arte* 65, no. 8: 45–54.

Guzzo, P.G., and L. Fergola. 2000. *Oplontis: la villa di Poppea.* Milan.

Hales, S. 2003. *The Roman Social Order and Roman Social Identity.* Cambridge.

Hall, M. 2000. *Archaeology and the Modern World: Colonial Transcripts in South Africa and the Chesapeake.* London and New York.

– 2008. 'Ambiguity and Contradiction in the Archaeology of Slavery,' *Archaeological Dialogues* 15, no. 2: 128–30.

Handler, J.S., F.W. Lange, and R.V. Riordan. 1978. *Plantation Slavery in Barbados: An Archaeological and Historical Investigation.* Cambridge, MA.

Harnack, A. 1962. *The Mission and Expansion of Christianity in the First Three Centuries.* New York.

Harper, J. 1972. 'Slaves and Freedmen in Imperial Rome,' *AJPh* 93: 341–2.

Harris, J., and B. Fleischman. 1994. *A Passion for Antiquities: Ancient Art from the Collection of Barbara and Lawrence Fleischman.* Malibu.

Harris, M.D. 2003. *Colored Pictures: Race and Visual Representation.* Chapel Hill.

Harris, W.V. 1980. 'Towards a Study of the Roman Slave Trade,' in J.H. D'Arms and E.C. Kopff, eds., *The Seaborne Commerce of Ancient Rome: Studies of Archaeology and History.* MAAR vol. 36., 117–40. Rome.

– 1989. *Ancient Literacy.* Cambridge, MA.

– 1994. 'Child-exposure in the Roman Empire,' *JRS* 84: 1–22.

– 1999. 'Demography, Geography and the Sources of Roman Slaves,' *JRS* 89: 62–75.

Hartman, S.V. 1997. *Scenes of Subjection: Terror, Slavery, and Self-Making in Nineteenth-Century America*. New York and Oxford.

Hasegawa, K. 2005. *The Familia Urbana during the Early Empire: A Study of Columbaria Inscriptions.* BAR International Series 1440. Oxford.

Haynes, S. 1985. *Etruscan Bronzes*. London.

Heilmeyer, W.D. 1996. *Der Jüngling von Salamis: Technische Untersuchungen zu römischen Grossbronzen*. Mainz.

Helbig, W. 1966. *Führer durch die öffentlichen Sammlungen klassischer Altertümer in Rom* (2nd ed. by Hermine Speier) II: *Die Städtischen Sammlungen: Kapitolinische Museen und Museo Barracco*. Tübingen.

Helttula, A. 1973. 'Onomastica,' in V. Väänänen, ed., *Le iscrizioni della necropoli dell'Autoparco Vaticano*, 139–55. Rome.

Hempel, H.L. 1963. *Enciclopedia dell'arte antica classica ed orientale V*. Venice.

Henig, M. 1978. *A Corpus of Roman Engraved Gemstones from British Sites*. Oxford.

– 1994. *Classical Gems – Ancient and Modern Intaglios and Cameos in the Fitzwilliam Museum, Cambridge*. Cambridge.

Henzen, W., et al., eds. 1884. *Ephemeris Epigraphica: C.I.L. Supplementum* V. Berlin.

Herrmann, P. 1904–50. *Denkmäler der Malerei des Altertums*. Munich.

Herrmann-Otto, E. 1994. *Ex ancilla natus*. Stuttgart.

Hiller, H. 1994. 'Zum Xantener Bronzeknaben,' *Akten der 10. Internationalen Tagung über antike Bronzen, Freiburg, 18.–22. Juli 1988*, 201–10. Stuttgart.

Himmelmann, N. 1971. *Archäologisches zum Problem der griechischen Sklaverei*. Mainz.

Hodgson, N. 2002. '"Where did they put the horses?" Revisited: The Recent Discovery of Cavalry Barracks in the Roman Forts at Wallsend and South Shields on Hadrian's Wall,' in Philip Freeman et al., eds., *Limes XVIII.2: Proceedings of the XVIIIth International Congress of Roman Frontier Studies, Held in Amman, Jordan (September 2000)*, BAR International series 1084.II. Oxford.

Hoffmann, B. 1997. 'Zenturionenquartiere in römischen Legionslagern,' in W. Groenman van Waateringe et al., eds., *Roman Frontier Studies 1995*, 195–8. Oxford.

Hölscher, T. 1987. *Römische Bildsprache als semantisches System*. Heidelberg. *The Language of Images in Roman Art*, A. Snodgrass and A. Künzl-Snodgrass, trans. Cambridge.

– 2003. 'Images of War in Greece and Rome: Between Military Practice, Public Memory, and Cultural Symbolism,' *JRS* 93: 1–17.

– 2006. 'The Transformation of Victory into Power: From Event to Structure,' in S. Dillon and K. Welch, eds., *Representations of War in Ancient Rome*, 27–48. Cambridge.

Hope, V.M. 2003. 'Remembering Rome: Memory, funerary monuments and the Roman soldier,' in H. Williams, ed., *Archaeologies of Remembrance: Death and Memory in Past Societies*, 113–40. New York.

Hopkins, K. 1978. *Conquerors and Slaves: Sociological Studies in Roman History*, vol. 1. Cambridge.

– 1983. *Death and Renewal: Sociological Studies in Roman History*, vol. 2. Cambridge.

Horsfall, N. 1995. 'Rome without Spectacles,' *G&R* 42: 49–56.

Hunt, A.S., and C.C. Edgar, eds. 1936. *Select Papyri. Vol. 1: Non-Literary Papyri, Private Documents*. Cambridge, MA.

Icard-Gianolio, N. 1994. 'Psyche,' in *Lexicon Iconographicum Mythologiae Classicae* 7, 569–84. Zurich and Munich.

Iozzo, M., ed. 1999. *'Qual era tutto rotto': L'enigma dell'Idolino di Pesaro, Indagini per un restauro*. Florence.

Isaac, R. 1999. *The Transformation of Virginia, 1740–1790*. Chapel Hill.

Işkan, H. 1998. 'Der bronzene Jüngling aus dem Schwarzen Meer,' *Antike Plastik* 26: 91–9.

James, S.L. 2003. *Learned Girls and Male Persuasion: Gender and Reading in Roman Love Elegy*. Berkeley.

Jantzen, U. 1958. *Griechische Griff-Phialen*. Berlin.

Jashemski, W.F. 1979–93. *The Gardens of Pompeii, Herculaneum and the Villas Destroyed by Vesuvius*, 2 vols. New Rochelle.

– 1987. 'Recently Excavated Gardens and Cultivated Land of the Villas at Boscoreale and Oplontis,' in E.B. MacDougall, ed., *Ancient Roman Villa Gardens*, 33–75. Washington, DC.

Johnson, A.P. 2006. 'The Blackness of Ethiopians: Classical Ethnography and Eusebius's Commentary on the Psalms,' *HThR* 99: 165–86.

Joshel, S.R. 1992. *Work, Identity and Legal Status at Rome: A Study of the Occupational Inscriptions*. London & Norman, OK.

– 2011. 'Slavery in Roman Literature,' in P. Cartledge and K. Bradley, eds., *The Cambridge World History of Slavery Volume 1*, 214–40. Cambridge.

The J. Paul Getty Museum Handbook of the Antiquities Collection. 2002. Los Angeles.

Kajanto, I. 1963. *Onomastic Studies in the Early Christian Inscriptions of Rome and Carthage*. Acta IRF II.1. Helsinki.

– 1965. *The Latin Cognomina*. Helsinki.

– 1968. 'The Significance of Non-Latin *Cognomina*,' *Latomus* 27: 517–34.

Kajava, M. 1988. Review of Kleiner, 1987. *Arctos* 22: 248–56.

Kalveram, K. 1995. *Die Antikensammlung des Kardinals Scipione Borghese*. Worms.

Kampen, N. 1981. *Image and Status: Roman Working Women in Ostia*. Berlin.

Kandler, M., ed. 1997. *Das Auxiliarkastell Carnuntum II: Forschungen seit 1989.* Vienna.

Karanastassi, P. 1992. 'Nemesis,' in *Lexicon Iconographicum Mythologiae Classicae* 6, 733–62. Zurich and Munich.

Kaschnitz-Weinberg, G. 1937. *Sculture del Magazzino del Museo Vaticano.* Rome.

Kaye, A.E. 2007. *Joining Places: Slave Neighborhood in the Old South.* Chapel Hill.

Keegan, P. 2010. 'Blogging Rome: Graffiti as Speech-Act and Cultural Discourse,' in J.A. Bairdand C. Taylor, eds., 165–91. London and New York.

Keene Congdon, L.O. 1981. *Caryatid Mirrors of Ancient Greece.* Mainz.

Kemp, G. Van der. 1978. *Versailles.* Versailles.

Kimball, F. 1951. 'The Reception of the Art of Herculaneum in France,' in G. Mylonas, ed., *Studies Presented to D.M.O. Robinson*, vol. 2, 1254–6. St Louis.

Kleijwegt, M. 2006. 'Freed Slaves, Self-Presentation and Corporate Identity in the Roman World,' in M. Kleijwegt, ed., *The Faces of Freedom: The Manumission and Emancipation of Slaves in the Old World and New World Slavery*, 89–115. Leiden and Boston.

Kleiner, D.E.E. 1977. *Roman Group Portraiture.* New York.

– 1987. *Roman Imperial Funerary Altars with Portraits.* Rome.

Knittlmayer, B., and W.-D. Heilmeyer. 1998. *Die Antikensammlung: Altes Museum Pergamonmuseum.* Berlin.

Kockel, V. 1993. *Porträtreliefs stadtrömischer Grabbauten. Ein Beitrag zur Geschichte und zum Verständnis des spätrepublikanisch-frühkaiserzeitlichen Privatporträts.* Mainz.

Kolendo, J. 1979. 'Éléments pour une enquête sur l'iconographie des esclaves dans l'art hellénistique et romain,' in M. Capozza, ed., *Schiavitù, manomissione e classi dipendenti nel mondo antico*, 161–74. Rome.

– 1981. 'L'esclavage et la vie sexuelle des hommes libres à Rome,' *Index: Quaderni camerti di studi romanistici* 10: 288–97.

Kopplin, M. 1987. '"Was fremd und seltsam ist": Exotica in Kunst- und Wunderkammern,' in H. Pollig, ed., *Exotische Welten, Europäische Phantasien*, 296–317. Stuttgart.

Kozloff, A.P., and D.G. Mitten, eds. 1988. *The Gods Delight: The Human Figure in Classical Bronze.* Cleveland.

Krüger, M.-L. 1970. *Die Reliefs des Stadtgebietes von Carnuntum, I: Die figürlichen Reliefs. CSIR Österreich I.3, Carnuntum.* Vienna.

Kunze, M. 1992. *Die Antikensammlung im Pergamonmuseum und in Charlottenburg.* Mainz.

Laes, C. 2003. 'Desperately Different? *Delicia* Children in the Roman Household,' in D. Balch, and C. Osiek, eds., *Early Christian Families in Context: An Interdisciplinary Dialogue*, 298–326. Grand Rapids.

– 2010. '*Delicia*-children Revisited: The Evidence of Statius' Silvae,' in V. Dasen, and T. Späth, eds., *Children, Memory, and Family Identity in Roman Culture*, 245–72. Oxford.

– 2011. *Children in the Roman Empire*. Cambridge.

Lafon, X. 2001. *Villa Maritima. Recherches sur les villas littorales de l'Italie, BEFAR 307*. Rome.

Laken, L. 2003. 'Zebrapatterns in Campanian Wall Painting: A Matter of Function,' *BABesch* 78: 167–89.

Lamb, W. 1929. *Greek and Roman Bronzes*. London and New York.

Lancha, J. 1983. 'L'iconographie d'Hylas dans les mosaiques romaines,' in R. Farioli Campanati, ed., *III colloquio internazionale sul mosaico antico: Ravenna 6–10 settembre 1980*, 381–92. Ravenna.

Lanciani, R. 1979. *The Ruins and Excavations of Ancient Rome*. New York.

Langner, M. 1999. *Antike Graffitizeichnungen. Motive, Gestaltung und Bedeutung*. Wiesbaden.

Laurence, R. 1994. *Roman Pompeii: Space and Society*. London and New York.

Leach, E.W. 2004. *The Social Life of Painting in Ancient Rome and on the Bay of Naples*. Cambridge and New York.

Leiwo, M. 2002. 'From Contact to Mixture: Bilingual Inscriptions from Italy,' in J.N. Adams, M. Janse, and S. Swain, eds., *Bilingualism in Ancient Society: Language Contact and the Written Text*, 168–94. Oxford.

– 2003. 'Greek or Latin, or Something in Between? The Jews in Venusia and Their Language,' in H. Solin, M, Leiwo, and H. Halla-aho, eds., *Latin vulgaire – latin tardif* VI (Actes du colloque international Helsinki 2000), 253–64. Hildesheim, Zurich, and New York.

Lenski, N. 2011. 'Captivity and Romano-Barbarian Interchange,' in R.W. Mathisen and D. Shanzer, eds., *Romans, Barbarians and the Transformation of the Roman World*, 185–98. Farnham.

Levi, D. 1947. *Antioch Mosaic Pavements*. Princeton.

Lilja, S. 1965. *The Roman Elegists' Attitude to Women*. Helsinki.

Ling, R. 1997. *The Insula of the Menander at Pompeii. Volume I: The Structures*. Oxford.

Lippold, G. 1936. *Die Skulpturen des vaticanischen Museums* Band III 2. Berlin.

Lo Cascio, E. 2002. 'Considerazioni sul numero e sulle fonti di approvvigionamento degli schiavi in età imperiale,' *Antiquitas* 26: 51–65.

López Barja de Quiroga, P. 1995. 'Freedmen Social Mobility in Roman Italy,' *Historia* 44: 326–48.

– 1998. 'Junian Latins: status and number,' *Athenaeum* 86: 133–63.

Lugli, G. 1957. *La tecnica edilizia romana*. Rome.

Lyne, R.O.A.M. 1979. '*Servitium amoris*,' *CQ* 29: 117–30.

MacKinnon, M. 2007. 'Osteological Research in Classical Archaeology,' *AJA* 111: 473–504.

Madden, J. 1996. 'Slavery in the Roman Empire: Numbers and Origins,' *Classics Ireland* 3: 109–28.

Maderna-Lauter, K. 1991. 'Polyklet in Rom,' in H. Beck, P.C. Bol, and M. Bückling, eds., *Polyklet. Der Bildhauer der griechischen Klassik*, 328–92. Mainz.

Manzella, I. di Stefano. 2008. 'Q(uinti) n(epos) o Q(uinti) n(ostri)? Tre are della famiglia degli Antigoni nel Monumentum Volusiorum, fra datio loci e permissus,' in *Epigrafia 2006. Atti della XIVe rencontre sur l'épigraphie in onore di Silvio Panciera con altri contributi di colleghi, allievi e collaboratori* (Rome), M. L. Caldelli, G. L. Gregori, and S. Orlandi, eds., 299–322.

Maiuri, A. 1925a. 'L'Efebo di Via dell'Abbondanza a Pompei,' *BA* 5, no. 1: 337–53.

– 1925b. 'La raffigurazione del "placentarius" in quattro bronzetti pompeiani,' *BA* 5, no. 1: 268–75.

– 1927. 'Casa dell'Efebo in Bronzo, Reg. I, Ins. VII, Casa nn. 10–12,' *NSA*: 32–83.

– 1933. *La Casa del Menandro e il suo tesoro de argenteria*. Rome.

Marabini Moevs, M.T. 2008. 'Per una storia del gusto: riconsiderazioni sul Calice Warren,' *Bollettino d'Arte* 146: 1–16.

Marshall, C.W. 2006. *The Stagecraft and Performance of Roman Comedy*. Cambridge.

Marshall, F.H. 1909. 'Some Recent Acquisitions of the British Museum,' *JRS* 29: 151–67.

Marti, B.M. 1936. 'Proskynesis and adorare,' *Language* 12, no. 4: 272–82.

Marucchi, O. 1910. *Epigrafia cristiana: trattato elementare con una silloge di antiche iscrizioni cristiane principalmente di Roma*. Milan.

Marzano, A. 2007. *Roman Villas in Central Italy: A Social and Economic Study*. Leiden.

Mastroroberto, M. 2001. *In Stabiano: cultura e archeologia da Stabia; la città e il territorio tra l'età arcaica e l'età romana – catalogo della mostra, Castellamare di Stabia, palazzetto del mare 4 novembre 2000–31 gennaio 2001*, 113. Naples.

Mattingly, D.J. 2008. 'Comparative Advantage. Roman Slavery and Imperialism,' *Archaeological Dialogues* 15, no. 2: 135–9.

Mattusch, C.C. 1996. *Classical Bronzes: The Art and Craft of Greek and Roman Statuary*. Ithaca.

– 2008. *Pompeii and the Roman Villa: Art and Culture around the Bay of Naples*. New York.

Matz, F., and F. von Duhn. 1881. *Antike Bildwerke in Rom mit Ausschluss der grösseren Sammlungen*. Leipzig (repr. Rome 1968).

McCarthy, K. 1998. 'Servitium amoris: Amor servitii,' in S. Joshel and S. Murnaghan, eds., *Women and Slaves in Greco-Roman Culture: Differential Equations*, 174–92. London and New York.

– 2000. *Slaves, Masters and the Art of Authority in Plautine Comedy*. Princeton.

McDonnell, M. 1996. 'Writing, Copying, and Autograph Manuscripts in Ancient Rome,' *CQ*: 469–91.

McGinn, T.A.J. 2004. *The Economy of Prostitution in the Roman World.* Ann Arbor.

Merola, F.R. 1990. *Servo parere.* Camerino.

Mertens, J.R. 1990. 'The Human Figure in Classical Bronze-working: Some Perspectives,' in *Small Bronze Sculpture from the Ancient World: Papers Delivered at a Symposium Organized by the Departments of Antiquities Conservation and Held at the J. Paul Getty Museum, March 16–19, 1989,* 85–102. Malibu.

Métraux, G.P.R. 1998. '*Villa Rustica Alimentaria et Annonaria,*' in A. Frazer, ed., *The Roman Villa: Villa Urbana. Symposium on Classical Architecture,* 1–19. Philadelphia.

Micheli, M.E. 1992. 'Eroti in gabbia. Storia di uno motivo iconografico' *Prospettiva* 65: 2–14.

Michon, E. 1933. 'Éphèbe couronné: Nouvelle statue de bronze trouvée à Volubilis,' *MMAI* 33: 119–34.

Millar, F. 1984. 'Condemnation to Hard Labour in the Roman Empire, from the Julio-Claudians to Constantine,' *PBSR* 39: 124–47.

Miller, S.N. 1922. *The Roman Fort at Balmuidy.* Glasgow.

Mitten, D.G., and S.F. Doeringer. 1967. *Master Bronzes from the Classical World.* Mainz.

Mohler, S.L. 1937. 'The *Iuvenes* and Roman Education,' *TAPA* 68: 442–79.

– 1940. 'Slave Education in the Roman Empire,' *TAPA* 71: 262–80.

Mommsen, T. 1864. 'Die römischen Eigennamen der republikanischen und augusteischen Zeit,' in *Römische Forschungen* I: 1–68.

Moorman, E.M. 1988. *La pittura parietale romana come fonte di conoscenza per la scultura antica.* Assen and Maastricht.

Moreno, P., and A. Viacava. 2003. *I marmi antichi della Galleria Borghese.* Rome.

Morgan, P.D. 1998. *Slave Counterpoint: Black Culture in the Eighteenth-Century Chesapeake and Low Country.* Chapel Hill and London.

Morley, J. 1999. *The History of Furniture: Twenty-five Centuries of Style and Design in the Western Tradition.* Boston.

Morris, I. 1998. 'Remaining Visible: The Archaeology of the Excluded in Classical Athens,' in S.R. Joshel and S. Murnaghan, eds., *Women and Slaves in Greco-Roman Culture,* 193–220. London and New York.

Mosser, M. 2003. *Die Steindenkmäler der legio XV Apollinaris.* Vienna.

Mouritsen, H. 2004. 'Freedmen and Freeborn in the Necropolis of Imperial Ostia,' *ZPE* 150: 281–304.

– 2005. 'Freedmen and Decurions: Epitaphs and Social History in Imperial Italy,' *JRS* 95: 38–63.

– 2011a. *The Freedman in the Roman World.* Cambridge.

– 2011b. 'Die Inschriften aus der Insula I 10 im Pompeji,' in H. Meller and J.-A.- Dickmann, eds., *Pompeji – Nola – Herculaneum Katastrofen am Vesuv,* 277–83. Munich.

– forthcoming. 'The Inscriptions of the Insula of the Menander,' in H. Mouritsen, J.M. Reynolds, and A. Varone, eds., *The Insula of the Menander Vol. 5: The Wall Inscriptions*. Oxford.

Mühlenbrock, J., and D. Richter. 2004. *Verschüttet vom Vesuv. Die letzen Stunden von Herculaneum*. Mainz.

Mullins, P. 2008. 'The Politics of an Archaeology of Global Capacity,' *Archaeological Dialogues* 15, no. 2: 123–7.

Murgatroyd, P. 1981. '*Servitum amoris* and the Roman Elegists,' *Latomus* 49: 589–606.

Muth, S. 1998. *Erleben von Raum – Leben im Raum. Zur Funktion mythologischer Mosaikbilder in der römisch-kaiserzeitlichen Wohnarchitektur*. Heidelberg.

Néraudau, J.-P. 1984. *Être enfant à Rome*. Paris.

Neugebauer, K.A. 1924. *Führer durch das Antiquarium Berlin*, Tom I. *Bronzen*. Berlin.

Nielsen, H.S. 1990. '*Delicia* in Roman Literature and the Urban Inscriptions,' *Analecta Romana Instituti Danici* 19: 79–88.

Noelke, P. 1998. 'Grabreliefs mit Mahldarstellung in den germanisch-gallischen Provinzen – soziale und religiöse Aspekte,' in P. Fasold et al., eds., *Bestattungssitte und kulturelle Identität: Grabanlagen und Grabbeigaben der frühen römischen Kaiserzeit in Italien und den Nordwest-Provinzen. Kolloquium in Xanten vom 16. Bis 18. Februar 1995*, 399–418. Cologne.

Oliver, A. 1993. 'An Incense Burner in the Form of an Actor as a Slave on an Altar,' in J. Arce and F. Burkhalter, eds., *Bronces y religion romana: Actas del XI congreso internacional de bronces antiguos, Madrid, Mayo-Junio, 1990*. Madrid.

Orr, D. 1978. 'Roman Domestic Religion: The Evidence of Household Shrines,' in W. Haase, ed., *ANRW* 16, no. 2: 1557–91.

Ortalli, J., ed. 2006. *Vivere in villa. Le Qualità delle residenze agresti in età romana*. Florence.

Ostenberg, I. 2009. *Staging the World: Spoils, Captives, and Representations in the Roman Triumphal Procession*. Oxford.

Palmer, R.E.A. 1978. 'Silvanus, Sylvester, and the Chair of St. Peter,' *Proceedings of the American Philosophical Society* 122, no. 4: 222–47.

Parker, H. 1989. 'Crucially Funny or Tranio on the Couch: The *Servus Callidus* and Jokes about Torture,' *TAPA* 119: 233–46.

Pasquier, A., and J.-L. Martinez, eds. 2007. *Praxitèle*. Paris.

Patterson, O. 1982. *Slavery and Social Death: A Comparative Study*. Cambridge, MA.

Pavolini, C. 1993. *Caput Africae I*. Rome.

Pedicini, L., et al. 1989. *Le collezioni del museo nazionale archeologico di Napoli: La scultura greco-romana, le sculture antiche della Collezione Farnese, le collezioni monetali, le orificerie, la collezione glittica*. Rome.

Petersen, L. Hackworth. 2006. *The Freedman in Roman Art and Art History*. Cambridge and New York.

Pflug, H. 1989. *Römische Porträtstelen in Oberitalien*. Mainz.

Piccottini, G. 1972. *Die Rundmedaillons und Nischenporträts des Stadtgebietes von Virunum. CSIR Österreich* II.2, Virunum. Vienna.

– 1977. *Die Dienerinnen- und Dienerreliefs des Stadtgebietes von Virunum: Corpus Signorum Imperii Romani, Österreich* II.3. Vienna.

Pitts, L.F., and J.K. St Joseph. 1985. *Inchtuthil*. London.

Pollini, J. 1999. 'The Warren Cup: Homoerotic Love and Symposial Rhetoric in Silver,' *Art Bulletin* 81, no. 1: 21–52.

– 2002. *Gallo-Roman Bronzes and the Process of Romanization: The Cobannus Hoard*. Leiden.

– 2003. 'Slave-boys for Sexual and Religious Service: Images of Pleasure and Devotion,' in A.J. Boyle and W. J. Dominick, eds., *Flavian Rome: Culture, Image, Text*, 149–66. Leiden.

Portella, I.D. 2000. *Subterranean Rome*. Cologne.

Potter, R.A. 1998. *Spectacular Vernaculars: Hip-Hop and the Politics of Postmodernism*. New York.

Poulsen, F. 1933. *Sculptures antiques de musées de province espagnols*. Copenhagen.

Prowse, T., et al. 2007. 'Isotopic Evidence for Age-related Immigration to Imperial Rome,' *American Journal of Physical Anthropology* 132: 510–19.

Pugliese Carratelli, G., ed. 1990–2003. *Pompei: Pitture e mosaici*, 10 vols. Rome.

– ed. 1995. *Pitture e mosaici – immagine di Pompei nei secoli XVIII e XIX*. Rome.

Purcell, N. 1988. Review of Tchernia, *Le Vin de l'Italie romaine: essai sur l'histoire économique d'après les amphores* (1986), and Carandini, *Settefinestre* (1985). *JRS* 78: 194–8.

– 1995. 'The Roman Villa and the Landscape of Production,' in T.J. Cornell and K. Lomas, eds., *Urban Society in Italy*, 151–79. New York.

Rahms, H. 1994. 'Kunstbeute zum zweiten Mal gerettet: "Eros", "Dionysos" und andere Schätze aus dem Wrack von Mahdia,' *AW* 25: 360–4, 391–2.

Rawson, B. 1986. 'Children in the Roman Family,' in B. Rawson, ed., *The Family in Ancient Rome: New Perspectives*, 170–200. London and Sidney.

– ed. 1991. *Marriage, Divorce and Children in Ancient Rome*. Oxford and Canberra.

– 2003. *Children and Childhood in Roman Italy*. Oxford.

Rawson B., and P.R.C. Weaver, eds. 1997. *The Roman Family: Status, Sentiment, Space*. Oxford.

Rediscovering Pompeii, Exhibition by IBM-Italia, New York City, 12 July–15 September 1990. 1990. Rome.

Reil, T. 1913. *Beitrage Zur Kenntnis des Gewerbes im hellenistischen Ägypten*. Diss. Leipzig.

Reinach, S. 1884. *Description raisonnée du Musée de Saint-Germain-en-Laye: Bronzes figurés de la Gaule romaine*, 3 vols. Paris.

Reynolds, P.K.B. 1926. *The Vigiles of Imperial Rome*. London.

Rhomiopoulou, K. 2002. 'A Roman Bronze Lamp in the Form of a Barbarian Prisoner,' in C.C. Mattusch, A. Brauer, and S.E. Knudsen, eds., *From the Parts to the Whole: Acta of the 13th International Bronze Congress, May 28–June 1, 1996* II. 171–4. Portsmouth.

Richardson, L. 1992. *A New Topographical Dictionary of Ancient Rome*. Baltimore.

Richlin, A. 1992. *The Gardens of Priapus*. New York.

Richmond, I.A. 1962. 'The Roman Siege-Works of Masada,' *JRS* 52: 143–55.

Richter, G.M.A. 1921. 'Classical Accessions,' *MMAB* 16: 32–9.

– 1953. *Handbook of the Greek Collection*. Cambridge.

– 1971. *Engraved Gems of the Romans*. Edinburgh.

Ridgway, B.S. 2002. *Hellenistic Sculpture III: The Styles of ca. 100–31 B.C.* Madison.

Rinaldi Tufi, S. 1988. *Militari romani sul Reno: L'iconografia degli 'Stehende Soldaten' nelle stele funerarie del I secolo D. C.* Rome.

Riposati, M., ed. 1991. *Il Marocco e Roma: I grandi bronzi dal Museo di Rabat, Roma-Campidoglio, Palazzo dei Conservatori*. Rome.

Ritter, S. 2005. 'Zur kommunikativen Funktion Pompejanisher Gelagebilder: Die Bilder aus der Casa del Triclinio und ihr Kontext,' *JDAI* 120: 301–72.

Robinson, D.M. 1941. *Excavations at Olynthus. Part X, Metal and Minor Miscellaneous Finds*. Johns Hopkins University Studies in Archaeology 31. Baltimore.

Robinson, H.R. 1975. *The Armour of Imperial Rome*. New York.

Robinson, O.F. 1981. 'Slaves and the Criminal Law,' *Zeitschrift für Rechtsgeschichte* 98: 213–54.

Roller, M.B. 2006. *Dining Posture in Ancient Rome*. Princeton.

Rolley, C. 1986. *Greek Bronzes*. R. Howell, trans. London.

Rosenblum, R. 1969. *Transformations in Late Eighteenth Century Art*, 2nd ed. Princeton.

Rossiter, J.J. 1978. *Roman Farm Buildings*. Oxford.

– 1981. 'Wine and Oil Pressing at Roman Farms in Italy,' *Phoenix* 35, no. 4: 345–61.

Rostovtzeff, M.I. 1926. *Social and Economic History of the Roman Empire*. Oxford (2nd ed. rev. by P.M. Fraser, 1957).

Roth, J. 1999. *The Logistics of the Roman Army at War (264 B.C. – A.D. 235)*. Leiden.

Roth, U. 2004. 'Inscribed Meaning: The Vilica and the Villa Economy,' *PBSR* 72: 101–24.

– 2005. 'To Have and To Be: Food, Status and the *Peculium* of Agricultural Slaves,' *JRA* 18: 278–92.

– 2007. *Thinking Tools: Agricultural Slavery between Evidence and Models*. London.

Roxan, M. 1991. 'Women on the Frontiers,' in V.A. Maxfield and M.J. Dobson, eds., *Roman Frontier Studies 1989*, 462–7. Exeter.

Rumpf, A. 1939. 'Der Idolino,' *CA* 19–20: 17–27.

Sacco, G. 1997. *Le iscrizioni dei cristiani in Vaticano*. Vatican City.

Saller, R.P. 1994. *Patriarchy, Property and Death in the Roman Family*. Cambridge.

Saller, R.P., and B. Shaw. 1984. 'Tombstones and Roman Family Relations in the Principate: Civilians, Soldiers and Slaves,' *JRS* 74: 124–56.

Salskov Roberts, H. 2002. 'A Bronze Statue with Hook-Like Hands Found in Denmark,' in A. Giumlia-Mair, ed., *I bronzi antichi: Produzione e tecnologia, Atti del XV Congresso Internazionale sui Bronzi Antichi, 22–26 maggio 2001*, 456–1. Montagnac.

Sams, G.K. 1976. *Small Sculptures in Bronze from the Classical World: An Exhibit in Honor of Emeline Hill Richardson*. Chapel Hill.

Samson, R. 1989. 'Rural Slavery, Inscriptions, Archaeology and Marx,' *Historia* 38: 99–110.

Scheidel, W. 1996. Review of E. Herrmann-Otto, *Ex ancilla natus: Untersuchungen zu den 'hausgeborenen' Sklaven und Sklavinnen im Westen des römischen Kaiserreiches. Tyche* 11: 274–8

– 1997. 'Quantifying the Sources of Slaves in the Roman Empire,' *JRS* 87: 159–69.

– 1999. 'The Slave Population of Roman Italy: Speculation and Constraints,' *Topoi* 9: 129–44.

– 2002. Review of Leonhard Schumacher's *Sklaverei in der Antike: Alltag und Schicksal der Unfreien. BMCR* 2002.09.19.

– 2003. 'The Archaeology of Ancient Slavery,' *JRA* 16: 577–81.

– 2005. 'Human Mobility in Roman Italy, II: The Slave Population,' *JRS* 95: 64–79.

– 2008. 'The Comparative Economics of Slavery in the Greco-Roman World,' in E. Dal Lago and C. Katsari, eds., *Slave Systems, Ancient and Modern*, 105–26. Cambridge.

Schildgen, R., ed. 2000. *Ethnic Notions: Black Images in the White Mind, An Exhibition of Racist Stereotype and Caricature from the Collection of Janette Faulkner*. Berkeley.

Schlamm, C. 1992. *The Metamorphoses of Apuleius*. Chapel Hill.

Schmidt, E. 1982. *Geschichte der Karyatide*. Beiträge zur Archäologie 13. Würzburg.

Schmidt-Colinet, A. 1977. *Antike Stützfiguren. Untersuchungen zu Typus und Bedeutung der menschengestaltigen Architecturstütze in griechischer und römischer Kunst*. Frankfurt.

Schneider, R.M. 1986. *Bunte Barbaren: Orientalenstatuen aus farbigem Marmor in der römischen Repräsentationskunst*. Worms.

Schober, A. 1926. 'Zum neuen Epheben aus Pompeji,' *Belvedere* 9–10: 109–12.

Schumacher, L. 2001. *Sklaverei in der Antike. Alltag und Schicksal der Unfreien*. Munich.

Sebesta, J.L., and L. Bonfante, eds. 2001. *The World of Roman Costume*. Madison.

Segal, E. 1968. *Roman Laughter: The Comedy of Plautus*. Cambridge, MA.

Sena Chiesa, G. 1960. *Gemme del Museo Nazionale di Aquileia*. Aquileia.

Sgubini Moretti, A.M. 1998. Fastosa rusticatio: *la villa dei Volusii a Lucus Feroniae*. Rome.

Sharpe, J. 1995. 'Something Akin to Freedom: The Case of Mary Prince,' *Differences* 8, no. 1: 31–56.

– 2003. *Ghosts of Slavery: A Literary Archaeology of Black Women's Lives*. Minneapolis and London.

Sichtermann, H. 1969. 'Eros Glykypikros,' *RM* 76: 266–306.

Simmonds, L. 1987. 'Slave Higglering in Jamaica 1780–1834,' *Jamaica Journal* 20, no. 1: 31–8.

Simon, E. 2000. 'Der bestrafte Cupido and Psyche.' *Ktema* 25: 143–8.

Simpson, G. 2000. *Roman Weapons, Tools, Bronze Equipment and Brooches from Neuss – Novaesium Excavations 1955–1972 (BAR International Series 862)*. Oxford.

Singleton, T., ed. 1985. *The Archaeology of Slave and Plantation Life*. Orlando.

– 1999. *'I, Too, Am America' – Archaeological Studies of African-American Life*. Charlottesville.

Slater, W.J.S. 1974. 'Pueri, turba minuta,' *BICS* 21: 133–40.

Smith, R.R.R. 2002. 'The Use of Images: Visual History and Ancient History,' in T.P. Wiseman, ed., *Classics in Progress: Essays on Ancient Greece and Rome*, 59–102. New York.

Snowden, F.M. 1970. *Blacks in Antiquity*. Cambridge, MA.

– 1976. 'Iconographical Evidence on the Black Populations in Greco-Roman Antiquity,' in J. Vercoutter, J. Leclant, F.M. Snowden, and J. Desanges, eds., *The Image of the Black in Western Art, Vol. 1: From the Pharaohs to the Fall of the Roman Empire*, 133–245. New York.

Sogliano, A. 1898. 'La casa dei Vettii in Pompei,' *Monumenti antichi dell'Accademia dei Lincei* 8: cols. 233–416.

– 1901. 'L'Efebo in bronzo rinvenuto in Pompei,' *MAL* 10: 641–54.

Solin, H. 1970. 'L'interpretazione delle iscrizioni parietali.' Faenza.

– 1971. *Beiträge zur Kenntnis der griechischen Personnenamen in Rom I*. Helsinki.

– 1990. *Namenpaare. Eine Studie zur römischen Namengebung*. Helsinki.

– 1996a. *Die stadtrömischen Sklavennamen. Ein Namenbuch I-III. Forschungen zur antiken Sklaverei, Beiheft 2*. Stuttgart.

– 1996b. 'Namen im Alten Rom,' in E. Eichler et al., eds., *Namenforschung. Name. Studies Les noms propres* 2, 1041–8. Berlin and New York.

– 2001. 'Griechische und römische Sklavennamen. Eine vergleichende Untersuchung,' in H. Bellen and H. Heinen, eds., *Fünfzig Jahre Forschungen zur antiken Sklaverei an der Mainzer Akademie 1950–2000*, 307–30. Stuttgart.

– 2002. 'Zur Entwicklung des römischen Namensystems,' in H. Beck et al., eds., *Person und Name*. Ergänzungsband zum Reallexikon der Germanischen Altertumskunde 32, 1–17. Berlin and New York.

– 2003a. *Die griechischen Personennamen in Rom. Ein Namenbuch*². Berlin and New York.

– 2003b. 'Le trasformazioni dei nomi personali tra antichità e medioevo,' in F. De Rubeis and W. Pohl, eds., *Le scritture dai monasteri*. Acta IRF 29, 15–45. Rome.

– 2006. 'Episcopus und Verwandtes. Lexicographisches und Namenkundliches aus der christlichen *Frühzeit* Roms,' *Philologus* 150: 232–50.

– 2007. 'Mobilità socio-geografica nell'impero romano. Orientali in Occidente. Considerazioni isagogiche,' in M. Mayer Olivé et al., eds., *Acta XII Congressus Internationalis Epigraphiae Graecae et Latinae (Barcelona 2002)* II, 1363–79. Barcelona.

– 2009. 'Nomi greci nel mondo romano,' in E. Caffarelli and P. Poccetti, eds., *L'onomastica di Roma. Ventotto secoli di nomi*. Quaderni Italiani di Rivista Italiana di Onomastica 2, 61–84. Rome.

Solin, H., and M. Itkonen-Kaila. 1966. *Graffiti del Palatino I. Paedagogium*. Helsinki.

Solin, H., O. Salomies, and U.-M. Liertz, eds. 1995. *Acta Colloquii Epigraphici Latini Helsingiae 3.–6. Sept. 1991 habiti* (Commentationes Humanarum Litterarum 104). Helsinki.

Sommer, C.S. 1995. 'Where Did They Put the Horses? Überlegungen zu Aufbau und Stärke römischer Auxiliartruppen und deren Unterbringung in den Kastellen,' in W. Czysz, ed., *Provinzialrömische Forschungen. Festschrift für Günter Ulbert zum 65. Geburtstag*, 149–168. Espelkamp.

Speidel, M. 1989. 'The Soldiers' Servants,' *Ancient Society* 20: 238–47.

– 1992. *Roman Army Studies* II. Stuttgart.

– 1994. *Die Denkmäler der Kaiserreiter: Equites singulares Augusti*. Bonn.

Spier, J. 1992. *Ancient Gems and Finger Rings – Catalogue of the Collections, The J. Paul Getty Museum*. Malibu.

Starr, R.J. 1990–1. 'Lectores and Book Reading,' *CJ* 86: 337–43.

Steinby, E.M., ed. 1999. *Lexicon Topigraphicum Urbis Romae IV*. Rome.

Stemmer, K., ed. 1995. *Standorte. Kontext und Funktion antiker Skluptur*. Berlin.

Stibbe, C.M. 2000. *The Sons of Hephaistos: Aspects of the Archaic Greek Bronze Industry*. Rome.

Stuveras, R. 1969. *Le putto dans l'art romain*. Collection Latomus 99. Brussels.

Szilágy, J. 1956. *Aquincum*. Budapest.

Taylor, L.R. 1961. 'Freedmen and Freeborn in the Epitaphs of Imperial Rome,' *AJPh* 82: 113–32.

Terrenato, N. 2001. 'The Auditorium Site in Rome and the Origins of the Villa,' *JRA* 14: 5–32.

Thomas, M.L., and J.R. Clarke. 2007. 'The Oplontis Project 2005–2006: Observations on the Construction History of Villa A at Torre Annunziata,' *JRA* 17: 223–32.

– 2008. 'The Oplontis Project, 2005–2006: New Evidence for the Building History and Decorative Programs at Villa A, Torre Annunziata,' in M.P. Guidobaldi, ed., *Nuove ricerche archeologiche nell'area vesuviana (scavi 2003–2006)*. Atti del Convegno Internazionale, 1–3 febbraio 2007, 465–71. Rome.

– 2009. 'Evidence of Demolition and Remodeling at Villa A at Oplontis (Villa of Poppaea) after A.D. 45,' *JRA* 22: 201–9.

Thompson, F.H. 1994. 'Iron Age and Roman Slave-shackles,' *ArchJ* 150: 57–168.

– 2003. *The Archaeology of Greek and Roman Slavery*. London.

Thompson, L.A. 1989. *Romans and Blacks*. London.

Thylander, H. 1952. *Étude sur l'épigraphie latine*. Acta IRRS 8° 5. Lund.

Tomei, M.A. 1998. *Il Palatino*. Rome.

Treggiari, S. 1973. 'Domestic Staff at Rome in the Julio-Claudian Period, 27 B.C. to A.D. 68,' *Histoire sociale / Social History* 6: 241–55.

– 1975a. 'Family Life among the Staff of the Volusii,' *TAPhA* 105: 393–401.

– 1975b. 'Jobs in the household of Livia,' *PBSR* 43: 48–77.

Trillmich, W. 1976. *Das Torlonia-Mädchen: Zu Herkunft und Entstehung des kaiserzeitlichen Frauenporträts*. Göttingen.

Trümper, M. 2008. *Die 'Agora des Italiens' in Delos: Baugeschichte, Architektur, Ausstattung und Funktion einer späthellenistischen Porticus-Anlage*. Rahden.

Turner, P.A. 1994. *Ceramic Uncles and Celluloid Mammies: Black Images and Their Influence on Culture*. New York.

Väänänen, V. 1937. *La latin vulgaire des inscriptions pompéiennes*. Helsinki.

– 1962. *Graffiti di Pompei e di Roma*. Rome.

Valentini, R., and G. Zucchetti. 1940–53. *Codice topografico della città di Roma*. Rome.

Vallat, D. 2006. 'Bilingual Word-play on Personal Names in Martial,' in J. Booth and R. Maltby, eds., *What's in a Name? The Significance of Proper Names in Classical Latin Literature*, 121–43. Swansea.

Van Buren, A.W. 1923. 'Graffiti at Ostia,' *ClRev* 37: 163–4.

Varone, A. 1994. *Erotica pompeiana: iscrizioni d'amore sui muri di Pompei*. Rome.

Vercoutter, J., J. Leclant, F.M. Snowden, and J. Desanges, eds., *The Image of the Black in Western Art, Vol. 1: From the Pharaohs to the Fall of the Roman Empire*, 246–68. New York.

Visconti, C.L. 1868. *Sulla interpretazione della sigle V. D. N. dei graffiti palatini*. Rome.

– 1869. 'Di un nuovo graffito palatino,' *Giornale arcadico* 62: 159.

Visconti, P.E. 1867. *La Stazione della Coorte VII dei Vigili*. Rome.

Vlach, J.M. 1993. *Back of the Big House: The Architecture of Plantation Slavery*. Chapel Hill.

Vogt, J. 1974. *Slavery and the Ideal of Man*. Cambridge, MA.

Vollenweider, M-L. 1966. *Die Steinschneidekunst und ihre Künstler in spätrepublikanischer und augusteischer Zeit*. Baden-Baden.

von Petrikovits, H. 1965. 'Die Originalität der römischen Kunst am Rhein,' in *Le Rayonnement des civilisations grecque et romaine sur les cultures périphériques=Huitième Congrès International d'Archéologie classique (Paris, 1963)*, 145–52. Paris.

– 1975. *Die Innenbauten römischer Legionslager während der Prinzipatszeit*. Opladen.

– 1977. 'Verpflegunsbauten der Legion,' in J. Fitz, ed., *Limes: Akten des XI. Internationalen Limeskongresses: Székesfehérvár, 30.8.–6.9. 1976*, 633–4. Budapest.

Walker, S., and P. Higgs, eds. 2001. *Cleopatra of Egypt: From History to Myth*. Princeton.

Wallace-Hadrill, A. 1994. *Houses and Society in Pompeii and Herculaneum*. Princeton.

Wallace-Hadrill, A., and R. Laurence, eds. 1997. *Domestic Space in the Roman World. JRA* Suppl. 22, 183–195. Portsmouth.

Walters, H.B. 1915. *Select Bronzes, Greek, Roman, and Etruscan in the Departments of Antiquities*. London.

– 1921. *Catalogue of the Silver Plate (Greek, Etruscan, and Roman) in the British Museum*. London.

– 1926. *Catalogue of the Engraved Gems and Cameos, Greek, Etruscan, and Roman in the British Museum*. London.

Watson, A. 1987. *Roman Slave Law*. Baltimore and London.

Watson, P. 1992. 'Erotion: puella delicata?' *CQ* 42: 253–68.

Weaver, P.R.C. 1967. 'Social Mobility in the Early Roman Empire,' *Past and Present* 37, no. 1: 3–20.

– 1972. *Familia Caesaris: A Social Study of the Emperor's Freedmen and Slaves*. Cambridge.

– 1991. 'Children of Freedmen (and Freedwomen),' in B. Rawson, ed., *Marriage, Divorce and Children in Ancient Rome*, 166–90. Oxford.

– 2001. 'Reconstructing Lower-class Roman Families,' in S. Dixon, ed., *Childhood, Class and Kin in the Roman World*, 101–14. London and New York.

Webster, G. 1998. *The Roman Imperial Army of the First and Second Centuries A.D.*, 3rd ed. Norman.

– 2002. *The Legionary Fortress at Wroxeter: Excavations by Graham Webster 1955–85*. English Heritage Archaeological Reports 19. London.

Webster, J. 2001. 'Creolizing Roman Britain,' *AJA* 105.2: 209–25.

– 2003. 'Art as Resistance and Negotiation,' in S. Scott and J. Webster, eds., *Roman Imperialism and Provincial Art*, 24–51. Cambridge.

– 2005. 'Archaeologies of Slavery and Servitude. Bringing "New World" Perspectives to Roman Britain,' *JRA* 18: 161–79.

– 2008a. 'Less Beloved. Roman Archaeology, Slavery and the Failure to Compare,' *Archaeological Dialogues* 15, no. 2: 103–23.

– 2008b. 'Slavery, Archaeology and the Politics of Analogy,' *Archaeological Dialogues* 15, no. 2: 139–49.

Webster, T.B.L. 1995. *Monuments Illustrating New Comedy*, 3rd ed., rev. J.R. Green and A. Seeberg, 2 vols. London.

Wells, C.M. 1977. 'Where Did They Put the Horses? Cavalry Stables in the Early Empire,' in J. Fitz, ed., *Limes. Akten des 11. Internationalen Limeskongresses, Székesfehérvár, 30.8.–6.9.1976*, 659–65. Budapest.

Wells, P. 2004. *The Battle That Stopped Rome: Emperor Augustus, Arminius, and the Slaughter of the Legions in the Teutoburg Forest*. New York.

Welwei, K.-W. 1988. *Unfreie im antiken Kreigsdienst*: III: *Rom*. Stuttgart.

Westermann, W.L. 1955. *The Slave Systems of Greek and Roman Antiquity*. Baltimore.

White, K.D. 1970. *Roman Farming*. Ithaca.

Wiedemann, T.E.J. 1981. *Greek and Roman Slavery*. London.

– 1985. 'The Regularity of Manumission at Rome,' *CQ* 35: 162–75.

– 1997. *Greek and Roman Slavery*. London and New York.

Wiegels, R. 2002. 'Antikenlust. Der Caelius-Grabstein als Zeugnis frühneuzeitlicher Antikebegeisterung,' in R. Wiegels and W. Woesler, eds., *Antike neu entdeckt. Aspekte der Antike-Rezeption im 18. Jahrhundert unter besonderer Berücksichtigung der Osnabrücker Region. Kolloquium Osnabrück, 16–18 Februar 2000*, 35–70. Möhnesee.

Williams, C.A. 1999. *Roman Homosexuality: Ideologies of Masculinity in Classical Antiquity*. New York and Oxford.

Williams, D. 2006. *The Warren Cup*. London.

Wilson, L.M. 1938. *The Clothing of the Ancient Romans*. Baltimore.

Wiseman, T.P. 1985. *Catullus and His World*. Cambridge.

Wohlmayr, W. 2002. 'Individuum und Typus' am Beispiel eines römischen Tischträgers,' in A. Giumlia-Mair, ed., *I bronzi antichi: Produzione e tecnologia, Atti del XV Congresso Internazionale sui Bronzi Antichi, 22–26 maggio 2001*, 478–87. Montagnac.

Woolf, G. 1996. 'Monumental Writing and the Expansion of Roman Society in the Empire,' *JRS* 86: 22–39.

Wrede, H. 1981. *Consecratio in formam deorum. Vergöttlichte Privatpersonen in der römischen Kaiserzeit*. Mainz.

Wuilleumier. P., and A. Audin. 1952. *Les médaillons applique gallo-romains de la vallée du Rhône*. Paris.

Zanker, P. 1974. *Klassizistische Statuen: Studien zur Veränderung des Kunstgeschmacks in der römischen Kaiserzeit*. Mainz.

– 1975. 'Grabreliefs römischer Freigelassenen,' *JDAI* 90: 267–315.

– 1998. *Pompeii: Public and Private Life*. D. Lucas Schneider, trans. Cambridge, MA.

Zevi, F. 1996. 'La Casa di Giulio Polibio,' in M.R. Borriello et al., eds., *Pompei: Abitare sotto il Vesuvio*. 73–9. Ferrara.

Zimmer, G. 1982. *Römische Berufsdarstellungen*. Berlin.

Zwierlein-Diehl, E. 1969. *Antike Gemmen in Deutschland*. Munich.

– 1973. *Die antiken Gemmen des Kunsthistorischen Museums in Wien*. Munich.

– 1986. *Glaspasten im Martin-von-Wagner-Museum der Universität Würzburg*. Munich.

CONTRIBUTORS

Christer Bruun, Professor, Department of Classics, University of Toronto

Michele George, Associate Professor, Department of Classics, McMaster University

Sandra R. Joshel, Jon M. Bridgman Endowed Professor, Department of History, University of Washington

†Natalie Boymel Kampen, Professor emerita, Department of Art History, Barnard College, Columbia University

Peter Keegan, Lecturer in Roman History, Macquarie University

Noel Lenski, Associate Professor, Department of Classics, University of Colorado

Henrik Mouritsen, Professor of Roman History, Department of Classics, King's College London

INSCRIPTIONS

AE

1914, 253	194n21
1920, 75	192n4
1924, 40	192n4
1929, 106	194n21
1932, 50	194n21
1971, 88	176n14
1974, 475	197n52

CIL

III 536	96n39
III 940	41n50
IV 840	96n42
IV 2184	97n58
IV 2194	97n58
IV 2248	97n58
VI 2–3	24
VI 1039	94n8
VI 1052	94n8, 95n15
VI 1785 = 31931	96n37
VI 1884	96n39
VI 31863	96n39
VI 5931–60	65n22
VI 6242	44
VI 7290	95n15
VI 8658	27
VI 8663	94n9
VI 8817	153n55
VI 8867	150n29
VI 8948	96n39
VI 8956	153n55
VI 8977–9	95n16
VI 8982–87	94n8, 95n15
VI 8987	97n51
VI 9449	95n31
VI 9740	95n15
VI 10339 = 11.3806	94n9
VI 11315	26
VI 12306	26
VI 15329	26
VI 19633	31
VI 29563	31
VIII 827	150n29
VIII 1239	150n29
VIII 12355	150n29
X 4483	97n58
XI 3612	96n39
XI 3805	94n9
XIII 6960	195n30
XIII 7684	186
XIV 3537	96n41
XIV 3539	96n41
XV 118a	94n7
XV 1094h	94n7
XV 1449f	94n7

INDEX LOCORUM

INDEX

PHOENIX SUPPLEMENTARY VOLUMES